# VICTORIAN AMERICA

Geoffrey Blodgett

Richard D. Brown

Stanley Coben

Dee Garrison

David D. Hall

Claudia D. Johnson

D. H. Meyer

Gregory H. Singleton

Morris J. Vogel

# VICTORIAN
# AMERICA

Edited, with an Introductory Essay
by Daniel Walker Howe

 University of Pennsylvania Press/1976

# CONTENTS

# Overviews

# VICTORIAN CULTURE
# IN AMERICA

*DANIEL WALKER HOWE*

ON AUGUST 17, 1858, QUEEN VICTORIA AND PRESIDENT BUCHANAN EX-
changed a message in Morse code: "Europe and America are united by
telegraph. Glory to God in the highest. On earth peace and good-will toward
men." The new transatlantic cable soon malfunctioned and was not successfully re-laid until 1866. The message between the two heads of state,
however, typifies Victorian culture in its sense of Atlantic community, its
excitement in technology, its biblical rhetoric, and even in its premature
self-congratulation.

Victoria reigned in Britain from 1837 to 1901, and these sixty-four years
approximate the cultural dominion of what we call "Victorianism." How
Victorian culture arose in the United States, what it was like, and what has
happened to it are questions this collection of essays seeks to raise and discuss. The introductory essay sketches what is meant by regarding
American Victorianism as a culture and tries to show how that approach
can synthesize a great deal of what we know, and would like to know, about
American Victorianism. Of course nothing so pervasive and amorphous as
a culture comes into existence full blown or vanishes suddenly without a
trace; the dates, then, are but plausible conveniences. The period marked a
crucial—probably *the* crucial—transformation of the United States; it was
a time of industrialization, knowledge explosion, immigration and vast
population growth, urbanization, geographical expansion, changing race
relationships, and the greatest armed conflict on American soil. More and
more, students of American development are coming to examine the era as
a unit instead of respecting the conventional division of U.S. history at the
Civil War.

Using the name of a foreign monarch to describe an aspect of a country's
history implies some relationship between the two countries, and indeed a
close one existed between Britain and the United States in the nineteenth
century. Although the United States had become politically independent,

economic interdependence continued to characterize Anglo-American relations: each nation found the other a valuable customer, and maritime commerce increased, especially after the first steamship crossing of the Atlantic
in 1839. The cultural connection was, if anything, even closer than the economic one. Victorianism was a transatlantic culture—though in the largest
sense it was only an English-speaking subculture of Western civilization.
Inevitably, the English-speakers within the Western world shared many
common influences, which were reinforced by the expansion of printed communication during the 1830s and the subsequent laying of the transatlantic
cable. (British writings, unprotected by an international copyright law, were
freely and extensively reprinted in the United States.) Occasions like the
great conventions of the Evangelical Alliance held in London in 1846 and in
New York in 1873 exemplify the international quality of Victorian culture.[1]

The notion of an "American Victorianism" may also be taken to imply a
provincial status on the part of the United States vis-à-vis Britain; this in-
ference too is justified—with qualifications. At the beginning of the Victorian period reflective Americans worried lest their culture be insufficiently
distinctive to sustain a proper national identity. Yet American Victorianism
was not wholly a derivative culture; by the end of the Victorian era influence
had flowed in both directions across the Atlantic. American religious
leaders like Dwight Moody, writers like Longfellow, inventors like Morse,
and reformers like Dorothea Dix had contributed to the shaping of Victorian Britain.

Despite all they held in common, Victorianism in Britain and America developed within different contexts. The segment of British society identified
with bourgeois evangelicalism is usually thought the "most characteristically Victorian," and to it the origins of British Victorianism have been
traced.[2] In England such people lived at the periphery of polite society and
political power; in America they dominated economic, social, and political
institutions. Aristocratic culture patterns, against which middle-class Victorian standards often had to contend in Britain, were weak in the United
States. For this reason one could argue that Victorian culture was
experienced more intensely in the United States than in Victoria's homeland.[3] On the other hand, American Victorianism was not without its own
rivals and adversaries: the presence of so many ethnic minority groups gave

[1]On the Anglo-American cultural relationship, see Frank Thistlethwaite, *The Anglo-
American Connection in the Early Nineteenth Century* (Philadelphia: Univ. of Pennsylvania
Press, 1959); and Robert Kelley, *The Transatlantic Persuasion* (New York: Knopf, 1969). The
magnificent new study by David Brion Davis, *The Problem of Slavery in the Age of Revolution*
(Ithaca: Cornell Univ. Press, 1975) exemplifies the advantages of Anglo-American history.

[2]John Briggs and Ian Sellers, *Victorian Nonconformity* (New York: St. Martin's, 1974), p.
1; Maurice Quinlan, *Victorian Prelude* (New York: Columbia Univ. Press, 1941). See also
Ford K. Brown, *Fathers of the Victorians* (Cambridge, Eng.: Cambridge Univ. Press, 1961).

[3]How hard middle-class Victorianism had to struggle to impose its standards on Britain is
underlined in Morse Peckham, "Victorian Counterculture," *Victorian Studies,* 18 (March
1975), 257–76.

the United States a cultural diversity wider than anything known in Great Britain. The relationship of these groups to the dominant Victorian culture forms an important and still little understood chapter of American history.

The term "culture" stands in even greater need of exegesis than the term "Victorian." Sometimes, as we know, the word "culture" is applied narrowly to the prestigious arts; at the opposite extreme it can mean everything, material or otherwise, created by mankind. For our purposes, however, "culture" will be defined as an evolving system of beliefs, attitudes, and techniques, transmitted from generation to generation, and finding expression in innumerable activities people learn: religion, politics, child-rearing customs, the arts and professions, *inter alia.* During recent years, historians and other Americanists have been encouraged in their investigation of cultural systems by the example of anthropologists like Clifford Geertz. He and others see a culture as a distinctive heritage of ideas and values, providing people with nonmaterial resources to cope with life and a world view to make sense out of it.[4] We may define a society, on the other hand, as a structure of relationships among people. A third dimension of human existence, economy, would describe the relationship between society and the material resources it uses. All three may have varying degrees of articulation and formal organization. Each is essential to the other two: the cultural system is the collective memory of the group, and without it neither the social system nor the economic system could operate.

The distinction between culture and society is important to make for the study of Victorian America, because the two were frequently at odds with one another. Sometimes society, under the impact of urbanization, was changing faster than aspects of culture; at other times, cultural demands were ahead of social practice. Such discrepancies between culture and society make for an untidy picture; but Victorian culture was not simply a rationalization for the social structure, and the society was far from being a straight implementation of cultural ideals. Though we may seek for interrelationships among different aspects of culture and society (an enterprise sociologists term "functional analysis"), we must not always expect to find them.[5] Cecil Tate has recently distinguished between methodological holism

---

[4]See, e.g., Clifford Geertz, "Religion as a Cultural System," in *Anthropological Approaches to the Study of Religion,* ed. Michael Banton (New York: Praeger, 1966), pp. 1–46; Clifford Geertz, "The Impact of the Concept of Culture on the Concept of Man," in *Man in Adaptation: The Cultural Present,* ed. Yehudi Cohen (Chicago: Aldine, 1968), pp. 16–29; and Sidney Mintz, "Foreword," in *Afro-American Anthropology,* ed. Norman Whitten and John Szwed (New York: Free Press, 1970) pp. 1–16. The merits of "culture" as an interpretive construct are weighed in *The Idea of Culture in the Social Sciences,* ed. Louis Schneider and Charles Bonjean (Cambridge, Eng.: Cambridge Univ. Press, 1973).

[5]Even so eminent an exponent of functional analysis as Robert K. Merton has warned: "one cannot assume full integration of all societies. . . . We must be prepared to find a range of degrees of integration." See his *Social Theory and Social Structure* (Glencoe: Free Press, rev. ed., 1957), p. 36.

(willingness to investigate relationships even across conventional disci-
plinary boundaries) and ontological holism (the assumption that all aspects
of human life in a time and place form a synthesis). The first he commends;
the second he justly finds unwarranted.[6]

One problem with ontological holism is that it leaves no room for cultural
pluralism. This introductory essay was deliberately named "Victorian Culture in America," and not "The Culture of Victorian America." The latter title would have implied that there was only one culture in the United
States during the period between 1837 and 1901. In fact, of course, there
were a number of cultures and subcultures—some aboriginal Amerind,
some transplanted from the Old World and adapted to the New. As they
came into contact with each other they overlapped, and many a person
came under the influence of several. But there was one of these cultures that
exercised a kind of hegemony during the period of our focus, particularly
over the printed word, and this was American Victorianism.[7] I see no way
we can compile definitive statistics from this time as to what percentage of
the American people in, say, 1875 were participants in Victorian culture—
to some extent because that participation would be a matter of degree. Even
so, there seems sufficient justification for taking the dominance of Victorian
culture during this period as a basis for discussion.[8]

The Victorian age, on both sides of the Atlantic, was a time when people
were particularly self-conscious about their culture. Raymond Williams has
shown how ". . . the idea of culture, and the word itself in its general
modern uses, came into English thinking in the period which we commonly
describe as that of the Industrial Revolution."[9] (The use of "culture" as a
term in anthropology dates from 1848). The new awareness of culture is
understandable in an era of rapid change, when everything from art forms
to criminal law was being rethought, and habits of long standing came
under critical examination. It is this process of rethinking, this heightened
consciousness of consciousness itself, which lends justification to G. M.
Young's grand generalization: "Victorian history is before all things a history of opinion."[10] The re-evaluation of received opinion had of course been

[6]Cecil Tate, *The Search for a Method in American Studies* (Minneapolis: Univ. of Minnesota Press, 1973), p. 130.

[7]On the concept of cultural hegemony, see Eugene Genovese, *In Red and Black: Marxian
Explorations in Southern and Afro-American History* (New York: Pantheon Books, 1971), pp.
406–10.

[8]Steven Marcus, whose highly perceptive study of English pornography, *The Other Victorians* (New York: Basic Books, 1966), has done so much to call attention to nineteenth-
century counterculture, still affirms the "official" status of the canons his subjects defied—
indeed, their defiance presupposed the official culture. See esp. his pp. 1–33, 263, and 282–86.

[9]Raymond Williams, *Culture and Society* (London: Chatto & Windus, 1958), p. vii.

[10]G. M. Young, *Victorian England: Portrait of an Age*, 2d. ed. (London: Oxford Univ. Press,
1953), p. vi.

pioneered by the thinkers of the Enlightenment, who had also been innovative and programmatic. In the nineteenth century, however, the concept of public opinion had to be redefined in the Western world to take account of new means of communication and great increase in literacy. The Victorians' concern over culture was related to their concern over the emergence of mass society. An interest in Victorian culture, then, is something we share with the Victorians themselves.

Closely related to the increased sensitivity to culture was an intense preoccupation with national identity during the nineteenth century. Germany, where concern with *Kultur* reached its greatest sophistication, was forging its political nationality; the United States vindicated its national unity through bloody war. Certainly nationalism was a typical feature of American Victorianism—though many American Victorians were quite capable of criticizing their country. Nineteenth-century nationalism and cultural self-definition were in turn related to concern over economic growth and its consequences. We witness a somewhat analogous constellation of concerns in our own lifetime in the struggles for political independence, economic development, and cultural identification by the newer nations. Sometimes, especially in emerging nations, concern with culture becomes so explicit, integrated, and programmatic that the word "ideology" becomes appropriate.[11] Whether American Victorian culture was tightly organized enough to warrant terming it an ideology seems problematical.[12]

Central to the Victorian era in the Western world was modernization. We think of modernization primarily in terms of the economic and social realms, where we associate it with industrialization and urbanization. But in the course of these important transitions the cultural system is transformed as well; as E. P. Thompson puts it, "There is no such thing as economic growth which is not, at the same time, growth or change of a culture."[13] Indeed, if the initiative for modernization is located in scientific or technological change, its causes would lie within the cultural system. Thus, C. E. Black defines "modernization" as ". . . the process by which historically evolved institutions are adapted to the rapidly changing functions that reflect the unprecedented increase in man's knowledge, permitting control over his environment."[14] More satisfactory to most historians in the

[11]See Clifford Geertz, "Ideology as a Cultural System," in *Ideology and Discontent,* ed. David Apter (New York: Free Press, 1964), pp. 47–76.

[12]John Higham discusses nineteenth-century American national culture in "Hanging Together: Divergent Unities in American History," *Journal of American History,* 61 (June 1974), 5–28. He is willing to call it an "ideology," largely because it was so self-conscious, yet also grants it was "a large, loose faith."

[13]E. P. Thompson, "Time, Work-Discipline, and Industrial Capitalism," *Past and Present,* 38 (Dec. 1967), 97.

[14]C. E. Black, *The Dynamics of Modernization* (New York: Harper and Row, 1966), p. 7.

present state of our understanding would be a multivariant approach to modernization, stressing causal interconnections among economic resources, social structure, and cultural values, as well as knowledge of specific skills.[15]

Victorianism may be thought of as that culture which characterized the climactic era of modernization for the English-speakers. Modernization in Britain and the United States long antedated the accession of Victoria, of course. Among the English it was an extraordinarily protracted development, partly because they were the first people to undergo its industrial stages. The late eighteenth century witnessed one of a succession of industrial revolutions in Britain and a simultaneous political revolution in her colonies. In the seventeenth century, the Puritans had manifested many qualities that have been convincingly associated with incipient modernization. A case has also been made for the sixteenth-century "Tudor revolution," even further back in time, as the starting point of modernization. The significance of the Victorian era, then, lies not in its encompassing the whole of modernization but in being its exponential culmination.[16]

We have observed that not everyone who lived in the United States, even during the height of American Victorianism, was a Victorian. Among the many people with other cultural identities were American Indians, recent arrivals from the peasant societies of Europe and Asia, and the Spanish-speaking inhabitants of lands taken from Mexico. The extent to which Afro-American slaves came to share in American Victorian culture has been the subject of long controversy, but an impressive recent assessment concludes that they shaped a distinctive Afro-American culture by a creative synthesis of European and African forms.[17] It is important to remember that working-class native whites as well sometimes preserved cultural distinctiveness.[18] There were also intellectuals who were alienated: Walt Whitman, Herman Melville, and Edgar Allan Poe (to choose famous examples) all dissented from the norms of Victorianism sufficiently to be considered rebels rather than participants. Other intellectuals, like John Lothrop Motley and James Russell Lowell, were intensely Victorian.

[15]Today Marxian historians seem more willing than before to acknowledge the role of non-economic factors, and non-Marxians more willing to acknowledge the economic ones.

[16]On different phases of the long modernization of England, see Harold Perkin, *The Origins of Modern English Society, 1780–1880* (London: Routledge and Kegan Paul, 1969); David Little, *Religion, Order, and Law: A Study in Pre-Revolutionary England* (New York: Harper and Row, 1969); and G. R. Elton, *The Tudor Revolution in Government* (Cambridge, Eng.: Cambridge Univ. Press, 1953). The concept is applied to the United States in Richard D. Brown, "Modernization and the Modern Personality in Early America," *Journal of Interdisciplinary History,* 2 (Winter 1972), 201–228.

[17]Eugene D. Genovese, *Roll, Jordan, Roll: The World the Slaves Made* (New York: Pantheon, 1974).

[18]See, e.g., Bruce Laurie, "Life Styles of Philadelphia Artisans, 1820–1850," *Labor History* 15 (Summer 1974), 337–366.

There are various ways of trying to describe the boundaries of American Victorian culture. A convenient starting place is the characterization of it as Anglo-Saxon and Protestant. "Anglo-Saxon" does not do justice to the importance of the Scottish, Welsh, and Scots-Irish contributions to American Victorian culture (the Scottish being in some ways more important than the English), so the term "British-American" is preferable.[19] One must add that British-American Victorianism came under increasing German influence in the course of the nineteenth century, partly via German-American immigrants, partly through deliberate imitation of German models, especially in education and "high" culture.[20]

The description of Victorianism as essentially Protestant is useful in many respects. The fact that Samuel F. B. Morse was the son of the militant Calvinist leader Jedidiah Morse (and continued his father's fervent American nationalism) typifies a relationship between American Victorianism and evangelical Protestantism. The Victorian era was ushered in during the 1830s by what was probably the greatest evangelical revival in American history. During the twentieth century, the crumbling of Victorian culture has been associated with the failure of evangelical Protestantism to sustain its "culture-shaping power."[21] Yet, in the nineteenth century, Victorian culture was shaped at least as much by liberal Protestants, who had moved beyond their strict Reformation heritage, as by orthodox evangelicals. In such cases, evangelical Protestantism was a spiritual grandparent, rather than a parent, to the Victorian outlook.[22] Victorian culture also extended beyond the limits of the Protestant denominations: many Catholics and Jews manifested aspects of Victorianism, and intellectuals like William Graham Sumner did not abandon their Victorian cultural baggage overnight when they gave up their Protestant religion.

Victorian culture had a class derivation, as well as an ethno-religious one. It was bourgeois in origin, and the era of its flourishing coincides with that of the predominance of the bourgeoisie in Western civilization. The class within which Victorian culture took shape was largely a product of the industrial revolution—indeed, in some ways it was not much older than the industrial proletariat. Asa Briggs observes: "Two classes were in the process of formation in England in the late eighteenth and early nineteenth

[19]For one example of the importance of Scottish cultural inheritance, see Douglas Sloan, *The Scottish Enlightenment and the American College Ideal* (New York: Columbia Teachers College Press, 1971). In 1954 the editors of the *William and Mary Quarterly* devoted a special issue to the Scottish-American connection.

[20]See Henry Pochman, *German Culture in America* (Madison: Univ. of Wisconsin Press, 1957).

[21]Sydney Ahlstrom, *A Religious History of the American People* (New Haven: Yale Univ. Press, 1972), p. 8.

[22]On the relationship between liberal Protestantism and American Victorian culture, see Daniel Walker Howe, *The Unitarian Conscience* (Cambridge: Harvard Univ. Press, 1970).

centuries, and the concept of a 'middle class' . . . came first [before the working class]."[23] In the United States, a comparable bourgeoisie had emerged by the 1830s, generally different in composition from the merchant class of the preindustrial colonial era and dwarfing it in size.[24] There was less class-consciousness in America than in Britain; yet in both countries, a bourgeoisie and a proletariat were growing up along with the cities. Out of the greatly expanded context of urban life came a transformed social system, new cultural forms, a new material environment.[25] The cultural history of Victorianism is related to the social history of the new urban middle class: industrial as well as commercial, cosmopolitan in outlook, increasingly self-assertive, expressing its collective pride in literary and philanthropic organizations and in municipal improvement.[26]

Many patterns of Victorian culture (steady work, punctuality, compulsive behavior in general) were of direct practical utility to capitalist employers, and they were active agents in propagating them. Older artisan and peasant work habits often were suppressed through the efforts of the new industrialists.[27] But to the extent that such efforts were successful, working-class people were brought within the ambience of Victorian culture. A culture can reach out beyond the social group with which it originates and become a vital element in the consciousness of others (cf. the impact of Spanish culture on so many New World peoples). American Victorianism, then, had a life beyond the middle class, just as it had a life beyond British-Americans and Protestants.

Victorian culture patterns sometimes complemented the aspirations of the proletariat: "nineteenth-century sabbatarianism," Brian Harrison points out, "flourished on a genuine coincidence of interest between evangelicals and working men afraid of being exploited." Thus, conflict between

[23]For the impact of industrialization on British social structure, see Perkin, *op. cit.*, and E. P. Thompson, *The Making of the English Working Class* (London: Gollancz, 1963). The quotation of Asa Briggs is from his review of Thompson's book in *Labor History*, 6 (Winter 1965), 86.

[24]Edward Pessen's investigations of the upper reaches of this bourgeoisie have been collected in his *Riches, Class, and Power Before the Civil War* (Lexington, Mass.: D. C. Heath, 1973).

[25]Considerable attention is now being paid to urban history, as one can see from Leo F. Schnore, ed., *The New Urban History: Quantitative Explorations* (Princeton: Princeton University Press, 1975). However, as yet there is no overview of nineteenth-century American city life comparable to the two-volume compendium on Britain, *The Victorian City*, ed. H. J. Dyos and Michael Wolff (London: Routledge and Kegan Paul, 1973).

[26]See, e.g., Ronald Story, "Class and Culture in Boston: The Athenaeum, 1807–1860," *American Quarterly*, 27 (May 1975), 178–99. The English side of this process was illuminated for me by R. K. Webb, "The Provincial Assault, 1760–1860," a talk delivered at UCLA, February 12, 1975.

[27]On Britain, see Thompson, "Time, Work-Discipline, and Industrial Capitalism"; for the American side of the story, Herbert G. Gutman, "Work, Culture, and Society in Industrializing America," *American Historical Review*, 78 (June 1973), 531–88. These are two of the most rewarding essays on Victorian culture to appear in recent years.

Victorianism and other cultures did not necessarily coincide with conflict between classes.[28] Conversions to Victorianism were not invariably involuntary. Internalizing Victorian cultural values and techniques could bring tangible rewards, such as upward social mobility, and intangible ones as well, such as participation in a larger cultural matrix. Sometimes people retained the ability to appreciate and perpetuate their original cultural heritage as well as their new one. The millions who acquired Victorian culture, in whole or in part, were not merely passive. Many of them sought Victorian culture and adopted it eagerly, and their decision seems entitled to respect.[29] As the experiences of such people came within it, American Victorian culture was immeasurably enriched.

Alongside the new urban society there persisted a rural and small-town society more reminiscent of colonial times, within which one could find elements of the premodern folk culture of Elizabethan England and other Old World communities. As time passed, however, this society became ever more absorbed into the network of railways, print, and telegraphy which brought cosmopolitan Victorian culture to the countryside, permeating it with the values of modernization.[30] The rural society was expanding too, with the westward march of the frontier of white settlement. The continuing rural society was important not only for the people still living within it, but also as a source of many of the values the new urban bourgeoisie cherished. The cultural conservatism of the countryside counterbalanced the innovations of the growing cities in Victorian America, sometimes—as in the Jacksonian and Populist movements—actually rebelling against it.[31] The secret of the great strength of the Republican Party during the second half of the nineteenth century lay to a large extent in its ability to harmonize the rural and urban constituencies of American Victorian culture in its appeal to the values of modernization.[32]

If the social base of American Victorianism was broader than the urban middle class, the origins of most of its spokesmen were narrower. For the most active and articulate propagators of American Victorian culture came

[28]Brian Harrison, "Religion and Recreation in Nineteenth-Century England," *Past and Present*, 38 (Dec. 1967), 98–125; quotation from p. 105.

[29]For examples of working-class people adopting Victorian values for purposes of their own, see Paul Faler, "Cultural Aspects of the Industrial Revolution," *Labor History*, 15 (Summer 1974), 367–94.

[30]On the beginning of this process, see Richard D. Brown, "The Emergence of Urban Society in Rural Massachusetts," *Journal of American History*, 61 (June 1974), 29–51.

[31]The cultural conservatism of Jacksonianism and Populism has been described in Marvin Meyers, *The Jacksonian Persuasion* (Stanford: Stanford Univ. Press, 1957); and Richard Hofstadter, *The Age of Reform* (New York: Knopf, 1955), pp. 3–130. (Both movements had other dimensions as well, and economic issues were probably the major cause of their appearance.)

[32]Eric Foner's fine study *Free Soil, Free Labor, Free Men* (New York: Oxford Univ. Press, 1970) locates the young party in its cultural context.

from an identifiable segment within the bourgeoisie. This was a group of mostly Northern, mostly middle-income, mostly Whig-Republican, literary men and women whom Stow Persons has called "the American gentry."[33] These people were trying, very self-consciously, to humanize the emergent industrial-capitalist order by infusing it with a measure of social responsibility, strict personal morality, and respect for cultural standards. They thought of themselves as preserving certain patrician values while democratizing their application. They wanted to make the age-old concept of gentility an achieved, rather than an ascribed, status; they hoped to accomplish this through a massive educational and propaganda effort. Notwithstanding the name "gentry," this American social group had less in common with traditional European landed gentry than with the urban intellectual elite, mainly of Dissenting antecedents, that was emerging in Victorian Britain.[34] For all their professed devotion to tradition, many of the American gentry-intellectuals were upwardly mobile; for all their efforts at preservation, they were even more important as innovators than as conservators. Their British counterparts were more successful in establishing identity and power, but the American Victorian gentry nevertheless won a wide audience and no small number of achievements. The American group took shape in the antebellum period, out of the matrix of evangelical reform and the Protestant educational system. During the second half of the nineteenth century the gentry-intellectuals became gradually more secularized in America, as in Britain, and their attention shifted away from the meetinghouse and toward such institutions as the universities, private secondary schools, and the civil service.[35] In some cities, most notably Boston, the American gentry overlapped to a large extent with the wealthy capitalist class, forming a single social entity; elsewhere they were distinct, and the two groups were often critical of each other.

The difficulty entailed in identifying American Victorianism neatly with particular social groups simply underscores the importance of remembering that "culture" is different from "society." American Victo-

[33]Stow Persons, *The Decline of American Gentility* (New York: Columbia Univ. Press, 1973). See also John Tomsich, *A Genteel Endeavor: American Culture and Politics in the Gilded Age* (Stanford: Stanford Univ. Press, 1971), and R. Gordon Kelly, "Literature and the Historian," *American Quarterly,* 26 (May 1974), 141–59.

[34]See Noel Annan, "The Intellectual Aristocracy," in *Studies in Social History: A Tribute to G. M. Trevelyan,* ed. J. H. Plumb (London: Longmans, Green, 1955), pp. 251–87; and R. K. Webb, *Harriet Martineau: A Radical Victorian* (New York: Columbia Univ. Press, 1960), esp. chaps. 2 and 12.

[35]The innovative quality of the antebellum reformers is emphasized in Lois Banner, "Religious Benevolence as Social Control: A Critique of an Interpretation," *Journal of American History,* 60 (June 1973), 34–41. For new views of the postbellum gentry, see James McLachlan, *American Boarding Schools* (New York: Scribner's, 1970); and Hugh Hawkins, *Between Harvard and America: The Educational Leadership of Charles W. Eliot* (New York: Oxford Univ. Press, 1972).

rianism was not the exclusive attribute of any social group or groups within the United States; it was a set of cultural motifs. Rebellion against Victorian society did not make one a rebel against Victorian culture: many who protested vigorously against Victorian society—including abolitionists, feminists, and socialists—did şo in the name of important Victorian cultural values. "Culture" is necessarily an abstraction, and the "American Victorian" an ideal type. Living people shared the culture to a greater or lesser extent, but probably no one was ever the prototypical American Victorian.[36]

Within American Victorianism, particular cultural motifs were continually waxing and waning in importance; they reached their apexes of influence at different times. Perhaps there was a temporary balance among them in the mid-Victorian generation between 1850 and 1870, which has been called "the age of equipoise" in England. This would be an infelicitous term to apply to the era of secession and Civil War in this country, but the implication of its being a pivotal moment is, I think, useful. After this turning point, the Victorians became less religious, less optimistic, more concerned than ever to embody their cultural values in institutions.[37]

Some divisions that we take for granted within our own cultural system did not yet fully exist in America during the Victorian age. One of these is the dichotomy between "mass" and "high" culture. It was 1915 when Van Wyck Brooks complained that American culture was bifurcated into "low-brow" and "highbrow." Victorian authors with large readership like Longfellow, Horace Bushnell, and Harriet Beecher Stowe, however, had defied this classification, as had performers like Edwin Booth and the European visitor Jenny Lind. Nor did only a few great individuals transcend the categories; many long-since obscure writers like Lydia Sigourney and William Ware did too.[38] A historian of Victorian Britain has written: "I have no doubt but that there was a higher proportion of the population who had read and were prepared to discuss the novels of Dickens and the poems

---

[36]William G. McLoughlin makes out a strong case for Henry Ward Beecher, though at most Beecher could illustrate one version of Victorianism. See *The Meaning of Henry Ward Beecher: An Essay on the Shifting Values of Mid-Victorian America* (New York: Knopf, 1970).

[37]W. L. Burn has written *The Age of Equipoise: A Study of the Mid-Victorian Generation* (New York: W. W. Norton, 1964). American historians have also noted, as Burn does, that later Victorians became "more anxious to improve the institutional framework of society because [they were] more doubtful of the capacity of men to improve themselves" (p. 331). See George Fredrickson, *The Inner Civil War* (New York: Harper and Row, 1965), and John Higham, *From Boundlessness to Consolidation* (Ann Arbor: Univ. of Michigan Press, 1969).

[38]Van Wyck Brooks, *America's Coming of Age* (New York: B. W. Heubsch, 1915), esp. pp. 9–19. Yet Carl Bode's *Anatomy of American Popular Culture, 1840–1861* (Carbondale: Univ. of Southern Illinois Press, 1959), justly includes writers like Washington Irving and William H. Prescott, whom we might be tempted to term "high," along with Lydia Sigourney and Felicia Hemans, for all were in fact popular in their day.

of Tennyson than could be found to discuss the works of any particular
novelist or poet today."[39] Substitute Longfellow for Tennyson and the same
could be said of the Victorian United States. Lawyers and politicians typically strove to appear not only folksy but also erudite. Even an embittered
intellectual like Mark Twain addressed a popular audience. A distinctive
"mass" culture emerged gradually and against the opposition of the gentry;
one of its earliest forms was the minstrel show.[40] That which we would
regard as "high" culture was characteristically undifferentiated in the Victorian world; the specialized "expert" had not yet become prominent.
College professors taught what seems to us a bewildering variety of subjects; ladies and gentlemen of letters felt free to pontificate on all topics.
Only recently—mainly in the twentieth century—did scholarship and some
of the arts become so recondite and specialized, so consciously exclusive, as
to be inaccessible to all but a handful of initiates. When this happened, it
was a symptom of the disintegration of Victorian culture.

In discussing American Victorianism as a unity, however, we must never
lose sight of its multiplicity. Diversity and contradiction existed within
American Victorianism, as well as between it and its rival cultures. There
were different versions of American Victorianism, and they might be
considered subcultures of it. Different national origins played a continuing
role in distinguishing subcultures, sometimes keeping apart even groups
with a close affinity like the German-American Wesleyan denominations
and the British-American Methodists. An enumeration of important
subcultures within British-American Victorianism would have to include
the Yankee "Presbygationalists" whose intellectual capital was New
Haven, the Old School Calvinists (mostly Scots-Irish) whose intellectual
capital was Princeton, the Unitarians whose intellectual capital was Boston-
Cambridge (few in number but important in their literary-cultural impact);
the Methodists with a less well defined intellectual structure; and the Bap-
tists, fervent but bitterly divided among themselves.[41] Rivalries among
these subcultures were strong and help account for the proliferation of
colleges in the West. Yale and Princeton were particularly active "academic
imperialists," helping to found other colleges across the continent in an

[39] Burn, *Age of Equipoise*, p. 7.

[40] On the minstrel show, see Robert Toll, *Blacking Up* (New York: Oxford University Press,
1974); and Alexander Saxton, "Blackface Minstrelsy and Jacksonian Ideology," *American
Quarterly*, 27 (May 1975), 3–28.

[41] "Presbygational" was a nickname contemporaries coined by conflating "Presbyterian"
with "Congregational." Two excellent studies of subcultural conflicts among Protestants by
Bertram Wyatt-Brown are: "The Antimission Movement in the Jacksonian South," *Journal of
Southern History*, 36 (Nov. 1970), 501–529; and "Sabbatarian Politics and the Rise of the
Second Party System," *Journal of American History*, 58 (Sept. 1971), 316–41.

effort to propagate their ideals.[42] Before the end of the Victorian era, a blurring of these British-American subcultures was apparent, partly because denominational lines within Protestantism became less important, partly because New York City overcame all the older subcultural centers to establish itself as the intellectual capital of the United States.

Subcultures of American Victorianism sometimes acquired geographical loci. The pattern of Yankee settlement from New England through upstate New York, across the Great Lakes region to Iowa and Oregòn, created one such subcultural zone. Organized efforts at cultural dissemination like the Society for the Promotion of Collegiate and Theological Education at the West (the SPCTEW) helped shape this zone. Within it could be found certain types of architecture, local government, town planning, and repeated place names, as well as its typical religious and educational institutions. The zone was the homeland of countless "isms" from Sabbatarianism to antislavery and temperance.[43] But the Yankee "Presbygational" subculture did not enjoy undisputed sway even within its zone. Recent studies have alerted us to ways in which the electoral politics of the region manifested continued conflicts among a variety of rival ethno-religious groups.[44]

The most obvious geographical subculture of American Victorianism was the South. There a precapitalist mode of labor exploitation, chattel slavery, existed along with a large degree of capitalist "rationalization" of production and a general integration of the section into the world capitalist economy.[45] Until its "peculiar institution" came to be perceived as such a threat to the rest of the American nation that it had to be extirpated during the Civil War, the South developed considerable distinctiveness. The tone of Southern white culture was set by the large owners of land and slaves, the planters. Under their leadership, the South showed indications that it might evolve in the direction of a cultural system qualitatively different from the

---

[42]See John S. Whitehead, "A Steady Hand at the Helm: A Plan and Purpose for the American College, 1828-1870," undergraduate honors thesis, Yale Univ., 1967.

[43]A classic treatment of one portion of this zone is Whitney Cross, *The Burned-Over District* (Ithaca: Cornell Univ. Press, 1950). Richard Lyle Power, "Planting Corn Belt Culture," *Indiana Historical Society Publications*, 17 (1953) 1-196, contains interesting information.

[44]See Lee Benson, *The Concept of Jacksonian Democracy: New York as a Test Case* (Princeton: Princeton Univ. Press, 1961); Ronald P. Formisano, *The Birth of Mass Political Parties: Michigan, 1827-1861* (Princeton: Princeton Univ. Press, 1971); Michael F. Holt, *Forging a Majority: The Formation of the Republican Party in Pittsburgh, 1848-1860* (New Haven: Yale Univ. Press, 1969); and Paul Kleppner, *The Cross of Culture: A Social Analysis of Midwestern Politics, 1850-1900* (New York: Basic Books, 1970).

[45]The pre-capitalist aspects are emphasized in Eugene Genovese, *The Political Economy of Slavery* (New York: Pantheon, 1965); the capitalist aspects in Julia Floyd Smith, *Slavery and Plantation Growth in Antebellum Florida* (Gainesville, Fla.: Univ. of Florida Press, 1973); and Robert Fogel and Stanley Engerman, *Time on the Cross: The Economics of American Negro Slavery* (Boston: Little, Brown, 1974).

Victorianism of the North, based as that was upon urbanization rather than plantation life.[46]

However, the cultural ideals of the Southern planter class had much in common with those of Victorians in the Northern states. In the first place, they shared a predominantly British-American Protestant heritage. The Calvinistic world view, didactic rhetoric, and intense self-righteousness we associate with nineteenth-century Yankees were also not uncommon among the Southern planter class.[47] Both the Southern plar.ter gentry and the Northern bourgeois gentry hoped to preserve the good manners and patrician life style they associated with European tradition; both idealized women, at least within their own group. When the comparison is made between Southern planters and Northern capitalists, rather than Northern gentry, similarities still appear. Both these groups liked to think they were benefitting their workers, civilizing them. In reality, both groups were *nouveaux*.[48] The Confederacy lost its bid for national independence, and with that the possibility of cultural autonomy and the perpetuation of slavery. George Fitzhugh, former prophet of a "sociology for the South" based on slavery, then urged his section to industrialize.[49] The plantation became a cherished memory, lovingly embroidered, rather than an active agency promoting cultural differentiation. As a result the white South remained within the broad outlines of Victorianism rather than becoming an altogether separate culture. In the twentieth century, the Southern subculture of Victorianism has proved quite durable.[50]

The Victorian cultural community constituted an international reference group in the nineteenth-century world. If this reference group, as we have seen, was not precisely coterminous with social entities defined in terms of citizenship, class, religion, ancestry, or urban residence, then what did define it? One way to answer this question is to view Victorianism as a communications system. The communications system of Victorianism was

[46]Two perceptive explorations into Southern distinctiveness are C. Vann Woodward, "The Southern Ethic in a Puritan World," in his *American Counterpoint* (Boston: Little, Brown, 1971), pp. 13–46; and Donald G. Mathews, "Religion in the Old South: Speculations on Methodology," *South Atlantic Quarterly*, 73 (Winter 1974), 34–52.

[47]See the remarkable collection of private correspondence edited by Robert Manson Myers, *The Children of Pride* (New Haven: Yale Univ. Press, 1972).

[48]Even Genovese judiciously qualifies his claims for the distinctiveness of planter culture by calling it quasi-aristocratic rather than aristocratic, and by emphasizing its "pretentions and possibilities" for further divergence from bourgeois Victorianism rather than the extent to which this potential was actualized. *Political Economy of Slavery*, pp. 15 et passim. Further qualifications appear in his *The World the Slaveholders Made* (New York: Pantheon, 1969).

[49]See Kenneth Stampp, "Interpreting the Slaveholders' World," *Agricultural History*, 44 (October 1970), 407–12.

[50]See George B. Tindall, "Beyond the Mainstream: The Ethnic Southerners," *Journal of Southern History*, 40 (February 1974), 3–18.

based on the English language and the media of print and (in due course) the telegraph and telephone. Knowledge of English put one in potential contact with a particular cultural heritage, including law, religion, and science, and enabled one to deal with established political institutions in the United States. Literacy and exposure to instant long-distance communication magnified the impact language could have.[51] Since the electronic media did not achieve their major impact until the twentieth century, the nineteenth was characteristically an age of print. In 1811 the steam-powered printing press was invented. Its impact was enhanced by the economical manufacture of paper from wood pulp and improvements in the transportation system facilitating dissemination of printed materials. Magazines and novels became important vehicles for communication; newspapers and tracts proliferated. As more people (especially women and the working classes) received more schooling in the course of the nineteenth century, they came more effectively within this Victorian communications system. It was fitting that Victorian opinion leaders should place such a premium upon persuasion rather than strong government as a means of social control; they possessed greater access to the opinions of multitudes than had ever been possible before.[52]

To relate Victorian culture to a reference group is to call attention to its value system. Besides its communication system, Victorian culture was defined by this value system. Victorian values, like Victorian culture as a whole, represented a combination of premodern modes of thought (patriarchalism, English common law) with attitudes specifically linked to the modernization process. The former were the cultural inheritance of the English-speakers, the latter the adaptations made in that culture during a specific historical epoch. Victorian ideals associated with modernization taught people to work hard, to postpone gratification, to repress themselves sexually, to "improve" themselves, to be sober, conscientious, even compulsive. These values were not newly discovered at the accession of Victoria, but they were commanding wider and more zealous support than ever be-

---

[51]Conversely, non-Victorian cultures in America attached importance to the preservation of languages other than English. See Joshua Fishman et al., *Language Loyalty in the United States: The Maintenance and Perpetuation of Non-English Mother Tongues by American Ethnic and Religious Groups* (The Hague: Mouton and Co., 1966). This volume treats only European languages and thus leaves out such linguistic minorities as the Chinese-Americans and the Navajo.

[52]The relationship of media of communication to society and culture is brilliantly and provocatively explored in Walter J. Ong, *Rhetoric, Romance, and Technology: Studies in the Interaction of Expression and Culture* (Ithaca: Cornell Univ. Press, 1971). The importance of "the printing revolution" upon the antislavery movement in the 1830s is noted in Leonard Richards, *"Gentlemen of Property and Standing": Anti-Abolition Mobs in Jacksonian America* (New York: Oxford Univ. Press, 1970), pp. 71–73.

fore, and for the rest of the century they exerted unprecedented influence on the shaping of British and American society.[53]

A well known Victorian value was competitiveness, an attitude reflecting the excitement and sense of power with which they faced the world. We usually think of this value in connection with the Victorian economic system, but it manifested itself in many other ways as well. Party politics finally achieved acceptance at the beginning of the Victorian period; it was conceptualized as a political competition by a culture that endorsed competition. American Victorians gloried in the pattern of denominationalism— unique to the United States—that encouraged religious competition. The Victorians' educational practices frequently relied on "emulation," a word they always used to mean desire to excel in rivalry, never in its twentieth-century sense of imitation.[54] Even more than inter-personal competition, however, the Victorians valued what has been called "intra-personal competition," stressing mastery over the "bad passions" within oneself.[55]

Just as they valued rational order in the individual, the Victorians valued it in society at large. Within this order, they hoped, competition might be structured and contained. Avid exponents of order in the Victorian world included some of the capitalist entrepreneurs and some of the socialist utopians (the early Victorian Scotsman Robert Owen was both). The institutional creations of the Victorians—economic, educational, philanthropic, political—were as remarkable as their technological creations. Most of all, however, the Victorians pursued order in their personal lives. Here they could practice humanistic self-cultivation, Protestant self-denial, and/or bourgeois self-control, all in the name of regulated self-improvement. Order in the individual and order in society were, of course, mutually reinforcing in Victorian civilization.[56]

The intellectual origins of the Victorians' high valuation on rational order can be traced to the Enlightenment and the Newtonian cosmology that went with it. Victorians pursued order not only in society and the individual but also in the universe around them: not only through municipal police departments and self-imposed schedules but also through the development of

---

[53]Ruth Miller Elson, *Guardians of Tradition: American Schoolbooks in the Nineteenth Century* (Lincoln: Univ. of Nebraska Press, 1964), is a convenient guide to many Victorian values. The author points out that the schoolbooks depict life as troubled and complex, but values as clear (p. 339). Cf. J[ohn]. F. C. Harrison, *The Early Victorians* (London: Weidenfeld and Nicholson, 1971), pp. 134–145, on Britain.

[54]The OED does not mention the latter definition of "emulation." Its entries for words beginning with the letter "E" were prepared between 1888 and 1893.

[55]Michael Katz, *The Irony of Early School Reform* (Cambridge: Harvard University Press, 1968), p. 56.

[56]See Trygvie Tholfsen, "The Intellectual Origins of Mid-Victorian Stability," *Political Science Quarterly*, 86 (March 1971), 57–91.

classical physics.[57] Their concentration on rational order explains why rebellion against Victorian culture so often took the form of anti-rational,
order-defying romanticism. The greatest scientific discovery of *dis*order to
occur during the nineteenth century, Darwin's theory of evolution, proved
profoundly subversive. Despite all efforts to reconcile it with optimism and
harmony, it ultimately played an important role in the destruction of the
Victorian world view. The end of the Victorian era of belief in objective
order is appropriately marked by the publication of Einstein's theory of
relativity in 1905.

To some extent the Victorian preoccupation with order probably reflected a need for psychological stability amidst the rapid changes occurring
during the nineteenth century. One must be cautious about thinking of this
impulse toward order as simply "conservative," however. Orderliness is not
the same thing as permanence or immobility. Many manifestations of the
Victorian desire for order were innovations at the time: prohibition of al-
cohol and the founding of penitentiaries, for example. Even Victorian
prudery was an innovation.[58]

A high valuation on time was also central to Victorianism. Though we
think of them as thrifty, Victorians in the United States were more
remarkable for trying to save time than for conserving material resources:
the civilization they built destroyed forests and bison, topsoil and whales.
More and more Victorians came to engage in conspicuous consumption as
the nineteenth century wore on, despite reproaches from the gentry-
intellectuals. Because labor was often expensive and raw material cheap, the
American environment accentuated an emphasis on time-thrift and time-
accounting rather than husbanding materials. The adoption of standard
time zones in the United States in 1883, undertaken at the initiative of the
railroads, was a landmark of Victorian modernization and standardization.
The American Victorians manifested an extreme form of "future-
orientation"; their ambition, their interest in education, their willingness to
reinvest profits, all show their concern with planning ahead and using time
wisely. It is no accident that their great civil war was fought between
American Victorians over rival visions of the future of the country, over the
expansion of slavery into new territories, rather than over the actual
presence of the institution.

[57]See Richard Olson, *Scottish Philosophy and British Physics: A Study in the Foundations
of the Victorian Scientific Style* (Princeton: Princeton Univ. Press, 1975).
[58]See, e.g., David Rothman, *The Discovery of the Asylum* (Boston: Little, Brown, 1971); and
David Pivar, *Purity Crusade: Sexual Morality and Social Control, 1868-1900* (Westport, Ct.:
Greenwood Press, 1973). Pivar calls his purity crusaders "a modernizing elite." The Victorian
pursuit of rational order led eventually to the general institutional bureaucratization which is
the theme of Robert Wiebe, *The Search for Order, 1877-1920* (New York: Hill and Wang,
1967).

The Victorians' chosen methods of social control manifest both the value they placed on rational order and their future-orientation. There had been a long tradition of violence in Anglo-American culture dating back to pre-modern times, and this continued to manifest itself, especially in frontier areas and in dealings with peoples of different ethnic background.[59] But the tendency of Victorian culture was away from sanctioning the use of violence in human relationships, and toward the substitution of persuasion as a means of social control. American Victorian reformers deplored physical violence in such varied contexts as schools, families, ships, plantations, and insane asylums. Of course the American Victorians were still capable of resorting to coercion, as their suppression of labor organizers and Mormon polygamists illustrates. The new kinds of social control they introduced, however, often addressed the mind rather than the body (solitary confinement rather than flogging) and the future rather than the present (hope of "success" rather than higher wages). Through such means the Victorians sought to stimulate the individual's capacity for prudential calculation and moral guilt.

Two classic conceptualizations of the values of modernization Victorians embraced have been offered by Ferdinand Tönnies and Max Weber. Tönnies described a transition from Gemeinschaft to Gesellschaft; Weber a transition from "the Protestant ethic" to "the spirit of capitalism." Since their day our sense of the complexity of these developments (which, to do them justice, Tönnies and Weber recognized too) has deepened. Scholars become ever less willing to oversimplify or romanticize preindustrial societies and ever less willing to glorify our own. Most of us now feel more comfortable speaking of "modernization"—that is, of a process—than of modernity as the end point on an evolutionary scale. Indeed, if the "modern" age is that of the Victorians, we are no longer sure whether we still live in it or in some "post-modern" world whose character is not yet clear. In one respect the effect of Weber's writing was unfortunate: by focusing attention on the earlier phases of modernization during the sixteenth through the eighteenth centuries, he distracted it from the full-blown modernization of the Victorian age.[60] Too often the characteristics of the Victorians have been attributed to the Puritans. But the categories of Tönnies and Weber retain usefulness, particularly if we remember that they were intended as ideal types and that their authors were penetrating critics of the process they

[59]This powerful tradition and its representation in American literature are discussed in Richard Slotkin, *Regeneration Through Violence: The Mythology of the American Frontier* (Middletown: Wesleyan Univ. Press, 1973).

[60]Recent scholarship emphasizes the slow pace of modernization in pre-Revolutionary America. See Kenneth Lockridge, *Literacy in Colonial New England* (New York: W. W. Norton, 1974); and J. E.. Crowley, *This Sheba, Self: The Conceptualization of Economic Life in Eighteenth-Century America* (Baltimore: Johns Hopkins Univ. Press, 1974).

described. More recent social scientists have enhanced our understanding of how much the Victorians had in common with other modernizing peoples.[61] Today socialist as well as capitalist states in pursuit of economic development try to promote time-thrift and industrious habits among their populations.

Victorian culture, as already noted, was a composite: traditional, pre-modern patterns continued to exist alongside new ones and often interacted creatively with them. One powerful aspect of tradition in Victorian America was the Christian religion. Those who crusaded for Victorian reforms in the United States were thinking of not only a new institutional rationality but also, usually, the will of Christ. We are reminded that the nineteenth century was both a time of secularization and a great age of Christian missions.[62] But between the beginning and the end of Victoria's reign one senses—especially among the most sophisticated—a definite weakening of the hold of religious tradition. Such changes and internal anomalies within Victorian culture could give rise to what has been well termed "cultural strain."[63]

Whether or not they were allaying secret doubts and confusions, the Victorians took their values seriously—indeed, their "seriousness" was one of their most distinguishing characteristics, noted by themselves and their contemporaries. Victorian seriousness reflected a sense of moral urgency.[64] Victorian terminology, laden with words like "duty" and "virtue," has a ring of intolerable self-righteousness to our ears; the moral seriousness of the Victorians seems narrow-minded or, alternatively, hypocritical. It is the Victorian reformers who most often bear the brunt of our resentment. Historians need to begin with the recognition that such a self-righteous tone was not peculiar to reformers, being also common among political conservatives and moderates in Victorian America. Self-righteousness was as typical of Daniel Webster, Jefferson Davis, or Grover Cleveland as of Horace Mann or Charles Sumner. It was rooted in the assumption of the objectivity and universality of moral principles, which were conceptualized in much the same fashion as the laws of classical physics. This view of morality was expressed most specifically in the Scottish "common sense" philosophy, synthesizing Protestantism with the Enlightenment, that

[61]On values common to modernizing peoples, see the essays in S. N. Eisenstadt, ed., *The Protestant Ethic and Modernization: A Comparative View* (New York: Basic Books, 1968), esp. part III.

[62]Paul Carter, *The Spiritual Crisis of the Gilded Age* (DeKalb: Northern Illinois Univ. Press, 1971), chap. 1.

[63]See William R. Hutchison, "Cultural Strain and Protestant Liberalism," *American Historical Review*, 76 (April 1971), 386–411.

[64]Walter Houghton, in his superb description of British Victorianism, calls this characteristic "earnestness." *The Victorian Frame of Mind* (New Haven: Yale Univ. Press, 1957), pp. 218–262.

reigned in the English-speaking world until the later nineteenth century.[65] Today it is more common to regard values as human constructs. Much of what we find objectionable in the Victorians, however, may be termed a self-righteousness of style—the forensic, hortatory style of leadership and expression Victorian society accepted. The educational system, with its emphasis on classics, moral philosophy, declamations, and idealized heroes, fostered this style. The dangers of self-righteousness to the human spirit within this cultural ambience did not escape notice at the time, for many Victorians were highly introspective and given to self-reproach. Conscientious Victorians strove to purge vice wherever they recognized it, in others or in themselves. Many charges of their later critics—including that of self-righteousness—were actually anticipated in the Victorians' own self-criticism.[66]

Since the Victorians were so serious about their morality, and so committed to persuasion as a means of propagating it, Victorian culture was profoundly didactic. With their high degree of cultural self-consciousness, the Victorians were well aware that their culture was but one of many. They responded to this diversity with a cultural competitiveness fully worthy of their other modes of competitiveness. They sought converts aggressively in their colonies and in the working classes at home. American Victorians, seeking to bring everyone within their own culture, were not unlike many of their European middle-class contemporaries: British liberals hoped to bridge the gulf between the "two nations of Englishmen" by means of education; German liberals hoped to assimilate the Jews. The Dawes Severalty Act of 1887 represented a major assault on American Indian tribal cultures and an attempt to impose Victorian values upon them. But Victorian didacticism was not directed only at members of other classes and ethnic groups; the Victorians also sought converts among the children in their own families. Quite likely their didactic rhetoric served at times to persuade themselves as well.

Victorian didacticism could take many forms. It can be found in the academic moralizing of Francis Wayland but also in the burning indignation of Theodore Dwight Weld; in Horace Greeley and in Anthony Comstock; in *Godey's Ladies' Book* and in Chautauqua. Didacticism permeated so much of Victorian life and characterized so many Victorian accomplishments that it is impossible to do more here than suggest a few of its manifestations. The nineteenth century was a time of the expansion of education at all

[65]See D. H. Meyer, *The Instructed Conscience: The Shaping of the American National Ethic* (Philadelphia: Univ. of Pennsylvania Press, 1972); and Henry F. May, *The Enlightenment in America* (New York: Oxford Univ. Press, 1976), Part IV: "The Didactic Enlightenment."

[66]See Jerome Buckley, *The Victorian Temper* (Cambridge: Harvard Univ. Press, 1951), chap. 1; Victorian self-righteousness and self-criticism would both repay further study.

levels, public and private, denominational and secular. It witnessed establishment of school systems for whites and blacks in the South and West, the origin of many new types of institutions for professional and vocational training, the opening of higher education to women.[67] The multiplication of schools is typical of modernizing societies, but its consequences in the particular Victorian context were many and diverse. One of the most significant was that the enormous expansion of school teaching opened up important professional opportunities for women.[68]

In addition to the educational system, other public institutions—prisons, poorhouses, insane asylums—also came to profess didactic objectives. The churches too (at least the British-American Protestant ones) became generally more concerned with moral or spiritual uplift and less with theology or ecclesiology. Foreign missions, not one of the more successful aspects of Protestantism in earlier centuries, reached their apex in the nineteenth. Even the South's "peculiar institution" was extolled by its apologists for having didactic aspects. In fact, before its demise, the slave system does seem to have begun to show greater concern for the spiritual and material welfare of those held in bondage (as well as for the maintenance of order) than had been typical in colonial times.[69] What inspired Victorian didacticism—and Victorian self-criticism—was not only moral absolutism but also a faith in redemption. Ignorance and sin could be remedied, given sufficient discipline and will.

Didacticism characterized Victorian expression as well as Victorian institutions. Through the printed media, Victorian writers sought to shape the quality of life for themselves and others. It was a great age of prescriptive writing of all kinds: child-rearing manuals, books on household management, etiquette books, even joke books to tell people how to be funny. It was also an age when poetry and fiction legitimated themselves by the morals they taught. "Art for art's sake" was not a principle widely accepted among American Victorians; literature and the other arts were expected to benefit society by elevating or instructing their audience.[70] Thus didacticism harnessed the Victorian communications system to the Victorian value system. Improvements in the technology of communications came to the

[67]The literature of educational history is voluminous; I shall mention here only the distinguished study of Laurence R. Veysey, *The Emergence of the American University* (Chicago: Univ. of Chicago Press, 1961).

[68]Other consequences of the development of educational institutions in nineteenth-century America are weighed in Daniel Calhoun's fascinating cultural study, *The Intelligence of a People* (Princeton: Princeton Univ. Press, 1973).

[69]Such was the argument persuasively presented by Willie Lee Rose in "The Rise of Slavery as a 'Domestic' Institution," an address delivered at Yale University, April 30, 1973.

[70]For an interesting reinterpretation of one kind of didactic writing popular in the Victorian age, see Richard Weiss, *The American Myth of Success* (New York: Basic Books, 1969), pp. 3–127.

aid of Victorians determined to disseminate their values as widely as possible.

But it was not only the new media that transmitted Victorian values. The age-old practice of oratory enjoyed a kind of Indian summer in the United States during the mid-nineteenth century. Preachers, politicians, lawyers, and travelling lecturers basked in the glory accorded eloquence. After the deaths of John Quincy Adams, Webster, and Clay, however, the second half of the century witnessed a decline in American oratory. It became more identified with the "elocution" of schoolboys than with shaping the national destiny. At the end of the century the oratory of William Jennings Bryan hearkened back to an earlier American culture that had relied more on face-to-face contact.

Victorian didacticism should be distinguished from racism, in spite of the fact that both assume a posture of superiority vis-à-vis others. One is predicated upon a belief in cultural superiority, the other is an unwarranted belief in biological superiority. We are often startled by the prevalence of racial and ethnic stereotypes among even enlightened Victorians, though as historians we should not be. These attitudes represented an amalgam of traditional ethnocentric habits with modern nationalism and racism. They tended to restrict rather than reinforce didacticism, for while Victorian didacticism assumed that everyone would benefit by acquiring Victorian culture, the stereotypes supposed that some people were incapable of doing so, at least beyond an elementary stage. Hence the experience of many people that even after having acquired the appropriate culture they were denied full participation in Victorian society. The Victorians' perception of outsiders tended to be a confused mingling of hostility with didactic paternalism; they looked at someone of another race and saw him, in Kipling's words, "half devil and half child." The conflict between didacticism and racism, between assimilation and rejection of others, turned out to be one of the most tragic contradictions within American Victorian culture.

The intended product of Victorian didacticism was a person who would no longer need reminding of his duties, who would have internalized a powerful sense of obligation and could then safely be left to his own volitions. Such a person has been described by David Riesman as "inner-directed," possessed of a moral gyroscope that would function even amidst the unfamiliar surroundings in which Victorians so often found themselves. A society composed of such persons, the Victorians hoped, could get along with a minimum of government; thus the Victorian political ideal of liberalism was linked to moral seriousness on the private level. The Victorians also expected that the individual self-assertion of such persons, hard working and conscientious, would be the most effective way to promote the general material welfare. The Victorians themselves called the quality they sought to create "character." This was not a set of rote responses but an intangible strength of purpose, combining self-reliance, self-discipline, and responsibility. Victorian educators sought to mold character through the carefully balanced development of various human faculties.[71] To a considerable extent the person of character always remained more of an ideal than a reality: in practice there were always plenty of people—even adults—in need of further exhortation.[72] The ideal was important, however; it explains why such Victorian institutions as the English public school and the American prep school devoted so much attention to character-building discipline.

Highly self-conscious of their culture, Victorians were also highly self-conscious about its transmission. Communication across space, while valuable, was insufficient for their didactic purposes. They were fascinated by the techniques of persuasion and instruction, of self-improvement and the improvement of others. One of the most revealing of Victorian institutions was the normal school, or teacher training college (1839); one of the most revealing of Victorian documents was Horace Bushnell's *Christian Nurture* (1847), sanctifying proper child-rearing practice as a conversion ordinance. Mere rational presentation was not powerful enough as an instrument of cultural transmission and social control. Out of Victorian interest in the arts of persuasion came the cultivation of emotional manipulation. Drawing upon the writings of eighteenth-century rhetoricians, Victorians appealed to the "heart" as well as the "head" in their literature, their pedagogy, their preaching, and their politics. Victorian writers, teachers, ministers, and politicians became expert at influencing others through the invocation of the proper sentiments. In authentic Victorianism (as distinguished from romantic rebelliousness), however, the emotions always remained complementary and subordinate to rational order.

Of course the most important locus for cultural transmission in Victorian society was the home, and the Victorians acknowledged this with their cult of domesticity. The home was conceived as an orderly and secure place where children were indoctrinated with the proper values before being sent forth to make their way in a rapidly-changing world. The American family underwent far-reaching changes in the course of the nineteenth century, and a new group of social historians of the family is currently

[71]A widely-used teacher's manual put it this way: "Education is developing, in due order and proportion, whatever is good and desirable in human nature." John L. Hart, *In the School-Room* (Philadelphia: Eldrige and Brother, 1868), p. 276.

[72]See T. Scott Miyakawa, *Protestants and Pioneers: Individualism and Conformity on the American Frontier* (Chicago: Univ. of Chicago Press, 1964). The discrepancy between didactic ideal and social fact is also noted in Carl Degler, "What Ought to Be and What Was: Women's Sexuality in the Nineteenth Century," *American Historical Review*, 79 (Dec. 1974), 1467–90.

examining these.[73] Apparently, as the home became less a center of economic production with the decline of family farms and handcrafts, it was left free to concentrate more than ever upon the socialization of the children. The emphasis shifted from the home as a place of productive activity to the home as a place of family community. The successful introduction of the Christmas tree and the myth of Santa Claus into an intensely Protestant culture which had previously made a point of not celebrating the Nativity was made possible by, and indeed typified, this new Victorian perspective on home life.

A prominent feature of the Victorian cult of domesticity was the exaltation of motherhood. The high esteem accorded the status of motherhood in Victorian culture was a logical consequence of the importance assigned the mother as an agent of cultural transmission. The mother was an acknowledged guardian of moral, religious, and other cultural values among American Victorians, and the home was her sphere of influence. She was expected to operate to a large extent through emotional conditioning, conceding to her husband superiority in the ultimately more important domain of reason.[74] What was innovative in Victorian culture, however, was not the final supremacy of the father in the family, for that had characterized Western civilization since time out of mind; it was the new importance accorded the mother's position. In the nineteenth century the cult of domesticity played a major part in enhancing the dignity of womanhood. Though it seems somewhat paradoxical to us, Victorian domesticity represented a phase in the modernizing liberation of women from their traditional subjugation.[75] The participation of women in nineteenth-century religious, educational, and reform movements, and after 1869 in electoral politics, was ultimately aided more than inhibited by the recognized role of women as moral preceptors within the framework of Victorian didacticism.

One useful approach to the history of women in the nineteenth century is to study their particular subculture of Victorianism. The innovations in printing and in women's education brought with them the emergence of an enormous new audience of women readers, who were served to a large extent by a new group of women writers. There was a women's communi-

[73]Some of this work is in unpublished dissertations: Mary P. Ryan, "American Society and the Cult of Domesticity, 1830–1860," Univ. of California, Santa Barbara, 1971; Robert Mc-Glone,"Suffer the Children: The Emergence of Modern Middle-Class Family Life, 1820–1870," UCLA, 1971; Kirk Jeffrey, "The Middle-Class American Family in the Urban Context, 1830–1870," Stanford Univ., 1972.

[74]The use of emotional manipulation in Victorian child-rearing is discussed in Calhoun, *op. cit.*, pp. 156–88. See also Peter Slater, "Views of Children and of Child-Rearing During the Early National Period," Diss. Univ. of California, Berkeley, 1970.

[75]The complexities and contradictions of the situation are well delineated in Kathryn Kish Sklar, *Catharine Beecher: A Study in American Domesticity* (New Haven: Yale Univ. Press, 1973).

cation network in middle-class Victorian society.[76] Often this feminine Victorianism operated as complementary, even compensatory, in relation to masculine Victorianism, emphasizing values like security and sentiment. In the hands of women like Harriet Beecher Stowe and Sarah Josepha Hale, these could be powerful appeals. A few women boldly espoused the same ideals as Victorian men. They argued for women's rights on the basis of such Victorian values as individual autonomy, self-development, subordination of sensuality, contractualism (applying it to marriage), and the work ethic. Opting whole-heartedly for modernization against traditionalism, these nineteenth-century femininists were probably the most consistent of all Victorians. They challenged the Victorian social order in the name of important Victorian cultural values.[77]

This essay has defined American Victorianism in cultural terms and argued that Victorian culture must be understood primarily with reference to its values. The value system is presumably central to any culture, but especially so when it is as explicit and propagated with such earnestness as among the Victorians. The Victorians habitually expressed themselves in moral terms, as the Puritans did in religious terms. Having made the effort to recover a feeling for the Puritan categories, historians should now be willing to try to recover a sense of the Victorian ones. If historians who do not believe in the God of Calvin can cope with the professions of the New England Puritans, there can be a comparable effort to understand the Victorians—even by historians who do not believe in "chastity" or "sobriety."

The essays that follow address a number of important issues in the rise and decline of Victorian culture in America. Richard D. Brown leads off with a description of the Victorian era as a time when the long, slow modernization of American society and culture reached a climax. He interprets the ethnic and regional animosities among Americans in the nineteenth century as in part the outcome of differential rates of modernization. The Victorian era was a time of both evangelical activism and secularization, as the next two essays remind us. Gregory H. Singleton shows the contribution antebellum Protestant voluntary organizations made to shaping a modernized society and culture that would later be dominated by giant secular corporations. Yet the America of 1900 was not what the evangelical moralists of the 1830s had wanted, he emphasizes, for the consequences of their activities were as much inadvertent as intentional. D. H. Meyer discusses one of the greatest cultural strains within Victorianism: the crisis of religious faith. He lays bare the strange "mixture of doubt and

[76]On the Victorian women's literary subculture, see two essays by Ann Douglas: "Why Women Wrote," *American Quarterly*, 23 (Spring 1971), 3–24; and "Heaven Our Home," *ibid.*, 26 (Dec. 1974), 296–315.
[77]Ross Paulson, *Women's Suffrage and Prohibition* (Glenview, Ill.: Scott, Foresman, 1973), is a brief but wide-ranging study relating both movements to modernization.

certainty" that characterized the intellectual community of the later nineteenth century.

David D. Hall's essay offers a new perspective on the mid-Victorian group we usually call "mugwumps," locating them within their transatlantic cultural matrix. Instead of viewing them simply as conservatives, he sees them as innovators, secularizers, and modernizers. Geoffrey Blodgett calls for placing the political history of the so-called Gilded Age in a cultural context. He invites us to "climb inside the minds of those strange Victorian Americans and look out at the world through their eyes." Claudia Johnson relates a little-studied example of cultural change in Victorian America: the suppression of prostitution in legitimate theaters. This she takes as illustrating new attitudes toward both morals and art in the Victorian epoch. The impersonal hospital we know today is partly an outgrowth of an austere Victorian philanthrophy, Morris Vogel reminds us. In his description of two medical facilities of the 1870s, we can see the tendency for Victorian didacticism to pass into discipline and a preoccupation with imposing order.

The last two essays address issues relating to the decline in power of American Victorianism. Dee Garrison describes the emergence of a mass culture that did not defer to Victorian canons. She argues that dissatisfaction with Victorian sex roles and sex inhibitions underlay the rise of this "immoral" culture. Stanley Coben tells of the massive assault against Victorian values and assumptions mounted during the 1920s by academics, artists, ethnic separatists, and other cultural rebels. By the end of Coben's story, American Victorianism has lost its cultural hegemony.

The present is an auspicious moment for Victorian studies. The Victorians themselves were so caught up in the excitement of their era and its dramatic changes that they usually glorified it in their scholarship, interpreting previous eras as incomplete stages en route to their own. The result we call "Whig history." Then came a period in the twentieth century when intellectuals were struggling against the restraints of Victorian convention, and consequently debunking was in fashion. Now, it would seem, the time is ripe for a kind of understanding that can go beyond an immediate need to celebrate or derogate, that can take a fresh look at the characteristics and dynamics of American Victorian culture.[78] Only then, when we have imaginatively recreated the world the Victorians experienced, and at the same time put that world into a perspective of our own, will we be in a position to comprehend the true nature of their achievement.

[78]Good recent reassessments include Daniel Horowitz, "Genteel Observers: New England Economic Writers and Industrialization," *New England Quarterly,* 48 (March 1975), 65–83; and Richard Allan Gerber, "The Liberal Republicans of 1872," *Journal of American History,* 62 (June 1975), 40–73. Americanists could take as a model Brian Harrison, *Drink and the Victorians* (London: Faber and Faber, 1971).

# MODERNIZATION: A VICTORIAN CLIMAX

*RICHARD D. BROWN*

THE TERM "MODERNIZATION," RECENTLY IN VOGUE AMONG SOCIAL scientists, is clearly external to Victorian culture. It does not appear in the writings of nineteenth-century Americans. Most often we find it employed in the analysis of contemporary societies where centuries-old social and economic structures are being supplanted by "modern," western ways. The concept of modernization has appealed to social scientists because it transforms historical development into a process, allowing cross-cultural comparisons. Within this framework the diverse experiences of people in Japan, India, Brazil, and Iran achieve some measure of comparability.[1]

The most obvious, visible manifestations of modernization, evident in these four nations and in many others, have been urban and industrial development. Few doubt that industrial cities are modern. More generally, however, modernization is understood as a process in which people turn to new, more productive methods in virtually all economic spheres. Sustaining these changes in economic activity is a value structure emphasizing rationality, specialization, efficiency, cosmopolitanism, and an interest in a future that can be better than the present in material and social terms. Such a value structure, while manifest in the economy, obviously possesses more than purely economic consequences. Politics, the family, the community, indeed society in general, *become* modern as components of this value structure are internalized by a population.

The internalization of these values is the central attribute of people who

---

[1] One basic discussion of the idea by James S. Coleman, Daniel Lerner, and Ronald P. Dore appears in the *International Encyclopedia of the Social Sciences,* David L. Sills, ed. (New York: Macmillan and The Free Press, 1968), X, 387–409. Studies employing the concept abound in political science and sociology. See, e.g., John Brode, ed., *The Process of Modernization—An Annotated Bibliography* (Cambridge, Mass.: Harvard Univ. Press, 1969); Myron Weiner, ed., *Modernization: The Dynamics of Growth* (New York: Basic Books, 1966); Cyril E. Black, *The Dynamics of Modernization* (New York: Harper, 1966); and Marion Levy, *Modernization and the Structure of Societies* (Princeton, N.J.: Princeton Univ. Press, 1966).

are said to possess modern personalities. In this context "personality" is used loosely, in a social sense, referring only to generalized traits—not the individual psychological characteristics that give every person a distinct personality. Like the idea of "national character," "modern personality" refers to values and traits that are broadly shared. Individuals who differ widely in tastes and in temperament can equally share in the group of values associated with the modern personality.

Because modernization has been so closely associated with urbanization and industrialization, they are sometimes viewed as synonyms. The fact that they overlap in some respects—specialization, for example, is a key part of all of them—leads some to conclude erroneously that they are indistinguishable. In fact urbanization refers primarily to settlement patterns that are not necessarily modern or industrial: witness medieval Rome, Paris, or London. Industrialization, which is surely a manifestation of modernization and operates according to some of its core values such as efficiency and innovation, is a more restricted phenomenon. It refers only to modes of production and has, in many instances, been carried on as well in the countryside as in the city. The idea of modernization, however, is far broader, comprehending not only production but also such diverse phenomena as scientific analysis, rapid communications, even a symphony orchestra.[2]

Modernization and modern personality appear in sharper relief when they are contrasted to traditional society and personality. Perhaps no entirely traditional society still exists, owing to the economic and cultural imperialism of modern nations which have penetrated every quarter of the world in search of raw materials, bringing transistor radios along. But if one thinks of Iran before the discovery of oil, or of mid-nineteenth century India or Sicily, then one is approaching a traditional society where the people and their values recall a past stretching back many centuries. Here the past was the chief guide, not aspirations for the future. Here face-to-face relationships within a patriarchal authority structure dominated. Here punctuality and efficiency were disruptive, alien values. In their own terms, these societies were rational, but rational analysis was not vigorously applied to production for the purpose of maximum yields. In these traditional societies people adjusted themselves to accommodate the natural environment rather than seeking to control and direct nature.[3]

[2]E. A. Wrigley, "The Process of Modernization and the Industrial Revolution in England," *Journal of Interdisciplinary History,* 3 (Autumn 1972), 225–60, considers the synonymous use of "modernization" and "industrialization."

[3]See Ann K. S. Lambton, "Persia: The Breakdown of Society," in *The Cambridge History of Islam,* P. M. Holt, Ann K. S. Lambton, Bernard Lewis, eds. (Cambridge, Eng.: Cambridge Univ. Press, 1970), I, 430–67; Ann K. S. Lambton, *Landlord and Peasant in Persia* (London: Oxford Univ. Press, 1953); K. Ishwaran, *Tradition and Economy in Village India* (London:

When one turns to Victorian America, it may not be immediately clear where and whether it fits within this schema. We have some difficulty in seeing the "Victorians" as modern, since they seem so stuffy, hidebound, repressed, and old-fashioned. Their romantic sentimentalism and cultivation of the patriarchal family, as well as their reliance on human and animal-powered agriculture, seem to set them apart from modern rationality and productivity. Yet such surface impressions are misleading. Actually the rush of modernization was evident in nearly every facet of Victorian society, rural and urban, agricultural and industrial. Manifestations of the broad involvement in the modern personality abound, whether one looks at common working people or the wealthy and educated elite. Indeed it may well be that the most traditional-seeming aspects of Victorian culture, the patriarchalism and the misty-eyed idealization of the past, were actually self-conscious attempts to soften the hard edges of modernization, to reduce its psychological stresses.

Although Victorians did not use the word "modernization," they were certainly aware of many phenomena that would now be associated with it. Some, indeed, like education, technological development, and rising production, they liked to celebrate as "progress" toward a brighter future. Insofar as the orators of the first half of the nineteenth century proclaimed an official American outlook, it was a vision of major advances. The nineteenth century would be a better era, morally, socially, and materially, than times past.[4] Many believed that the fruition of a fully modern society—highly efficient, educated, prosperous, orderly, and secure—lay almost within reach. This quasi-official ideology did have critics who, at the extremes, yearned for either the order of hereditary aristocracy or the individual liberty of natural anarchy.[5] But few enlisted under these banners. Instead a massive commitment to modernization, glorified as "progress," pervaded American society.

Although I have argued elsewhere that the basic components of the modern personality syndrome had been broadly established in America by 1800, it is important to emphasize that the legacy of the Revolution was

---

Routledge and Kegan Paul, 1966); Milton B. Singer, *Traditional India: Structure and Change* (Philadelphia: American Folklore Society, 1959); Denis Mack Smith, *Modern Sicily, After 1713* (New York: Viking, 1968), vol. 3 of Moses I. Finley, *A History of Sicily,* 3 vols.

[4]See Clarence Mondale, "Daniel Webster and Technology," *American Quarterly,* 14 (Spring 1962), 37–47, and Leo Marx, *The Machine in the Garden: Technology and the Pastoral Ideal in America* (New York: Oxford Univ. Press, 1964), 209–14.

[5]Belief in an aristocratic social order was most often articulated by Southerners, George Fitzhugh for example, but elite New Yorkers, James Fenimore Cooper and Chancellor James Kent among others, also expressed reservations about democratic society and admired aristocratic social values. The anarchist critique is associated with Adin Ballou, Henry David Thoreau, Josiah Warren, and some of their contemporaries. See Leonard I. Krimerman and Lewis Perry, eds., *Patterns of Anarchism* (New York: Anchor Books, 1966).

equivocal in significant ways.[6] Notwithstanding the modern, self-conscious rationality of the Founding Fathers, and the crucial role of the Revolution in creating the foundations of modern, parliamentary democracy, the Revolution and its leaders were also oriented toward traditional society. Bernard Bailyn has demonstrated convincingly that Revolutionary ideology was certainly backward-looking in the first instance. The radical English Whigs who nourished American rhetoric were reactionary in their attachment to the mythic Saxon constitution and in their grounding of politics in the realm of particularistic "rights, privileges, and liberties."[7] For them the state itself was barely legitimate, and they perceived it primarily in negative terms. Their proceduralism cut both ways, reinforcing modernization by its prohibition on censorship in favor of free communications, retarding it by elevating precedent and procedure, rather than functionalism, as dominant political values.

When one considers the Constitution of 1787 and the political contests of the early national period, it is apparent that the Revolution underwrote both traditional and modern political elements. The declared purposes of government were defensive, to preserve an existing, decentralized structure of political and social relationships. The actual governing arrangements of the period, as well as the political debates of ratification and afterwards, placed no premium on efficiency, and very little on uniformity. Beneath the grandeur of republican rhetoric lay a substantial commitment to the *status quo ante* of 1763.

This traditionalism is especially noticeable in the social-political theory of both the Federalists and Jeffersonians. Although one emphasized commercial leadership and the other an agricultural elite responsible to the people, they agreed that the "best people" should conduct public business, and that their social and economic inferiors should generally defer to their wisdom. By modelling their theory on the republicanism of classical antiquity, they assumed that society would maintain a continuity with the hierarchic, deferential forms of the colonial era.[8]

Yet the Revolution and the Constitution also reflected and stimulated

[6]See Richard D. Brown, "Modernization and the Modern Personality in Early America, 1600–1865: A Sketch of a Synthesis," *Journal of Interdisciplinary History*, 2 (Winter 1972), 201–28, esp. 213.

[7]*The Ideological Origins of the American Revolution* (Cambridge, Mass.: Harvard Univ. Press, 1967).

[8]These assertions are my own, but they have been influenced by: Roger H. Brown, *The Republic in Peril: 1812* (New York: Norton, 1971); Richard Buel, Jr., *Securing the Revolution: Ideology in American Politics, 1789–1815* (Ithaca, N.Y.: Cornell Univ. Press, 1972); Richard Hofstadter, *The Idea of a Party System: The Rise of Legitimate Opposition in the United States, 1780–1840* (Berkeley: Univ. of California Press, 1972); Gordon S. Wood, *The Creation of the American Republic, 1776–1787* (Chapel Hill, N.C.: Univ. of North Carolina Press, 1969).

modernization. The elimination of hereditary monarchy in favor of a broadly-based republic was obviously modern. Equally important, the Revolution generated a transformation in attitudes away from particularistic "rights and liberties," so that "Rights" and "Liberty" became universals. The pledge that "life, liberty, and the pursuit of happiness" was the birthright of all white men ripped away the old colonial lid on popular aspirations. Modern ambitions for individual, family, and collective achievement were sanctioned and reinforced by a Revolution that had begun as an argument over the traditional definition of an Englishman's rights. The Constitution itself, as the deliberate, self-conscious offspring of the most erudite political science of its day, was essentially modern. From its opening preamble to its last article, the Constitution was the antithesis of the organic, inherited system of government characteristic of traditional societies. Its origins were not lost in the mists of time, nor was it the work of legendary sages or divinities. Everyone knew that it was made in Philadelphia between May and September, 1787, by the delegates who signed their names to it. It was a government made in a test-tube.

This government looked toward the future to the degree that it was national, in its provision for the admission of future states, and in its anticipation of change through amendments. It was modern in that the tripartite division it established was functional—executive, legislative, judicial—and not based on a traditional stratified social order as were the King, Lords, and Commons of Britain. In the premiums it placed on competition, both electoral and between the branches of government, the modern values of its creators were evident. Notwithstanding their traditional rhetoric of disinterested wisdom, the Founding Fathers set up a structure where policy would be the outcome of continual competitions for office and among officeholders. Building such dynamic, competitive values into the fundamental law of the nation gave a substantial impetus to further modernization.

Broadly conceived, the Revolution's significance for promoting modernization and the modern personality was immense. By opening the trans-Appalachian West to American settlement and by including it in the political system, the Revolution initiated key alterations in the economic, social, and political networks of the United States. Expansion, economic and political, accelerated modernization. Migration, to the frontiers and to cities, reinforced and extended public attachments to modern values.

Evangelical protestantism, which also flourished during the early national era, possessed similarly mixed implications for modernization. Recalling the divine omnipotence of sixteenth-century Calvinism, its rhetoric seemed to abase mankind and to require his uncomplaining acceptance of the world and his humble estate in it. Yet at the same time evangelicalism exalted individual piety and called upon Christians to remake society. Ultimately a faith that had once been rooted in Calvinism would be led by spokesmen such as Charles Grandison Finney, who proclaimed the prospects of perfection to throngs of aspiring, improving citizens. Such attitudes in religion reinforced the modernization of the political order and of secular society generally.

Population growth was a fundamental element in transforming America. Between 1780 and 1820 the total population of the United States more than tripled (343%), growing from 2.8 million to 9.6 million. The number of states nearly doubled as eleven new states joined the original thirteen. Theoretically these additions need not have affected modernization. Conceivably this growth could represent merely an expansion of existing arrangements, the same old *status quo,* but bigger. Much of the expansion that had occurred in the colonial period had actually followed this pattern as localistic, quasitraditional settlements proliferated.[9] In the early nineteenth century, however, expansion meant dramatic changes. The economic impulses that sustained the expansion required the rapid creation of transportation facilities, first via roads and rivers, then supplemented by canals and railroads. Western settlers seldom expected to remain subsistence farmers for more than a few years. They demanded, and within the space of a generation obtained, access to a national marketing network.

The prospect of economic rewards was clearly fundamental to the modernization of early nineteenth-century America. The geographic mobility that fed the frontiers and the cities was inspired by hopes of prosperity, as were many political decisions. The sales policy on public lands was oriented toward a relatively rapid transfer of real estate to private hands for development, in contrast to British policy which had preserved the interior for Indians and the fur trade. Public aid for national roads, for turnpikes and canals was based on similar motives.[10]

The drive for productivity sped American technology from mediocrity to superiority within two generations. The assembly-line technique of manufacture with interchangeable parts was invented simultaneously in Britain and the United States before 1810, but because it was so rapidly adopted in

[9]These statistics are drawn from U.S. Bureau of the Census, *Historical Statistics of the United States: Colonial Times to 1957* (Washington D.C.: U.S. Dept. of Commerce, 1960), 7, 13. The rate of population growth was quite similar from 1700 to 1740 (354%), 1740 to 1780 (312%), and 1780 to 1820 (343%).

[10]One standard discussion of these phenomena is Edward C. Kirkland, *A History of American Economic Life,* 4th ed., (New York: Appleton-Century-Crofts, 1969), chs. IV, VI. Kirkland incorporates the views of Carter Goodrich, "American Development Policy: The Case of Internal Improvements," *Journal of Economic History,* 16 (Dec. 1956), 449–60. James Willard Hurst's seminal essays, "The Release of Energy," "The Control of Environment," and "The Balance of Power," treat these issues at a more general, abstract level in *Law and the Conditions of Freedom in the Nineteenth-Century United States* (Madison, Wisc.: Univ. of Wisconsin Press, 1956).

New England it became known as the "American System" by the 1830s. Products once requiring artisan handcraft—clocks, textile machinery, and even steam engines—became assembly-line output. By the 1850s English visitors found that American levels of mechanization and standardization led the world when it came to woodwork, shoes, plows and mowing machines, files, nuts, bolts, screws, nails, locks, clocks, watches, pistols, typewriters, sewing machines, and railroad locomotives. By this time Americans found it both feasible and economic to produce their own machine tools instead of importing them.[11]

Yet modern economic motives were not the only forces shaping American expansion. Modern political objectives were also vital. President Jefferson, the purchaser of Louisiana, dreamed of the United States as a vast "empire of liberty."[12] Nationalism was an integral part of public policy. This is especially evident in communications legislation. Interstate travel was subsidized by new transportation facilities, and an immense new postal system was created. The colonies, in 1774, had possessed only one post office, but by 1789 the Congress had created 75. In the next decade the number climbed to 903, and by 1810 there were 2,300 post offices. Fifty years later, in 1860, the United States had over 28,000 post offices serving the public.[13] Coupled with the expansion of the postal system was a postal rate structure that subsidized newspaper deliveries, encouraging interstate expansion of the press. The Revolutionary ideological commitment to an informed citizenry, as well as commercial objectives, sustained these policies. Their success is partially confirmed by the rapidity of communications even before the advent of electronic telegraphy. By 1840 virtually the entire region east of the Mississippi River was less than two weeks away from news sources in Boston, New York, Philadelphia, and Washington. Most of the population, in fact, lived within one week of the latest national news.[14]

The American eagerness for modern communications was tied directly to a wide variety of common activities. Frequent elections, which were written into state and national constitutions, tended to generate electoral competition which initially provided much of the support for a rapidly expanding press. The Revolutionary ideal of the active citizen, reinforced by the energetic piety of the second Awakening, and facilitated by increasing concen-

---

[11]H. J. Habakkuk, *American and British Technology in the Nineteenth Century* (Cambridge, Eng.: Cambridge Univ. Press, 1962), 4, 104, 105; Peter Temin, "Steam and Waterpower in the Early Nineteenth Century," in Robert W. Fogel and Stanley L. Engerman, eds., *The Reinterpretation of American Economic History* (New York: Harper, 1971), 228–37.
[12]A concise discussion of Jefferson's views on the "empire of liberty" is in Merrill D. Peterson, *Thomas Jefferson and the New Nation: A Biography* (New York: Oxford Univ. Press, 1970), 745–46.
[13]*Historical Statistics of the U.S.*, 497.
[14]Allan R. Pred, *Urban Growth and the Circulation of Information: The United States System of Cities, 1790–1840* (Cambridge, Mass.: Harvard Univ. Press, 1973), esp. ch. 2.

trations of people engaged in non-agricultural pursuits, led to a dramatic proliferation of voluntary associations.[15] Such associations, which were often joined in county, state, or even national leagues, were in many instances the communications organizations for special concerns. Their enormous potential for influencing public opinion, and policy, was evident in the temperance crusade which, by the 1850s, produced restrictions on liquor sales in more than a dozen states. The temperance drive itself, with its emphasis on the efficient, productive life, was a testament to the widespread internalization of modern values among native Protestants. The sedative beverages of eighteenth-century colonial workingmen, beer and rum, were proscribed by the temperance movement.[16]

A similar spirit was evident in the drive for public education. An informed, pious, and productive citizenry had to be capable of reading, writing, and arithmetic. As a result Americans spent tax dollars on education, as well as subsidizing it with public land grants. By the middle of the century the school attendance figures in the United States as a whole surpassed all the major industrial nations, and the record for the Northern states led the world. Such an investment in mass education not only promoted modernization, but testified to the modern, future-oriented values the American public already possessed.[17] Americans were modern before they were Victorian.

Under these circumstances it is next to impossible to distinguish causes from effects. If American society had not already been substantially committed to modern values the dynamism of the post-Revolutionary generation would have been absent, and the economic, political, and social innovations of that era would have been stillborn. Yet these innovations, themselves effects of modernization, were also sources of its further development. Market agriculture and commercialization were mutually reinforcing, and they exercised a continuing influence on communications and on popular attitudes. Electoral competition and political parties had simi-

[15]See Richard D. Brown, "The Emergence of Voluntary Associations in Massachusetts, 1760–1830," *Journal of Voluntary Action Research,* 2 (1973), 64–73, and "The Emergence of Urban Society in Rural Massachusetts, 1760–1820," *Journal of American History,* 61 (June 1974), 29–51.

[16]Alice Felt Tyler, *Freedom's Ferment: Phases of American Social History from the Colonial Period to the Outbreak of the Civil War* (Minneapolis: Univ. of Minnesota Press, 1944), ch: 13, "The Temperance Crusade," still provides a good overview; also see Joseph Gusfield, *Symbolic Crusade: Status Politics and the American Temperance Movement* (Urbana: Univ. of Illinois Press, 1963).

[17]Douglass North, "Capital Formation in the United States during the Early Period of Industrialization: A Re-examination of the Issues," in Robert W. Fogel and Stanley L. Engerman, eds., *The Reinterpretation of American Economic History* (New York: Harper, 1971), 274–84; Albert Fishlow, "The Common School Revival: Fact or Fancy?" in Henry Rosovsky, ed., *Industrialization in Two Systems: Essays in Honor of Alexander Gerschenkron* (New York: Wiley, 1966), 40–67.

larly wide-ranging consequences. Voluntary associations and mass
education were no less important in extending the influence of modern
values and reinforcing modernization. In practice, yesterday's effect was
tomorrow's cause.

Did "Victorian" culture reinforce modernization? Certainly its concern
for punctuality, order, and time-thrift were modern, as was the future-
orientation of many Victorian thinkers, whether preachers like Channing,
philosophers like Ralph Waldo Emerson, or politicians like Daniel Webster.
But Victorian individualism was ambiguous. Champions of the individual
were suspicious of large-scale enterprises, and opposed to bureaucracy,
conformity, and discipline. Here they were reacting against the threats
posed by modernization. Yet at the same time they generally expected high
levels of achievement from their fellow citizens, and were intolerant of
waste and the accumulated injustices of the past. Romantic individualism
was not in the mainstream of the push for modernization, but its self-conscious adherents did share substantially in the modern personality.

So far, I have written as if modernization was a relatively uniform, national phenomenon. In fact, however, it moved at an uneven pace. Within
any given state the localities that were close to the long-distance communications network were normally more heavily involved in national economic
and political affairs, and more modern, than their neighbors that had less
access.[18] In the nation as a whole it was the Northeast whose native population was most fully modernized. Among these people literacy was all but
universal, and the ideal of the thrifty, mobile, active citizen was supreme.
During the 1840s and 1850s, however, a more traditional population of
peasant immigrants (mostly Irish) were entering the Northeast. Their attitudes toward time-thrift, education, and temperance values were at odds
with most of the native population. As a result there was substantial tension
that was only partially based on the age-old antagonisms of Protestants and
Catholics. Nativist rhetoric appealed to the values of a modern citizenry; it
was not bigotry pure and simple. Insofar as immigrants behaved like
modern, middle-class Yankees they were acceptable. "Americanization,"
as the nativists proclaimed it, was similar to the internalization of modern
values.[19] Perhaps one of the reasons for the keenness of nativist anxiety was
that the immigrants retained a traditional network of values and relationships that the natives themselves had been working so hard to escape. Irish
patterns of community, family, and church allegiance, and even their

---

[18]Brown, "Emergence of Urban Culture," 29–51; Pred, *Urban Growth,* ch. 2; Jackson
Turner Main, *The Anti-Federalists: Critics of the Constitution, 1781–1788* (Chicago: Quad-
rangle, 1964), 269–74.

[19]Oscar Handlin, *Boston's Immigrants,* rev. and enl. ed. (New York: Atheneum, 1974), chs.
V, VI, and VII.

convivial tavern-haunting, were much too reminiscent of the Yankees' own grandfathers' era. To natives, they represented regression.

In the free West, where the economic emphasis was on agriculture, the picture was also mixed. Where settlement had been established for a decade or more, market agriculture predominated. In the areas of most recent settlement, subsistence farming prevailed, but with the expectation of future profits and specialization. In this region urban growth, sustained first by commerce, then by the food processing industries with augmentation by the manufacture of farm implements, was extremely rapid. Within the space of a single generation tiny frontier outposts like Cincinnati grew to be cities of tens of thousands, performing a wide range of specialized functions, fully enmeshed in the national communications network, and possessing heterogeneous populations. In this region immigrants from rural backgrounds were often quickly transformed into freeholding farmers, and the entrepreneurial, time-thrifty spirit with which they carried out their settlement made their "Americanization" a comparatively easy process. Some immigrants retained some old ways, but they never seemed to threaten the native population with a regression to traditional society.

It was the direction of the South that was most ambiguous from the perspective of modernization. On the one hand its large-scale plantation system, especially as applied to the cotton crop, represented the most fully modern, highly specialized, industrial agriculture anywhere. Fogel and Engerman would claim that the "productivity" of Southern agriculture in general made it more modern than that of the North.[20] Yet Fogel's and Engerman's statistics are questionable, and even if they did definitely establish higher Southern productivity it remains true that Southern society, and slavery in particular, possessed fundamental characteristics that were traditional.[21] Southern ideology emphasized traditional values like honor, loyalty, and family, not time-thrift or an active citizenry. It sanctioned a quasi-aristocratic, hierarchical social structure in which heredity and "breeding" counted at least as much as talent.[22] This self-conscious re-

[20]Robert William Fogel and Stanley L. Engerman, *Time on the Cross: The Economics of American Negro Slavery* (Boston: Little, Brown, 1974), 192–96.

[21]Two notable critiques of Fogel and Engerman are by Paul A. David and Peter Temin: "Slavery: The Progressive Institution," *Journal of Economic History,* 34 (1974), 739–83; "*Time on the Cross:* Two Views—Capitalist Masters, Bourgeois Slaves," *Journal of Interdisciplinary History,* 5 (Winter 1975), 445–58. Another, Herbert G. Gutman, *Slavery and the Numbers Game: A Critique of Time on the Cross* (Urbana, Ill.: Univ. of Illinois Press, 1975), virtually demolishes much of the book.

[22]Eugene D. Genovese, *The Political Economy of Slavery: Studies in the Economy and Society of the Slave South* (New York: Random House, 1967), chs. 1 and 8; and *The World the Slaveholders Made* (New York: Random House, 1971); John Hope Franklin, *The Militant South* (Cambridge, Mass.: Harvard Univ. Press, 1956); Carl Degler, "The Two Cultures and the Civil War," in *The Development of American Culture,* Stanley Coben and Lorman Ratner, eds. (Englewood Cliffs, N.J.: Prentice-Hall, 1970), 92–119.

jection of bourgeois modernity was surely defensive, and it could not wholly block white Southerners from participating in national social patterns, but it did reduce such participation. Looking at school budgets alone demonstrates that Southern social policy was far less oriented to social mobility than the North, and far more committed to extending the social hierarchy of the old Southeast to the new Southwest. The weakness of the temperance movement in the South also suggests the continuation of old standards of social conduct. Yankees were outraged by Irish inebriation; Southerners laughed at drunkenness among their slaves and even encouraged it.[23]

And why not? Slavery, notwithstanding its rational, capitalist elements, was grounded on the concept of the slave as serf, as the most traditional of people. Owners never expected slaves to be thrifty with time, or to be literate, active citizens. They were deliberately kept traditional, isolated from communications and politics, and primarily confined to the agricultural technology of the sixteenth century. Deference, indeed outright dependence on patriarchal owners, was the model of political socialization for slaves. In its slave system the Victorian South did more than merely pay lip service to the traditional ideals of medieval Europe; it organized a major part of its culture around the exploitation of a traditional agricultural laboring population.[24]

The Southern states, and their white populations, did experience substantial modernization in many of the same ways as the North. Yet the pace was slower, retarded by a quasi-traditional ideology, by comparatively low investments in transportation and education, and most of all by the central commitment to the maintenance of a traditional slave labor force.[25] Relatively speaking, Southern political life was localistic and deferential, and in spite of specialized, commercial crop production, a subsistence manorialism was widely practiced. Modernization in this region was retarded by the continuing attractiveness and utility of numerous traditional social, political, and economic arrangements to the dominant class.

The great public crisis for Victorian Americans was the Civil War. To claim that the war was a conflict generated by modernization would be reductionist. The war was such a complex set of events that virtually any unitary explanation of it requires the use of a prism that permits viewing only

[23]Kenneth M. Stampp, *The Peculiar Institution: Slavery in the Ante-Bellum South* (New York: Knopf, 1956), 170; Frederick Douglass, *Narrative of the Life of Frederick Douglass, An American Slave,* Benjamin Quarles, ed. (Cambridge, Mass.: Harvard Univ. Press, 1967), 106–08; Eugene D. Genovese, *Roll, Jordan, Roll: The World the Slaves Made* (New York: Pantheon, 1974), "De Big Times," 566–84.

[24]Stampp, *Peculiar Institution;* Genovese, *Political Economy, World Slaveholders Made.*

[25]On railroad investment see: Milton S. Heath, "Public Railroad Construction and the Development of Private Enterprise in the South before 1861," reprinted in *Views of American Economic Growth: The Agricultural Era,* Thomas C. Cochran and Thomas B. Brewer, eds. (New York: McGraw-Hill, 1966), 150–60.

one stream of light, only one kind of data. Yet one important element in the
conflict was surely modernization. For the United States was a nation
passing through a rapid process of modernization, and at different rates in
various regions. These differences placed intolerable strains on a political
system that had not yet resolved its internal contradictions.

Consider. The immediate political and constitutional issues that served as
the explicit *casus belli* for the war were chiefly those of national supremacy
and unionism versus state sovereignty and secessionism. When the Republicans asserted the absolute bonds of the nation at gunpoint, they were laying
the foundation for modern, centralized national government. The South, by
asserting state autonomy and erecting a Confederacy in which that independence was preserved, stood for the localistic particularism of a traditional, pre-national state. The fact that the debate over the Constitution
came down to a battle over central supremacy suggests that regional tensions accompanying modernization were more than peripheral.

The slavery question, the most explosive issue morally and emotionally,
was also a conflict of modernization. For in their eagerness to assure the
safety of their peculiar institution, Southerners were out to preserve traditional values and a traditional mode of production. Loyalty and the acceptance of suffering, paternalism, and protection were the ideals of a labor
system that sought to hold 37 per cent of the Southern population in a permanent, hereditary, nonliterate, localistic dependence. Northerners, who
had little liking for blacks, found such a system outrageous because it
threatened the modern labor ideals they cherished. A free, competitive
labor system wherein efficient production relied on the personal responsibility and self-interest of workers was a cardinal principle of modernization
in Victorian America. For some of the same reasons that they found Irish
peasant immigrants so alarming, Northerners were eager to see slavery set
on the road to extinction. The survival of slavery symbolized a broader
conflict between traditional and modern society. For the dominant classes
in the North and the West modernization was attractive. It reinforced and
legitimated their roles and their influence in society. But in the South it
challenged the dominant class in vital ways. For these reasons, among
others, secession was attractive to many Southerners and anathema to
most people in the North.[26]

Such differences in modernization between the North and the South were
partially responsible for the conscious debates of the Civil War era. Yet in
some ways both sides were essentially modern. The war, one must recognize, was fought over the future of the United States, not its past. This was

[26]The paragraph echoes Eric Foner, *Free Soil, Free Labor, Free Men: The Ideology of the
Republican Party Before the Civil War* (New York: Oxford Univ. Press, 1970), and Genovese,
*Political Economy* and *World the Slaveholders Made.*

not an ancient blood feud based on old wrongs or old boundaries. All parties agreed that the United States would continue to grow in size and to develop; their battle was over the terms of that expansion and the future character of the United States of America. This forward-looking, anticipatory quality in the conflict is a further indication that the war was integrally related to American modernization.

Mobilization itself was a great modernizer for both sides. In the Civil War the North and the South created armies on a scale previously unknown in America. The organization and logistics required to raise, supply, and move these hundreds of thousands of men elevated government planning and bureaucracy to new levels. Within the armies specialization, whether in fighting units like artillery, or in support activities such as transportation, was more elaborate than ever before. Behind the lines, both sides devoted more resources to the specialized industries that supplied the armies. In the North especially this had a modernizing effect on the production of weapons, textiles, and machine tools. The "productivity" of guns themselves was raised as the Yankees introduced breech-loading, repeating rifles midway in the war, and machine guns at its conclusion.[27]

Sustaining both military efforts was an ideological commitment on behalf of masses of people, a commitment that the opposing governments cultivated through the use of propaganda. The belief that God marches on "our" side is certainly traditional enough, but in the self-conscious elaborations of the Northern and Southern "causes" that dwelt on abstract ideals and the future, modern ideological warfare was evident. Ironically the South, which fought for states' rights, promoted a Southern nationalism that raised people's attachments above parochialism and toward general ideological abstractions. For both regions the war became a promoter of modern political mobilization.[28]

When the war ended in April 1865, the more "modern" side had won. The supremacy of the nation had been established, erasing the most fundamental contradictions of the prewar Constitution. The thirteenth, fourteenth, and fifteenth amendments prescribed the end of slavery and the be-

[27]A standard, though unsatisfactory, account of some technical and bureaucratic implications of the war may be found in J. G. Randall and David Donald, *The Civil War and Reconstruction* (Lexington, Mass.: Heath, 1969), chs. 17, 18, 19. A more suggestive treatment is Stephen Salsbury, "The Effect of the Civil War on American Industrial Development," in Ralph Andreano, ed., *The Economic Impact of the American Civil War* (Cambridge, Mass: Schenkman, 1962), 161–68. A description of the impact of the war on Northern and Southern industry is in Victor S. Clark, *History of Manufactures in the United States, II, 1860–1893,* (New York: McGraw-Hill, 1929), chs. 1–5.

[28]For the North see Frank Freidel, ed., *Union Pamphlets of the Civil War, 1861–1865* (Cambridge, Mass.: Harvard Univ. Press, 1967), introduction 1–24. On the South: E. Merton Coulter, *The Confederate States of America* (Baton Rouge, La.: Louisiana State Univ. Press, 1950), chs. IV, XX, XXI.

ginning of an era of equal manhood suffrage. Union victory had vindicated
the ideal of modern citizenship, while the wartime effort had yielded a more
modern social and economic order. The America of postwar Victorians was
to be modern.

Obviously society was still not entirely modern. Regional differences
survived the war, and within each region there were ethnic and occupational
groups whose traditional ways remained in place. Immigration from
Eastern and Southern Europe further increased the quasi-traditional population "awaiting" assimilation into modern society. But the process of
modernization that was to occur in late Victorian America was not something new. In the economy, in communications, in education, in politics,
modernization after the war proceeded along prewar lines, although now, of
course, the South was more fully integrated than ever before.

The defeat of the South was symbolic of the general closing off of traditional alternatives. The growth of bureaucracy and standardization became
common to education, the professions, and business enterprise. "Gen-
tlemen-scholars" like "gentlemen-merchants" and "gentlemen-public
officials" were a vanishing breed as specialists assumed leadership in one
field after another. Even the benefactions of philanthropy became subject to
the discipline of efficiency. At the other end of the social spectrum, the poor
and the physically and mentally incompetent were now managed by specialized bureaucracies staffed by people who assumed professional roles. In
manufacturing and in agriculture the family enterprise and the tradition of
sons following fathers were in retreat before the march of large-scale, impersonal production techniques. The machine had become the model not
merely for industry, but for society as well.[29]

These developments required more and more exacting standards of individual behavior; and it is here that the social and psychological necessities of
Victorian repressiveness become apparent. Traditional personal behavior,
with its unplanned, natural rhythms, did not fit comfortably within modern
society. Large-scale organizations, bureaucracies of all sorts, required uniformity and regularity. People had to fit within appropriate categories,
whatever their rank in the increasingly complex system of stratification. In
the professions, certification of some sort guaranteed a degree of uniformity
analogous to the system of manufacture by interchangeable parts.

[29]These themes are treated in many works, among them: Geoffrey Blodgett, *The Gentle
Reformers: Massachusetts Democrats in the Cleveland Era* (Cambridge, Mass.: Harvard
Univ. Press, 1966); George M. Frederickson, *The Inner Civil War: Northern Intellectuals and
the Crisis of the Union* (New York: Harper, 1968); Samuel P. Hays, "Political Parties and the
Community—Society Continuum," in *The American Party Systems: Stages of Political De-
velopment,* William Nisbet Chambers and Walter Dean Burnham, eds. (New York: Oxford
Univ. Press, 1967), 152–81; Daniel Horowitz, "Genteel Observers: New England Economic
Writers and Industrialization," *New England Quarterly,* 48 (March 1975), 65–83.

Education, both public and private, became largely devoted to "turning out" citizens certified for each niche in the social structure. Repression of emotions and spontaneous impulses in favor of punctuality, order, cleanliness, and devotion to duty was a social necessity. Victorians, eager to achieve the prosperity and physical security that modernization promised, were generally willing to put the spontaneous, sexually-relaxed, traditional world behind them so as to become, like the characters in Edward Bellamy's *Looking Backward* (1888), entirely rational, well-organized, secure beings.

It wasn't easy to stamp out the behavior patterns of generations. It was hard work; and in the sometimes compulsive zeal of Victorians for order and regularity, and to suppress passion, they seem to be overcompensating. They appear struggling to remake themselves and to disown elements of their upbringing that were part of them. Their reactions to immigrants and blacks were part of this struggle. In these submerged groups they saw the aspects of themselves that they were rejecting. They responded with excoriation, suppression, and the barbed humor of blackface and dialect jokes. For them modern behavior and respectability were nearly synonymous.

Still, not everyone, even among the most privileged ranks of society, gloried in the experience of modernization. Henry Adams, who came to take an increasingly gloomy view of the recent history of America, was only one of many who by the end of the century questioned the shibboleths of their youth. Indeed by 1900 a new determinism, in which man and society were inexorably controlled by natural forces, had achieved wide currency. Even the role of human rationality was being challenged. Society and nature were becoming more mysterious and less amenable to human willpower at the end of the century than they had been at the beginning, notwithstanding the swift development of the natural and social sciences. The belief in efficiency and productivity remained widespread, but now it was complemented by a nostalgic romanticization of the bucolic, pre-industrial past.

As time went on, and the inherent conflicts of capital and labor became manifest, doubts grew. The social realities of large-scale urban and industrial development, of mass immigration and mass politics, of agricultural mechanization and specialization, were not as rewarding as rhetoric had promised. Sharp movements of the business cycle intensified public anxiety. Although much of what was happening was the fruit of modernization—the increased scale and integration of activities, automation, and large impersonal bureaucracy in business and government— criticisms emerged. Labor complained, farmers complained, and even the most favored, educated, and wealthy found cause for dismay in the new, modern America. Romanticizing the colonial and Revolutionary eras, the

natural wilderness, and the beauties of European aristocratic art and culture, many Americans sought escapes from enveloping modernization.

By all appearances, no society has been entirely modern. Yet in Victorian
America modernization as a process reached a climax. The values
associated with the modern personality—rationality, specialization,
efficiency, cosmopolitanism, and optimistic expectations for the future—became a national orthodoxy at the same time that the social order was
coming under the domination of large-scale organizations in the economy
and in public life. Traditional ways of life were being reduced to the levels of
sub- or counter-cultures. If today the Victorians appear "old-fashioned," it
is not because they were traditional but because they tested the limits of
modernization, and we have become more skeptical of modern values and
social organization than our great-grandparents.

# Religion and Secularization

# PROTESTANT VOLUNTARY ORGANIZATIONS AND THE SHAPING OF VICTORIAN AMERICA

## GREGORY H. SINGLETON

SWAMI VIVEKANANDA, THE WORLDLY MYSTIC WHO FASCINATED VICTORIAN Americans at the 1893 World's Parliament of Religions in Chicago, informed a group of Midwesterners that he faced his greatest temptation in this country. When asked, "Who is she, Swami?" the Eastern sage laughingly responded, "Oh, it is not a lady, it is organization!"[1] Vivekananda was tempted, but nineteenth-century American Protestants had long since found organization irresistible.

The "voluntary principle" which emerged in the twilight of the Federal period and the dawn of the Jacksonian era has been a common item in our store of historical information since Winthrop Hudson and Sidney Mead brought it so clearly to our attention two decades ago. However, the principle and its manifestations—a host of organizations with a cluster of religious, moral, and social concerns—have been studied mainly in an ecclesiological context. This article attempts a new interpretation of voluntarism: an analysis of its role in promoting both deliberate cultural perpetuation and inadvertent social change in America during the Victorian period.

The "voluntary principle" must be seen primarily as a Northern phenomenon.[2] The expanding commercial structure of the North, the

---

[1] Paul A. Carter, *The Spiritual Crisis of the Gilded Age* (DeKalb: Northern Illinois Univ. Press, 1971), pp. 217–18.

[2] For the most insightful discussions of the voluntary principle, see Winthrop Hudson, *The Great Tradition of the American Churches* (New York: Harper, 1953), pp. 63–136; and Sidney E. Mead, *The Lively Experiment: The Shaping of Christianity in America* (New York: Harper, 1963), pp. 103–33. A recent summary definition of the term as used among church historians is in Sidney E. Ahlstrom, *A Religious History of the American People* (New Haven: Yale Univ. Press, 1972), pp. 382–83.

fluidity of migration patterns, and the tendency of immigrants to settle in this area resulted in a decline of deferential local social structures. In order to preserve traditional sociocultural dominance in American society and extend their social structures into the newly settled areas of the West, American Protestants (laity as well as clerics) joined in various forms of consociation. These united a group of Protestant denominations of British origin which functioned socially very much as an established church. Two immediate results followed. First, "voluntarism" provid·d a form of ethno-class identification during a period of increasing ethnic heterogeneity and economic differentiation. Second, it provided a basis for a rhetoric of individualism, expressed within the context of conformity to the social order. Both these results can be seen as short-range benefits for the participants, who were attempting to maintain traditional social arrangements in a rapidly expanding society. Another result was immediately beneficial, but ultimately became part of a cluster of trends which created a new social reality that made Protestant denominations peripheral. Sons of voluntaristic Protestants, who had been raised amid a cluster of organizational forms, turned their attention in the later nineteenth century to newer, more exciting organizational ventures in commerce, industry, and government.

The structure that developed in the nineteenth-century voluntarist denominations—national scope of organization, elements of a lay bureaucracy, establishment of "branches" in the expanding West—seems not unlike the corporate social structure operated by the "new" middle class at the turn of the century. It is the argument of this essay that Protestantism as a system of social organization facilitated the expansion of the American consciousness from localism to the nationalism implicit in the intricate structure of voluntarism, ultimately facilitating the emergence of a corporate society. In the new corporate society, all areas of economic, social, and political life became as specialized and structured as the "Protestant establishment" had become before the Civil War. Lyman Beecher, Robert Baird, and others were not spokesmen for the "organization man," nor were they addressing themselves to the efficiency of administration by professionals, trained managers, and technocrats. They did, however, provide organization models for a later generation.

The structural changes wrought by voluntarism can be seen most clearly by contrasting them with the social life of the dominant Protestant denominations between 1790 and 1820. Only a few secondary authorities are useful here.[3] Nevertheless, impressionistic suggestions from travelers' accounts,

---

[3]Some good work was done by an older generation of social historians, such as Whitney R. Cross, *The Burned Over District: The Social and Intellectual History of Enthusiastic Religion in Western New York, 1800-1850* (Ithaca, N.Y.: Cornell Univ. Press, 1950), and more recently by socio-political analysts such as David Hackett Fisher, *The Revolution of American*

newspapers, and a limited set of church rolls and records surviving from the period do allow for a partial reconstruction of the social organization of American churches.[4] What is most striking about the religious life of this period is the remarkable stability of social patterns between 1790 and 1820, which the Second Great Awakening did not fundamentally alter.[5] Protestant organization of religious life at this time was still localistic and deferential. Samuel Benninger, a Congregationalist minister from London who spent fourteen months in New England, New York, and Pennsylvania in 1806 and 1807, explained to his fellow Englishmen, "Whether Anglican or separatist, we [Englishmen] have a notion of Church and nation. In the American states, even Anglicans speak only of village and congregation."[6]

Studies of various British-origin confessional groups in the large seaport cities during this period indicate that even in the cosmopolitan communities of Boston and Philadelphia, religious life was organized primarily by congregation. There is very little evidence of activity involving a significant portion of the laity at the presbytery, diocese, or district level, and even less at synodical and national levels. In New York City in 1820, for example, less than five per cent of the total adult male population (over 18) appears on lists of lay boards at the congregational, city-wide, regional or national levels. Over three-quarters of the names collected from these lists are either found in Moses Beach's compilations of New York's men of wealth during the next decade, or are related to them. Furthermore, the structure of lay leadership in 1820 was not divided. Approximately eight out of ten of these men served in two distinct capacities (e.g., officer of a congregation and member of a city-wide benevolence or mission committee), and just under half served at three levels (e.g., delegate to a meeting of the presbytery, in addition to the examples given above). It is worth noting that of the lay

*Conservatism: The Federalist Party in the Era of Jeffersonian Democracy* (New York: Harper, 1965). The close analyses of social patterns which we have for the mid- and late nineteenth century, however, are generally not available. One of the few to appear recently, Bernard Farber, *Guardians of Virtue: Salem Families in 1800* (New York: Basic Books, 1972), surprisingly contains no information on local religious life, analytical or descriptive.

[4]For travelers' accounts and newspapers, I have relied heavily on the general materials relating to early and nineteenth-century America. The church rolls and records examined are those reprinted in the Massachusetts Historical Society *Collections* or the Essex Institute *Historical Collections*, or housed at Union Theological Seminary, New York City.

[5]For the Northern states, the Second Great Awakening was not so much a sectarian or individualistic fragmentation as a development of intensified concern among members of "established" denominations. See Donald G. Mathews, "The Second Great Awakening as an Organizing Process: An Hypothesis," *American Quarterly*, 21 (Spring 1969), 22–43. The higher growth rate in the Baptist and Methodist bodies during this period seems to have been less in the Northern states than in the South; see Edwin Scott Gaustad, *Historical Atlas of Religion in America* (New York: Harper, 1962), passim.

[6]Samuel Benninger, *An Account of a Visitation to America: With Observations, Facts, and Conversations Recorded Toward the Purpose of Truth* (London: Privately Published, 1807), p. 43.

officers in 1820, approximately one-quarter had held office for at least a
decade and approximately one-third were sons of office holders. Studies of
smaller towns and rural areas during this period indicate that the New York
pattern was not unique.[7]

Localism and generalized deference, however, were not to last. The
configuration of religious institutions changed rapidly between 1820 and
1860, while the extent of participation in them increased. In 1860 approximately twenty per cent of the adult Protestant population of New
York City can be found on lists of a wider variety of lay boards. Over half
had served as lay officers for less than five years. By that time, the
leadership community had become differentiated. Less than one-quarter of
the lay leaders served two distinct functions, and just over ten per cent
served three functions. Beyond the structure of leadership, approximately
one-third of New York's adult population were members of at least one of
the many church-related voluntary associations. Based on estimates of
British-origin denominational membership in 1860, perhaps as much as
forty-five per cent of New York's Protestants were involved in some form
of religious institution beyond the congregation. Prior to the 1820's, membership in ancillary ecclesiastical institutions was generally limited to those
who held office on a lay board. By 1860, in addition to various lay boards,
there was a minimum of eighty-seven voluntary associations available to
New York Protestants. That there was a change in level of organization as
well as structure is indicated by the fact that fifty-eight of these associations
were local affiliates of regional and national associations.[8]

Although the 1820 and 1860 data demonstrate the changing structure of
the Protestant community most dramatically, the emerging new pattern
can be seen quite clearly by 1830. Interdenominational membership in
citywide organizations (e.g., the New York Female Reform Association)

---

[7]This summary is based on an analysis of reports of the Presbytery of New York, Episcopal
Diocese of New York, Congregational Association, Methodist District, and Baptist Conference housed in the Union Theological Seminary Library, New York City, as well as reports
and lists of lay boards published in the local press between 1790 and 1820. Contemporary
printed material of various interdenominational lay boards, containing lists of members and
reports of activities, are housed at the New York Public Library. See "Checklist of New
York—its Clubs, Charities, Hospitals, etc., in the New York Public Library," *Bulletin of the
New York Public Library*, 5 (June 1901).

[8]This is a summary of statistical reconstructions based on denominational records and those
of twenty-three congregations (Presbyterian, Congregational, Methodist, Episcopal, Baptist,
and Dutch Reformed), housed at the Union Theological Seminary Library, supplemented by a
survey of local periodical material from this period, especially *The Evangelical Yearbook*,
which began publication in 1832, and was published under various titles until 1903. The latter
work made the distinction between American Protestant voluntary associations and non-
British-American religious "clubs" quite clear. The organizations listed are both national and
the more prominent local associations. Nativity was obtained by a random sample record
linkage with 1860 Manuscript Census Schedules for New York City housed at the New York
Historical Society on microfilm.

and in local affiliates of the new national organizations (e.g., the American Sunday School Union) was common even at that early date. The lack of data for most years between 1820 and 1860 does not allow for any detailed time-series analysis, but a few individual congregational records indicate that by the 1830's, lay offices were already held by representatives of a wider social base than had been the case in 1820. It would appear that the general unity of leadership found in 1820 had also changed by the 1850's. The new pattern was celebrated by an anonymous writer in the American Home Missionary Society *Annual Report* for 1857, who commented that "Christ's Army is the Church, and the soldiers are the laity, not the clergy (the error of Rome). It is fitting that each soldier should serve in his proper capacity, rather than depending on the few to serve all. In a true Christian nation, there are no drones."[9]

The story of the multifaceted institutions of social control and reform that sprang from the voluntary principle has been told many times, and there is no necessity to repeat it here.[10] But there was also a strong desire to extend the concept of Christian community from the Eastern states to the expanding West, and this requires some comment. In its *Annual Report* of 1829, the American Home Missionary Society noted that the center of American population was rapidly moving "beyond the Allegheny." Leave the future leader of the Republic without the Gospel, the report warned, and he will become a "ruffian giant."[11] There is an irony basic to voluntarism: though it appealed to the individual will, it operated through ever-larger organizations. This can be seen most clearly in the activities of the American Home Missionary Society. In order to preserve the stature of Protestant culture and of institutions related to a cohesive concept of the local community, and to extend the structure and values of that culture into frontier areas, the Society felt it necessary to depend increasingly on a national level of organization. T. Scott Miyakawa has skillfully pieced together isolated evidence from a wide variety of secondary sources to suggest that American Protestantism rapidly brought conformity to newly settled Western areas.[12]

[9] American Home Missionary Society, *Annual Report* (Philadelphia, 1857), p. 274.

[10] See, e.g., John R. Bodo, *The Protestant Clergy and Public Issues, 1812–1848* (Princeton: Princeton Univ. Press, 1954); Charles Foster, *An Errand of Mercy: The Evangelical United Front, 1790–1837* (Chapel Hill: North Carolina Univ. Press, 1960); Charles G. Cole, Jr., *The Social Ideas of the Northern Evangelists, 1820–1860* (New York: Columbia Univ. Press, 1954); Clifford S. Griffin, *Their Brothers' Keepers: Moral Stewardship in the United States, 1800–1865* (New Brunswick: Rutgers Univ. Press, 1960); and W. David Lewis, "The Reformer as Conservative: Protestant Counter-Subversion in the Early Republic," in *The Development of an American Culture* (Englewood Cliffs: Prentice-Hall, 1970), eds., Stanley Coben and Lorman Ratner. A recent critical review of this interpretation is Lois W. Banner, "Religious Benevolence as Social Control: A Critique of an Interpretation," *Journal of American History*, 60 (June, 1973), 23–41.

[11] American Home Missionary Society, *Annual Report* (Philadelphia, 1829).

[12] T. Scott Miyakawa, *Protestants and Pioneers: Individualism and Conformity on the American Frontier* (Chicago: Univ. of Chicago Press, 1964).

In Quincy, Illinois, for example, the American Home Missionary Society, the American Tract Society, and the American Sunday School Union were influential in rapidly establishing a voluntaristic social basis. During the period of migration from 1830 to roughly 1840, the residents of the new community were engaged in various personal and public building programs. The first public structure was a church of the "Presbygational" variety, and the first pastor was a Congregationalist minister supplied by the American Home Missionary Society, as were the second and third ministers. Religious educational materials were supplied by the American Tract Society and the American Sunday School Union. By 1843, there were in Quincy seventeen different missionary, reform, and benevolence organizations, fifteen of them affiliated with national associations. By 1860, there were fifty-nine voluntary associations, containing approximately ninety per cent of the adult population. Obviously, Quincy was a most Protestant town.[13] The success of the voluntaristic attempt to extend Northern Protestant culture westward was not limited to urban areas. Letters of members of a rural Presbyterian congregation in DeKalb County, Illinois, between 1843 and 1862, for example, contain many references to a full schedule of associational activity.[14]

It should not be assumed that the voluntary system was universally accepted by the membership of the American Protestant denominations, even in the North and West. In the 1830's a disenchanted former Presbyterian minister accused his fellow churchmen of what he called "Protestant Jesuitism"; and in the late 1850's a group of dissident members of the voluntaristic churches met in New York to call into question the hegemony exercised by their denominations in the United States.[15] One commentator claimed that "matters have come to such a pass that a peaceable man can hardly venture to eat or drink, to go to bed or get up, to correct his children or kiss his wife" without the benevolent guidance of at least one—probably

[13] Based on an analysis of the Manuscript Census Schedules, 1850–1880; Joseph T. Holmes, *Quincy in 1857* (Quincy: Privately Published, 1857); Pat H. Redmond, *History of Quincy and Its Men of Mark* (Quincy: Privately Published, 1869); S. B. Wycoff, *Directory: History and Statistics of the City of Quincy for the Years 1864–5* (Quincy: Privately Published, n.d.); David F. Wilcos, *The History of Quincy and Adams County* (Chicago: Ryersons, 1919); Quincy *Daily Herald*, 1837–73; Adams County *Whig*, 1834–57; Quincy *Register*, 1852–80.

[14] The letters are collected in Jennie M. Patten, *History of the Somonauk Presbyterian Church near Sandwich, DeKalb County, Illinois, With Ancestral Lines of the Early Members* (Chicago: Geographical Publishing Co., 1928), pp. 258–96.

[15] Calvin Colton, *Protestant Jesuitism: By a Protestant* (New York: Putnam, 1836). The proceedings of the meeting of the short-lived group, Young Men's Christian Union, were reported in *The Religious Aspects of the Age, With a Glance at the Church of the Present and the Church of the Future, Being Addresses Delivered at the Anniversary of the Young Men's Christian Union of New York, on the 13th and 14th Days of May, 1858* (New York: Privately Published, 1858).

more—church-related societies.[16] These examples, however, are important for their exceptionality. A more normative attitude was voiced by Robert Baird, who in 1856 claimed proudly that the voluntary principle had influenced "the character and habits of the people of the United States" in a way that a legally established church could not.[17]

Harmony did not always exist between or within constituent denominations, but the instances of doctrinal amelioration and institutional cooperation far exceeded the moments of antagonism.[18] Furthermore, it must be remembered that the most bitter and lasting schisms occurred between the Northern and Southern forces within the major denominations. Occasionally, also, a schism would occur in which a minority faction, believing the dominant denominations to be *too* church-like (in Troeltsch's sense) and too concerned with the matters of this world, would withdraw into deliberate sect-like organizations. Such a group was the Disciples of Christ, which, typical of this category of denominations, reentered into full associationalism and social contact with other British-origin Protestants shortly after mid-century.[19]

Thus arose a "benevolent empire" of Protestant organizations that provided models for secular organization in the second half of the nineteenth century. But the earlier generation not only set an example for the later; it also shaped its consciousness. The rhethoric of voluntarism continued to inform that later generation. The abundant literature on American nativism, for example, drew heavily upon this rhetoric, and there is no question that such sentiments survived the period of voluntary dominance.[20] The rhetoric contains much more than nativism, however, that is useful to the cultural historian. In a sermon before the Protestant Episcopal Diocese of Massachusetts in 1833 (which became a basic document in voluntary literature), the Reverend James Adams enunciated a definition of an organizational cul-

[16]Quoted in Stow Persons, *American Minds* (New York: Holt, Rinehart and Winston, 1958), p. 160.

[17]Robert Baird, *Religion in America: or an Account of the Origin, Relation to the State, and Present Condition of the Evangelical Churches in the United States. With Notices of the Unevangelical Denominations* (New York: Harper, 1856), p. 265.

[18]An example of interdenominational squabbles is found in Earl R. McCormac, "An Ecumenical Failure: The Development of Congregational Missions and Its Influence Upon Presbyterians," *Journal of Presbyterian History,* 44 (December 1966), 266–85.

[19]On the Disciples of Christ, see Winfred Ernest Garrison and Thomas DeGrott, *The Disciples of Christ, A History* (St. Louis: Christian Board of Publication, 1948). The most sophisticated analyses of the "sect to denomination" development in nineteenth-century America are Ruth B. Bordin, "The Sect to Denomination Process in America: The Freewill Baptist Experience," *Church History,* 34 (March 1965), 77–94, and Carl Obliger, *Strange Aberration: The Holiness Movement in Illinois* (Evanston: Institute for the Study of American Religion, 1973).

[20]See Ray Allen Billington, *The Protestant Crusade, 1800–1860* (New York: Macmillan 1938) and John R. Bodo, *The Protestant Clergy and Public Issues, 1812–1848* (Princeton: Princeton Univ. Press, 1954).

ture which was widely shared in contemporary literature. The key words in the definition were "community," "liberty," "law," and "order." All these values were assumed to have developed over centuries among the peoples of Anglo-Saxon origin. "We are accustomed to rejoice in the ancestry from which we are descended," said Adams, "and well we may, for our ancestors were illustrious men."[21] "Community" and "liberty" were not regarded as antithetic categories, but as the social and individual expressions of the Christian spirit. Adams saw the voluntary principle as the perfect embodiment of this spirit and claimed that:

> There is no possible form of individualism or social life which it is not fitted to meliorate and adorn. It not only extends to the more transient connections to which the business of life gives rise, but embraces and prescribes the duties springing from the great and more permanent relations of rulers and subjects, husbands and wives, parents and children, masters and servants. . . .[22]

"Law" was defined as the rules agreed upon by common assent, by which the community achieved this end, and "order" was the state of society in harmony with this principle. In this context, both the general civil order and the specific political institutions of the United States were interpreted by Adams as American Protestant by extension.[23] In addition to the general outline of Protestant culture provided by Adams, this literature stressed the importance of participation in organized community activities, individual betterment for the sake of the group, and the relationship of all organizations to a general spirit of fellowship and cooperation.[24]

The rhetoric of voluntarism indicates that the inclusion and exclusion categories associated with an earlier deferential America still existed, but with a difference.[25] Inclusion was possible for a greater number of people,

[21] James Adams, "The Relation of Christianity to Civil Government in the United States: A Sermon, preached in St. Michael's Church, Boston, February 13th, 1833, before the Convention of the Protestant Episcopal Church of the Diocese of Massachusetts," pamphlet in the Church History Collection, University of Chicago Library, p. 20.

[22] Ibid., p. 3.

[23] Ibid., pp. 24–26, 7–14.

[24] This is based on a systematic reading of the publications of the American Sunday School Union and the American Tract Society collected at the Newberry Library, Chicago.

[25] The magisterial works of Perry Miller on the ideological background of exclusivity and inclusivity, and the recent excellent works of social historians of Puritanism such as Kenneth Lockridge, John Demos, David H. Flaherty, and Stephen Foster are of course relevant to this subject. The concentration of colonial historians on the implications of the covenanted community in New England often obscures similar ideological and social trends that can be found in other Northern colonies. See Gary B. Nash, *Quakers and Politics: Pennsylvania, 1681–1726* (Princeton: Princeton Univ. Press, 1968); Frederick B. Tolles, *Meeting House and Counting House: The Quaker Merchants of Colonial Philadelphia, 1682–1753* (Chapel Hill: Univ. of North Carolina Press, 1948), esp. pp. 63–143; Richard James Hooker, "The American Church and the American Revolution" (doctoral dissertation, Univ. of Chicago, 1943), chs. 4 and 5; Guy S. Klett, *Presbyterians in Colonial Pennsylvania* (Philadelphia: Westminster Press, 1937) and Leonard John Trinterud, *The Forming of an American Tradition, a Re-examination of Colonial Presbyterianism* (Philadelphia: Westminster Press, 1949).

while exclusion was determined primarily along ethnic lines. As the United States became more heterogeneous, a direct participatory role in that society became obtainable by a greater proportion of an ethnically defined British-American Protestant community. I have stated the case in this way because of a recent trend in the historiography of voluntary associations toward interpreting them as agencies of social control and exclusionism. Of course, the benevolence and reform associations of nineteenth-century Boston, New York, and Philadelphia can be seen as organized efforts to define the increasing immigrant population as nonparticipants by designating them as objects of charity and as the groups in need of reform.[26] However, the activities of these organizations had internal structural meaning for the British-American Protestant community as well. Participation through the local church and the voluntary association became the behavioral expression of the ideology propounded in the Sunday School and Tract literature. This expansion of participatory possibilities within that community between 1820 and 1860 indicates that inclusionism may have been as strong a factor in the ethnic culture as the rhetoric indicates. Within the context of that community, there was every reason for the audience to feel a sense of deserved pride when they were told at the annual meeting of the Young Men's Christian Association at New York in 1856 that "Protestantism in America has divested itself of the old aristocratic notions of the rule of the many by the few. We have returned to the more ancient traditions of shared responsibilities."[27]

In the late nineteenth century another socio-economic system came into being, and along with it a new dominant typology. The "new" industrialists and the "new" middle class have been heralded as prototypical of modern America, born full grown from the rapid processes of urbanization, industrialization, and corporatization. Continuity with the structure and values of the old voluntary tradition, however, can be seen clearly in the corporate-business structure at the turn of the century, and there is evidence which suggests that the continuity was often familial as well as more broadly cultural. Using Blue Books and Social Registers from New York City and Chicago for the mid-1880's, the names of those individuals most associated with the new corporate social order (professionals, corporate managers, high-echelon municipal bureaucrats) were isolated. Based on the personal information given, and supplemented by obituaries, over seventy

---

[26]See, e.g., Bodo, *The Protestant Clergy and Public Issues;* Clifford Griffen, *Their Brothers' Keepers;* and Nathan I. Huggins, *Protestants Against Poverty: Boston's Charities, 1870–1900* (Westport, Conn.: Greenwood Press, 1971), pp. 3–56. For a criticism of this trend, see Carroll Smith Rosenberg, *Religion and the Rise of the American City: The New York City Mission Movement, 1812–1870* (Ithaca: Cornell Univ. Press, 1971).

[27]George D. Hallerton, "Speech Delivered on the First Day of June, 1856, to a Meeting of the Young Men's Christian Association of New York City" (manuscript), New York City Miscellany Collection, Union Theological Seminary Library.

per cent of these men in New York and just under sixty per cent in Chicago were members of one of the British-origin Protestant denominations. Slightly less than twenty per cent for New York and about eleven per cent in Chicago were members of voluntaristic associations or held lay offices. For the New York group, fifty-eight per cent of their fathers can be found on lay boards or in voluntary associations in the 1860's and 1870's. For the Chicago group, the figure is fifty-one per cent. The members of this corporate class tended toward class residential homogeneity and were much more heavily involved in professional and civic than church organizations.[28]

According to these data, the industrial bourgeoisie were primarily sons of Protestant laymen who had been active in church work. To assume that there is no important relationship between the social and religious world of voluntaristic fathers and the social and economic world of the corporate sons—as many scholarly treatments of the "new" middle class at least tacitly do—is to introduce an ahistorical notion that a child is nurtured by the future social trends of his adulthood rather than by the existing social world of his parents. It is unthinkable to suppose that the paternal examples of a structured Protestant enterprise and the rational division of responsibility achieved by mid-century were lost on children who became the formulators of the corporate society. Henry Drummond expressed the continuity when he wrote, in 1893, "The city, in many of its functions, is a greater Church than the Church. It is amid the whirr of its machinery and the discipline of its life that the souls of men are really made."[29]

The industrial bourgeoisie expressed a clear class-consciousness, not only in residential patterns but also in the various professional organizations and the increasing number of schools of business administration and engineering after the turn of the century. This class became increasingly heterogeneous in ethnic composition over time. (In this sense, the process generally called "assimilation" might be best understood functionally as *embourgeoisement*.) Both in constituency and general structure of values, however, the class was heavily influenced by the older culture of voluntary Protestant-

---

[28] Five Social Registers were surveyed for Chicago, and seven for New York. The name-specific data base contained occupational, residential and organizational affiliation information from the Social Registers, obituaries, and a variety of other directories. Information on name and location of fathers was also obtained from these sources. For New York, a combination linkage and retrieval process was used to identify fathers of the 1885 sample who appeared as lay officers or members of voluntary associations from the data base established from the ecclesiastical records discussed earlier. A similar procedure was used for Chicago, but the sources that remain from the 1860's and 1870's (housed primarily at the Newberry Library, McCormick Theological Seminary Library, the University of Chicago Library, and the Chicago Historical Society) are not nearly as complete as the New York material. This may be the reason for the variance between the Chicago and New York figures. In both cases, however, one is struck by the high degree of family persistence that is indicated by the data.

[29] *The City Without a Church* (New York: Harper, 1893).

ism. Professionalization, both in licensing and in the development of preparation through higher education and the foundation of professional associations, was, to some extent, an application of principles developed in earlier Protestant voluntary organizations.[30] The early writings of the new middle class stressed the values of professional community, especially the liberty and integrity of that community. The first graduating class of the Harvard Graduate School of Business Administration, for example, was told to "seek your own personal fortunes in the pursuit of the common good. You have been trained to function as effective individuals in organizations, and it is the organization of commerce, of industry, of government, and of our own affairs, rather than the disorganization of primitive and decadent societies, that is the glory of our heritage and the promise of our future."[31] The twentieth-century organization man continued the rhetoric of assumed dominance characteristic of the nineteenth-century British-American Protestant, along with the inclusionary and participatory values and the penchant for associational activities.

The theological *angst* of the turn of the century and the constant quest for religious "relevance" since that time suggest that the churches were merely passive victims of a rapidly changing social structure. In fact, however, they had pioneered the very changes they later lamented. If ecclesiastical spokesmen blamed a vague process called "secularization" rather than recognizing the new social order as the partial creation of their own institutions, they can be forgiven; delivering jeremiads was part of their job. The historian's job is something else, however.

The major thrust of this argument has been aimed at those social historians who maintain that the years between Appomattox and Versailles were an era of sudden transformation from *Gemeinschaft* to *Gesellschaft*, ushered in by a *new* middle class with a new set of values and a new concept of social organization. No one will question the profound changes in the economic, social, and political structure of the nation from 1880 to 1920. Most of us will agree that the notion of a corporate ideal in a liberal state was formulated during this period, and that the "new" middle class is a firmly

[30]See Robert Wiebe, *The Search for Order: 1877-1920* (New York: Hill & Wang, 1967), Ch. 5; *Medical Licensing in America, 1650-1965* (Baltimore: Johns Hopkins Univ. Press, 1967), pp. 213ff.; Roy Lubove, *The Professional Altruist: The Emergence of Social Work as a Career, 1880-1930* (Cambridge; Harvard Univ. Press, 1965); Raymond H. Merritt, *Engineering in American Society, 1850-1875* (Lexington: Univ. of Kentucky Press, 1969); Samuel Hays, "The Politics of Reform in Municipal Government in the Progressive Era," *Pacific Northwest Quarterly,* 55 (October 1964), 157–69; Melvin T. Copeland, *And Mark an Era: The Story of the Harvard Business School* (Boston: Atheneum, 1958); and Thomas M. Sutherland, "The Emergence of the Professional School, With Special Reference to Business Administration: 1880-1930" (doctoral dissertation, Stanford University, 1947).

[31]R. L. Groves, "Remarks to the Graduating Class of the School of Business Administration," *Harvard Graduate's Magazine,* (1912–13), 305.

entrenched social type. This article simply suggests that we too often over-look cultural and structural continuities enduring over a more extended period of time. The imposition of that social order which came to typify American corporate society did not await the emergence of post-Civil War industrialism; its origins can more properly be located in the second quarter of the nineteenth century. The structural transformation of Protestant institutions that occurred then resulted in the perpetuation of group dominance and the maintenance of cultural values, as its promoters desired. In the long run, however, the consequences took on a form that was not desired, nor even conceivable, by the early exponents of voluntarism. Our retrospective view affords us greater comprehension. If our Victorian forebears would be unable to recognize us as an extension of them, certainly we can recognize them in us.

# AMERICAN INTELLECTUALS
# AND THE
# VICTORIAN CRISIS OF FAITH

*D. H. MEYER*

OUR INTELLECTUAL INSTINCTS PULL US IN OPPOSITE DIRECTIONS, WILLIAM James observed in 1879. Once there was unity in higher thought: "Now our Science tells our Faith that she is shameful, and our Hopes that they are dupes; our Reverence for truth leads to conclusions that make all reverence a falsehood." James—who would, in the end, pronounce this a pluralistic universe—longed for unity. And if unity of truth were no longer possible, he would settle for unity of aspiration and purpose. The "miraculous achievement" for which we hope "must be a metaphysical achievement, the greatest of all time—the demonstration, namely, that all our different motives, rightly interpreted, pull one way." In this, as in many things, James spoke for his late Victorian age. Many desired unity, but could no longer find it in the universe about them. For James, unity and harmony are to be found, if at all, only in our heart and mind, our moral interior, our *Binnenleben,* as he once called it. And even that will be a "miraculous achievement."[1]

It is customary to think of "the Conflict between Religion and Science" as a distinguishing feature of the late nineteenth century, as we recall the dramatic confrontation over the theory of evolution between Thomas Henry Huxley, the champion of Darwinism, and Bishop Samuel Wilberforce, his orthodox adversary, on June 30, 1860. The sides were clearly drawn that day, and the issue seemed plain. But as we look back over the years we find that things were vastly more complicated than this scene would suggest. There were, to be sure, many who agreed with John William Draper that the battle between science and religion had begun, and that "on

[1]James, "Clifford's 'Lectures and Essays,' " *Collected Essays and Review* (London: Russell and Russell, 1920), p. 140; "Is Life Worth Living?" *The Will to Believe and Other Essays on Popular Philosophy* (London: Longmans, Green, 1897), pp. 61-62.

the one side there was a sentiment of disdain, on the other a sentiment of hatred."[2] Those who could see the matter in such simple terms were the lucky ones. For, in joining a crusade for either Truth or Faith, they could enjoy the zest of certitude. For many serious thinkers, however, as for William James, the real issue lay inward, within one's own mind. The "warfare" between science and religion was, for them, a matter of domestic tranquility, not of foreign policy. After the opening whoops and warcries of the 1860's and early 1870's, the clash between faith and reason stirred not jingo sentiments but a range of emotions, extending from the hopeful confidence that a new philosophical synthesis would create a truly scientific religion to deep anxiety and longing, what James called a mood of "speculative melancholy."[3]

This internal spiritual crisis as it affected American intellectuals in the later Victorian age concerns us in this essay. A word, first, is necessary to explain the term "intellectuals." In our century the word suggests many specific things, including an alienated elite attracted to esoteric ideas and, often, to radical politics. In the nineteenth century, although there were some alienated intellectuals, the person of ideas still typically regarded himself or herself as part of, indeed, as an exponent of, the wider culture. A term frequently used in the nineteenth century, the "educated class," perhaps serves better than "intellectuals," even though the term is, understandably, not often used today. It was the self-imposed duty of the educated class to recognize quality in life, thus to serve its society both as guide in matters of value and as critic of its society's goals and standards.[4] This could be a vexing assignment, particularly in the gilded society of the late nineteenth century. More: though champions of their society's higher culture, Victorian intellectuals frequently became sensitive to trends of thought and feeling of which the rest of the population was but dimly aware. For this reason—because intellectuals experience cultural tensions early— they are never truly representative of their society's mood at the moment. Certainly this is true of those involved in the crisis of faith in the late nineteenth century. Victorian intellectuals saw in the conflict between religion and science challenges and opportunities that were to become more widely evident only decades later.

To probe this Victorian crisis of faith, we must address three sets of questions. First, what was the precise nature of the crisis? What were the main issues involved? Second, what, if anything, makes the *American* crisis

[2] Draper, *History of the Conflict Between Religion and Science* (London: Kegan Paul, 1874), p. 303.

[3] James, "Is Life Worth Living?" *Will to Believe*, p. 42.

[4] See, for example, William James, "The Social Value of the College Bred," *Memories and Studies* (New York: Longmans, Green, 1911), pp. 307–325.

of faith unique? Third, what were the central spiritual concerns of those late nineteenth-century Americans who sought to make their intellectual home somewhere between agnosticism and positivism, at one extreme, and simple, uncritical faith, at the other?

\*     \*     \*

Intellectually, the Victorian crisis of faith involved a peculiar mixture of doubt and confidence. The Victorians saw themselves as transitional figures, stranded between medieval and modern perspectives, people wandering, as Matthew Arnold put it, ". . . between two worlds, one dead,/ The other powerless to be born."[5] The well-known "seriousness" and "earnestness" of the Victorians stem in part from their estimation of the worth of what they were losing and of the urgent necessity of replacing it. Among those concerned about religion and unwilling to abandon it altogether, there was a combined feeling of doubt, as old certainties vanished, and of hope that somehow, by dint of intellectual effort, a new unity of thought would be forthcoming. Until late in the nineteenth century it was widely assumed that truth is one. This assumption made the skeptics ferocious in attacking outworn theology and believers adamant in refuting the latest "errors" of science. For those in between, however, it meant that, bad as things looked, some new synthesis would appear on the horizon. All sides seemed to agree, nevertheless, that, although doubt was nothing new to the western world, the nature of Victorian doubt was different from anything that had gone before.

In the Victorian period doubt, certainly, was more thoroughgoing and unsettling than that of the previous century. It has been rightly said that the eighteenth-century *philosophes* rejected the Christian theology but not the Christian metaphysic.[6] They still needed God to explain the universe and account for the natural order. The deists directed their scorn at the more fantastic Christian beliefs and at clerical authority. The unbelief of the nineteenth century was more penetrating. "Doubt is mostly a modern thing," said the American liberal theologian Theodore Munger in 1887. In former times there was questioning and criticism but little "of what is now known as scepticism" and "not much mental perplexity." Modern doubt "destroys the sense of reality." It questions truth itself and "envelops all things in its

[5] "Stanzas from the Grande Chartreuse" (1855), *Poems of Matthew Arnold*, 3 vols. (London and New York: Macmillan, 1905–07), II, p. 214; see also Walter Houghton, *The Victorian Frame of Mind* (New Haven: Yale Univ. Press, 1957), pp. 1–23.

[6] See, for example, Noel Annan, *Leslie Stephen: His Thought and Character in Relation to His Time* (Cambridge, Mass.: Harvard Univ. Press, 1952), pp. 162–71; and Alasdair MacIntyre, "The Debate about God: Victorian Relevance and Contemporary Irrelevance," *The Religious Significance of Atheism* (New York: Columbia Univ. Press, 1969), pp. 3–20.

puzzle,—God, immortality, the value of life, the rewards of virtue, and operation of conscience; it puts quicksand under every step."[7] By the end of the century words like "agnosticism," "pessimism," and "indifferentism"—words absent from the philosophical vocabulary of all past centuries—had become common.[8]

How had this come to be? To most nineteenth-century thinkers the answer was clear: science, and the critical attitude inspired by science, had come to dominate the western imagination, not only providing thinkers with a coherent description of the natural world, but also offering itself as the model for rational inquiry, the standard by which all claims to empirical trust were to be tested. After Darwin had successfully brought the study of living things, including man, into the orbit of the new science, the wider cultural implications of the scientific revolution became clear to the entire intellectual community. Meanwhile, the age-old assumption that nature is an intelligently and purposefully designed system—fabricated by a benevolent Creator to serve Higher Ends—had eventually to be consigned to the rubbish heap. Purpose and order were replaced by randomness, chance, and the blind operation of natural laws. The "old argument of design in nature," Darwin himself concluded, "fails, now that the law of natural selection has been discovered." There is no more design in the variability of life forms, "than in the course which the wind blows."[9]

More was involved, however, than natural selection and evolution, to which superficial accommodation could be and was made. Underlying the change in biological *theory* was a more fundamental and gradual *change of mind* among western thinkers. This change of mind involved the restriction of attention to natural phenomena, which provide science with its only data, and consequent neglect of (and even denial of) things supernatural. More than this, it involved an increasingly emphatic insistence that we support *all* our assertions by critical observation and experiment, and that we limit our inquiries to matters that may be settled by an appeal to empirical evidence. The first of these trends has been called "naturalism." The second has been variously called "scientism" and "positivism." Together, they manifest a disposition to restrict the range of rational inquiry, to limit, in other words, what we rationally "know." The brilliant English geometer and atheist, William Kingdon Clifford, used the term "ethics of belief," to call attention to "the universal duty of questioning all that we believe." No evidence, he

---

[7]Theodore Munger, *The Appeal to Life* (Boston: Houghton, Mifflin, 1887), pp. 33–34.

[8]See John Theodore Merz, *A History of European Thought in the Nineteenth Century,* 4 vols. (New York: Dover, 1965; 1904–12), IV, pp. 307–8.

[9]*The Autobiography of Charles Darwin,* Nora Barlow, ed. (New York: Norton, 1958; 1887), p. 87. The extent of Darwin's own philosophical doubts is brilliantly discussed in Howard E. Grubner, *Darwin on Man: A Psychological Study of Scientific Creativity* (New York: Dutton, 1974).

said, "can justify us in believing the truth of a statement which is contrary to, or outside of, the uniformity of nature."[10] The eighteenth-century *philosophes* had tried to make science the norm of rationality and the standard of solid knowledge. The nineteenth century discovered what few *philosophes* really understood: namely, how narrow the range of science really is.

For some, the discovery of the narrow scope of science was a cause for celebration, for it promised to liberate the human mind, once and for all, from superstition and mystery, and to free man from the futile task of seeking answers to unanswerable questions. In 1869 Thomas Henry Huxley coined the term "agnostic" to identify his own attitude of resolute ignorance about ultimate things, putting his trust in "the constancy of the order of nature." "Doubt," he once affirmed, because it helps free the mind of error, "is a beneficent demon."[11] One of Huxley's American supporters, Robert G. Ingersoll, exhibited the more militant aspects of agnosticism. He made it clear to believers that his agnosticism was more than an individual case of cosmic bewilderment:

> The agnostic does not simply say, "I do not know." He goes another step, and he says, with great emphasis, that you do not know. . . . He is not satisfied with saying that you do not know,—he demonstrates that you do not know, and he drives you from the field of fact—he drives you from the realm of reason—he drives you from the light, into the darkness of conjecture—into the world of dreams and shadows, and compels you to say, at last, that your faith has no foundation in fact.[12]

"I do not know," and "*you* do not know." Like all moral principles worth their salt, the ethics of belief could be universalized and used to drive competing principles from the field. Doubt was no longer a matter of personal bafflement but a badge of intellectual honesty. Doubting was an obligation. Victorian faith may have been able to repulse the attack of Victorian science, but could it withstand the combined assault of Victorian science and Victorian moralism?

There was a more moderate version of agnosticism that attracted the attention of many British and American thinkers in the late nineteenth century. Herbert Spencer's agnosticism may be called benign and even reverent in the sense that it was not hostile toward religion. He contended that man has a "religious consciousness" that leads him to concern himself "with that which lies beyond the sphere of sense" with a mixture of scientific

---

[10]"Ethics of Belief" (1877), in Leslie Stephen and Frederick Pollock, eds., *Lectures and Essays of William Kingdon Clifford*, 2 vols. (London: Macmillan, 1879), II, pp. 177–211.

[11]Huxley, *Collected Essays*, 9 vols. (New York: Greenwood, 1968: 1898), IV, p. 47; IX, p. 56.

[12]"Reply to Dr. Lyman Abbott," *Works of Robert G. Ingersoll*, 13 vols. (New York: Dresden, 1909–15), IV, pp. 463–64.

wonder and religious awe.[13] Spencer argued, however, "that only in some highly abstract proposition can Religion and Science find a common ground."[14] And that common ground is religion's sense of the ultimate mysteriousness of the universe and science's modesty about knowing the essence of things. He used the term "the Unknowable" to identify this highly abstract common ground.[15] That was about as far as Spencer cared to carry the matter. To many of his critics, it was not far enough. Spencer's Unknowable, one American critic observed, is "pure mystery and negation." It is, "at best," a blank "infinite, at which we can only stare."[16] Trying to relate or give significant content to Spencer's Unknowable was akin, for many, to beating back the ocean with one's fists, or measuring eternity with a pocket watch.

Agnosticism, whether militant or mild, seemed anything but a liberating option to some thinkers. For them, moreover, doubt, though possibly demonic, was hardly a "beneficent demon." Many of the later Victorians regarded doubt less as a philosophical attitude than as a psychological discomfort—an emotion, as James put it, of "unrest."[17] As a pathological condition, doubt may intrude on a person's every mood, making it virtually impossible for one to trust in anything. Such doubt was a cultural ailment, not just a personal problem: it was the existential malady of the late nineteenth century. Behind this doubt was the growing suspicion that the universe was a far more strange and indifferent place than people formerly imagined. Thus, while some rejoiced in the limitations of science—its acknowledged incapacity to venture beyond the realm of natural phenomena—others were dismayed at the news. For to them it meant that, insofar as he remained committed to the standard of science and to the belief that truth is one, nineteenth-century man's universe had become incredibly shrunken. The major argument in James's famous essay, "The Will to Believe" (1896), is this: we have stopped proving things for which we cannot stop caring; are we, then, never justified in letting our cares carry us beyond our proofs? Have we no right to believe that which, as human beings with religious yearnings, we cannot help believing?[18]

[13]Spencer, "Religion: A Retrospect and Prospect," *Nineteenth Century,* 15 (Jan. 1884), 1–12.

[14]*First Principles* (New York: Appleton, 1896; 1862), p. 23.

[15]Ibid., pp. 3–126.

[16]Borden Parker Bowne, *Kant and Spencer: A Critical Exposition* (Port Washington, N.Y.: Kennikat Press, 1967; 1912), pp. 260–76. For a recent discussion of Spencer's Unknowable, see: J.D.Y. Peel, *Herbert Spencer: The Evolution of a Sociologist* (London: Heinemann Educational Books, 1971), pp. 127–30.

[17]*Principles of Psychology,* 2 vols. (New York: Holt, 1890), II, 184–85. For a more recent treatment of the subject, see Philip M. Helfaer, *The Psychology of Religious Doubt* (Boston: Beacon, 1972).

[18]*Will to Believe,* pp. 1–31.

The move to limit the scope of rational inquiry had disturbing results, in large part because of the seriousness with which the Victorians took the entire matter. The choice between belief and disbelief was a momentous one. The later Victorians had been brought up to take life, including life's ultimate questions, seriously. Once John Tyndall, the British physicist, disagreeing with a friend's cosmology while confessing his own indecision on the subject, was greeted with a snort of astonishment and contempt: "You surely must have a theory of the universe," he was told.[19] The later Victorians were perhaps the last generation among English-speaking intellectuals able to believe that man was capable of understanding his universe, just as they were the first generation collectively to suspect that he never would.

*   *   *

On this side of the Atlantic reflective American Victorians shared many of the religious concerns of their British cousins. In spite of the efforts of some Americans earlier in the century to erect a "barrier" against the "licentious and infidel speculations" which threatened to pour in "from Europe like a flood,"[20] there was no effective barrier against the scientific philosophy. In 1858 Horace Bushnell announced the appearance of a "new infidelity"—not the "rampant, crude-minded, and malignant scoffing" of the preceding century, but a naturalistic frame of mind that exhibits a concern for "genuine scholarship and philosophy," but insists on keeping "within the terms of mere nature itself." As a writer in *Harper's Monthly* observed that same year: "At present God is not so much denied as ignored."[21] The new infidelity was soft-spoken, serious-minded, and respectable. It did not flood the American mind; it seeped in.

Aside from the siege mentality of the early nineteenth century, there were other things that worked to distinguish American religious thought from that of European countries. First, the influence of American democracy on the nation's intellectual life and the intimate relation between higher thought and popular culture impressed foreign visitors to this country since the time of Tocqueville. Our middle-class society produced a middle-brow civilization that was widely literate rather than profoundly literary. As far as religious thought is concerned, all this implies that, while challenging new

[19]Quoted in Houghton, *Victorian Frame of Mind*, p. 104.
[20]Francis Bowen, *Lowell Lectures on the Application of Metaphysical and Ethical Science to the Evidence of Religion* (Boston: Little and Brown, 1849), pp. xii–xiii.
[21]Bushnell, *Nature and the Supernatural, as Together Constituting One System of God* (New York: Scribner, 1858), pp. 16–18; Editor's Table, *Harper's Monthly*, 16 (Jan. 1858), 262–66.

ideas might be regarded as dangerous to faith, morals, and social order, there would nonetheless be a tendency to accept them on a superficial level, blend them into mainstream thinking, and remain relatively unchanged by them. American philosophers, Morton White has argued, responding to the moral and emotional needs of their society, failed to develop a truly *critical* philosophical tradition. Instead, they tended to smooth away contradictions, stressing those features in any innovative system of ideas that would appeal to popular sentiments, comfort individual hearts, and support a general public philosophy.[22]

This process is well-illustrated in the remarkable career of John Fiske (1842–1901), the popular writer and lecturer, philosopher and historian, who was a follower of Spencer and an ardent champion of the theory of evolution—for which he gave Spencer a great deal of credit. Fiske—especially in the final two decades of his life—was passionate in his effort to reconcile final causes and immutable truths with the theory of evolution; and to allay the fears of good and pious Americans that the new science might seriously upset old beliefs. Science, he affirmed in his many books, ultimately supports both faith and morals. The theory of evolution, he reassured his audiences, "destroys the conception of the world as a machine. It makes God our constant refuge and support, and nature his true revelation. . . ."[23] The "lesson of evolution," Fiske soothed, ". . . is that through all these weary ages the Human Soul has not been cherishing in Religion a delusive phantom, but in spite of seemingly endless groping and stumbling it has been rising to the recognition of its essential kinship with the ever-living God."[24] The case of John Fiske shows how potentially dangerous new ideas could be blunted, modified, and absorbed into a general liberal religiousness. The challenge of nineteenth-century science could be successfully met because so few Americans were disposed scrupulously to spell out its implications.

Second, American religion was itself unique. America not only lacked an established church, but the country proudly celebrated its tradition of religious freedom and voluntarism, to the bewilderment of most British Anglicans who visited here.[25] Although there was considerable sectarian controversy early in the nineteenth century, the Americans had successfully compensated for their religious diversity by cultivating a kind of generalized

[22]Morton White, *Science and Sentiment in American Philosophy* (New York: Oxford Univ. Press, 1972), esp. pp. 290–310.

[23]Fiske, *A Century of Science and Other Essays* (Boston and New York: Houghton Mifflin, 1902), p. 60. On Fiske's career, see Milton Berman, *John Fiske: The Evolution of a Popularizer* (Cambridge, Mass.: Harvard Univ. Press, 1961).

[24]Fiske, *Through Nature to God* (Boston: Houghton Mifflin, 1899), p. 191.

[25]Richard L. Rapson, "The Religious Feeling of the American People," *Church History*, 35 (Sept. 1966), 312–13.

religious consciousness in both their institutional and their personal lives. On the institutional level, the Americans, regardless of "sect," gave common allegiance to what has been called a "civil religion," an official and general faith in a Supreme Being whose appeal was interdenominational and whose guidance could be ritually invoked on all public occasions. Although we were a religiously diverse people, we remained one nation "under God."[26] On the personal level, influenced by evangelical pietism and by a tradition of religious individualism that goes back to Jefferson and Franklin, many Americans became accustomed to thinking of "true" religion more as an inward matter than as an ecclesiastical affair. By 1880 that great mediator between high and low culture, the Reverend Henry Ward Beecher, could celebrate the fact that the divisive sectarianism of an earlier generation had given way to a spirit of cooperation and good will. The Americans, he announced, had learned that religion is not a matter primarily of doctrine or of institutional loyalty, but an intimate affair "of the heart."[27]

Even as the intellectual and the common, or popular, life seemed to blend in Victorian America, so did the religious and the secular life. Nineteenth-century observers seemed unable to decide whether the Americans were the most pious people on earth or the most worldly. Church attendance was high, and most Americans seemed anxious to avoid skepticism and infidelity. Yet it became evident to the more astute observers that much of American religion was *itself* secular—soothing the soul and charging the conscience, but offering little of what Matthew Arnold called "the discipline of awe and respect."[28] This kind of secularity, moreover, was noticeably on the increase by the middle of the century. The implication of all this for religious thought is evident: a secular religiosity that gains real meaning only in the individual heart and is most solemnly expressed in national rituals is singularly well-suited to withstand intellectual challenges. For one's personal faith is ultimately justified in one's subjective experience, despite "external" counter-evidence; and faith-in-general is a matter more of patriotic sentiment than of loyalty to some doctrinal system.

[26] Bellah's provocative essay of 1967 is reprinted in Russell E. Richey and Donald G. Jones, eds., *American Civil Religion* (New York: Harper and Row, 1974), pp. 21–44, along with essays on the subject by other scholars.

[27] Beecher, "William Ellery Channing," *Lectures and Orations of Henry Ward Beecher*, Newell Dwight Hillis, ed. (New York: AMS Press, Inc., 1970; 1930), pp. 171–73. See also: Langdon Gilkey, "Social and Intellectual Sources of Contemporary Protestant Thought in America," in Robert N. Bellah and William G. McLoughlin, eds., *Religion in America* (Boston: Beacon, 1968), pp. 145–48.

[28] Matthew Arnold, *Civilization in the United States* (Boston: Cupples and Hurd, 1888), p. 104. See also: Seymour Martin Lipset, *The First New Nation* (New York: Basic Books, 1963), pp. 140–69.

American civil religion was little affected, on a popular level, by the intellectual challenges of the later nineteenth century; but if personal religion were to remain a vital thing for deeply thinking people some accommodation had to be made with the leading ideas of the age. Counter-evidence to doctrines could be ignored, but the mood of uncertainty that it spawned could eat away at the experience that gave substance and meaning to religious life. The real enemy, as we noted, was not infidelity and atheism but doubt. The mood of doubt went far beyond the religious agnosticism of Spencer, Huxley, or Ingersoll. Although the formal intellectual issue was the existence or non-existence of God, the God-question was really only a convenient symbol for the growing feeling that, as Nietzsche put it, the highest values were losing their value, and that certainty was no longer possible in matters of ultimate concern.

The "quest for certainty" had dominated western philosophy since the time of the ancient Greeks. It is the search for immutable, rock-bottom Truths, manifested in Nature, on which we may confidently base all our most cherished beliefs. The scientific revolution that began with Copernicus and culminated in Darwin destroyed the connection between Nature and these Truths.[29] For those thinkers who were, unlike Huxley and Ingersoll, unwilling to abandon the quest for certainty, the question was: how can we accept the new science and still make metaphysical sense out of existence? Among American thinkers in this category, three concerns were particularly prominent. For convenience's sake, we may call them the need for cosmic comfort, the demand for a sense of cosmic momentousness, and the quest for cosmic unity. Although all were, in the broad sense, spiritual concerns, the first—the need for comfort—expressed a psychological need, while the others—the demand for momentousness and unity—expressed needs that were respectively moral and aesthetic. Each is worth examining in detail.

\* \* \*

"Who are we? Who cares for us? Is it all a vast and brazen hollowness?" Newman Smyth's questions were those of his generation. "We seem to ourselves as strangers and pilgrims here," Smyth lamented in 1877. "We feel alone in an alien world;—the soul wandering in orphanage of spirit, it knows not whither."[30]

[29]See John Dewey, *The Quest for Certainty* (New York: Putnam's, 1960; 1929), pp. 1–73, and his *Influence of Darwin on Philosophy* (Bloomington, Ind.: Indiana Univ. Press, 1965; 1910), pp. 1–19.
[30]Smyth, *The Religious Feeling: A Study for Faith* (New York: Scribner, Armstrong, 1877), pp. 111–13.

Americans of the late nineteenth century, like other Victorians, longed to feel at home in the universe, even in a universe described by Darwin. "The human soul," John Fiske said, "shrinks from the thought that it is without kith or kin in all this wide universe."[31] In an age when scientific analysis had put man out of touch spiritually with the world about him, the surest way to restore a sense of intimacy with the order of things seemed to lie within. When it became clear that natural theology was no longer capable of providing man with cosmic reassurance, thinkers turned inward, constructing what may be called a natural theology of the mind.[32]

The case of Borden Parker Bowne (1847–1910) nicely illustrates this shift in emphasis. Bowne, who taught at Boston University, was, like other American liberal theologians, influenced by Friedrich Schleiermacher (1768–1834), who had defended religion by tracing it back to the "inner life" and the feelings of utter dependence that one experiences. Bowne expanded Schleiermacher's description to include not only the feelings and emotions but *all* dimensions of human experience, intellectual, moral, and aesthetic, as well as emotional.[33] Thus armed, Bowne argued forcefully that, by holding too rigorously to the "scientific method" as the standard of rationality, in adhering too conscientiously to the ethic of belief, we are in fact restricting our right to make legitimate affirmations to confines that are narrower than our experience, in all its intellectual, moral, aesthetic, and emotional dimensions. Mankind is imposing a spiritual gag-rule on itself, denying its own nature—all in the name of science.[34] Science cannot satisfy the soul's appetite, he declared in 1905: our soul "longs to find God, to believe that it has not fallen into life headlong, to feel that it is in the hands of him that made it, and that he is ever near."[35]

Rejecting naturalistic agnosticism, Bowne intended to restore "the personal metaphysics" that the scientific philosophy had dismissed. He made human experience the starting- and end-point of thought, arguing that the universe is no vast machine but a living whole in which the natural and the supernatural join. The "cosmic order is no rival of God, but is simply the continuous manifestation and product of the divine activity."[36] Once we

---

[31] Fiske, *The Idea of God as Affected by Modern Knowledge* (Boston: Houghton, Mifflin Co., 1885), p. 138.

[32] In fact, natural theology had always looked in two directions—outward, to the natural order, and inward, into the human mind. The argument made in the present essay is merely that, after Darwin, the inward aspect of the natural-theology argument received greater emphasis: if there is a higher purpose to existence, it is to be found within the mind of man.

[33] Bowne, *Theism* (New York: American Book Co., 1902; 1887), p. 9. Schleiermacher's classic on the subject is *On Religion, Speeches to Its Cultured Despisers* (1799), John Oman, trans. (New York: Harper, 1958).

[34] Bowne, *Theism*, pp. 1–43.

[35] Bowne, *The Immanence of God* (Boston: Houghton, Mifflin, 1905), p. 118.

[36] Ibid., p. 27.

perceive the universe this way—from the angle of our total experience rather than of our scientific intellect only—we will recognize ourselves to be at home at last. For the divine presence is within and about us.

The inward emphasis in religion, of which Bowne's philosophy is but an example, reflects major themes in American evangelicalism and romanticism, and also illustrates the effort of western thinkers generally to retain a spiritual orientation in a world that was draining the supernatural of empirical significance, hence of meaning.[37] Human nature, if not physical nature, pointed toward the infinite and reestablished a sense of familiarity with the cosmos.

On another level, the quest for cosmic comfort reflects the prevailing nineteenth-century desire for stability and control in a time of rapid social change. As industrial society grew stranger and more inhospitable to human sentiments, Victorian people turned to institutions like the home and family for a reassuring and cozy sense of belonging, intimacy, and warmth. This feeling was, if possible, even more evident in America than abroad: in periodicals, novels, lectures, and sermons. Our greatest preachers—including William Ellery Channing, Henry Ward Beecher, Dwight L. Moody, and Phillips Brooks—in different ways all preached a message of acceptance and of intimacy between God and man. One senses an almost desperate quality in some of these statements, a kind of resolute coziness. In the social as in the natural order the old personal bonds between man and his world were being broken, because of technology, in the first instance, because of science, in the second. The longing for reassurance and for a more personal relation with the universe clearly was no merely speculative matter. It expressed some of the deepest needs of the age.

*    *    *

Can morality survive a decline in religious belief? This was the topic of a symposium in the first issue of the British literary journal, *The Nineteenth Century,* in 1877, and was a fundamental concern of the Victorian period. The French Revolution and its despotic aftermath had convinced the early nineteenth century that morality, hence the social order, depended on faith; that infidelity was as much a moral and social as a spiritual problem. By the mid-nineteenth century, however, the concern had shifted. Among the more thoughtful commentators, at least, the dread of godless anarchy diminished, and writers began to take a more serious look at the relation between faith and morals. James Martineau expressed the thinking of the latter part

[37] See Vernon Pratt (London: Macmillan, 1970), p. 11; Harry Blamires, *The Christian Mind* (New York: Seabury, 1963), and Merz, *European Thought,* IV, 307–08.

of the century when, in his contribution to the symposium, he observed that, should there be a decline in religion, morality "would lose, not its base, but its summit." Basic decency would probably remain, but moral grandeur would be lost: "To believe in an ever-living and perfect Mind, supreme over the universe, is to invest moral distinctions with immensity and eternity, and lift them from the provincial stage of human activity to the imperishable theatre of all being."[38]

The need to invest moral distinctions with immensity and eternity was, in part, a manifestation of the cosmic loneliness many felt. Were man's highest aspirations only vain illusions in a cold and indifferent universe? But more was involved than the dread that moral values are entirely earthbound. The dominant mood of the Victorian age, after all, was active and affirmative. When we believe "that a God is there," said William James, and that He takes an interest in our moral life, the "infinite perspective opens out," giving our moral life the fullness and robustness we demand of it. The capacity ". . . of the strenuous mood lies so deep down among our natural human possibilities that even if there were no metaphysical or traditional grounds for believing in a God, men would postulate one simply as a pretext for living hard, and getting out of the game of existence its keenest possibilities of zest."[39] This takes us well beyond the cosmic orphan's piteous search for reassurance and comfort. It is a feeling not of weakness but of strength—a strenuous, athletic mood. The demand for cosmic momentousness, in other words, concerns not our low periods and our dark nights of the soul, but our peak experiences and our most breathtaking hopes for a better tomorrow.

Although the Victorians disagreed about the relation of faith and morals, by the latter part of the century many would have agreed with Martineau that religion is more important to morality's summit than to its base. Some took the matter a step further and, along with the American educator and moralist, John Bascom, argued that religion "is not so much the foundation of morals, as morals is the foundation of religion."[40] The belief that morals are the foundation of religion was premised on the conviction that man is a moral being by nature, and that the universe is governed by moral laws that function and can be known in a way analogous to natural laws. This conviction, which was more systematically and elaborately set forth in America than abroad,[41] assumed that man is possessed of a conscience and a free

[38] Martineau, "The Influence upon Morality of a Decline in Religion," *Nineteenth Century*, 1 (April 1877), 343.
[39] "The Moral Philosopher and the Moral Life," *Will to Believe*, pp. 212–13.
[40] Bascom, "Atheism in Colleges," *North American Review*, 132 (January 1881), 38.
[41] For more detail see: D. H. Meyer, *The Instructed Conscience: The Shaping of the American National Ethic* (Philadelphia: Univ. of Pennsylvania Press, 1972).

will, that he can know and perform his moral duty. All this provided what seemed a sound basis both for morality and religion, for, as one writer on the subject observed, in giving us a conscience, God "has not left himself without a witness, in the breast of every man."[42] Indeed, it was a widely-shared conviction that the unbeliever, if he were open-minded, could be converted by an appeal to his own moral nature. More than this, for the believer himself the earnest pursuit of good character was one of the surest means of *spiritual* as well as moral growth. As we try to perfect our character, William Ellery Channing observed, we learn that human nature is "spiritual": the soul "is created to look beyond and above all material things." God has "imprinted on us the end of our being in giving us this central impulse towards himself." The idea of God, Channing said, is "an exhaustless spring of energy against weakness, of peace amid vicissitude, of courage to do and suffer, of undying hope, of immortal life."[43]

   In their search for cosmic comfort and reassurance, it may be said, the Victorians cried out God's name in loneliness and desperation. In their pursuit of the momentous, however, they sallied forth as soldiers prepared to do battle in His name. Met in this spirit, God is less a heavenly father than a cosmic partner. He is, as Matthew Arnold put it, an "enduring power, not ourselves, which makes for righteousness."[44] We serve Him by cooperating with Him in this grand cause. God, in turn, helps man by acting—as he did for Job—as his witness and vindicator. We demand to know, Josiah Royce said, "that, when we try to do right, we are not alone; that there is something outside of us that harmonizes with our own moral efforts by being itself in some way moral."[45] God supports us in our moral effort by giving our actions a significance that transcends our finitude, by placing them in the midst of eternity. In the final analysis it turns out that, although religion is founded on morals—that is, on man's moral nature—the moral life itself takes on its fullest meaning only when one realizes how firmly morality is rooted in religious experience. Henry Ward Beecher summed it up in 1882: "Morality is the indispensable ground of spiritual fervor. . . . An elevated morality blossoms into spirituality. And eminent spirituality sends down the elaborated sap into every leaf, fiber and root that helped create it." The creeds of the future, he said, will begin where the old ones ended: "upon the nature of man, his condition on earth, his social duties and civil obligations, the development of his reason, his spiritual nature. . . ." Our creeds, thus,

[42] Archibald Alexander, *Outlines of Moral Science* (New York: Scribner, 1852), p. 66.
    [43] Channing, "The Perfect Life," *Works of William Ellery Channing* (Boston: American Unitarian Association, 1903), pp. 979, 980.
    [44] Arnold, *Literature and Dogma* (New York: Macmillan, 1908; 1873), p. 52.
    [45] Royce, *The Religious Aspect of Philosophy* (New York: Harper, 1885), p. 219.

"will ascend from the known to the unknown." Beginning with ourselves, our moral nature, we reach out toward God.[46]

Not all Victorians were able to retain or recover their faith in God. W. F. Clifford found it sufficient to hope only for a general, "cosmic emotion," a sense of awe in contemplating the universe and of reverence in considering human nature.[47] His American critic, James, had to settle for an "as-if" posture and a sense of "on-the-wholeness," when faced head-on with the question of God—a vague sense of the personal responsiveness of at least some part of the universe to his strivings and defeats.[48] For the freethinker, Minot J. Savage, God represented orderliness and morality—"a power whose laws are so much a part of the universe that all good hinges on knowledge and obedience. . . ."[49] "God," for such people, was not the God of Abraham, Isaac, and Jacob, nor even the cosmic system-builder of the deists. If God existed at all, He existed as a vague hope to be acted upon or a principle of moral order. The point is that later Victorian thinkers were concerned that there be some moral responsiveness in the universe, or what Royce called a principle of "moral rationality" to existence, or at least something in the world worth getting excited about. Whether one was a believer, an agnostic, or an atheist, one wanted to feel that at least some of one's moral choices were still momentous.

\* \* \*

Stow Persons refers to the late nineteenth century as "an age of restatements." The doctrines of faith, many felt, could no longer be left to the clergy, who were ill-equipped to explain and defend them before the bar of science.[50] Those who still believed that the fight of faith was a good one frequently sought in a scientific theology the way to a positive yet credible religious affirmation. The advance of science, Octavius Brooks Frothingham declared in 1891, produced a "mental revolution" that made it necessary to reconsider all the fundamental questions of religion.[51] Not just the meaning of life but the very description of the universe was at stake. Some, like Henry Adams, were even wondering out loud if it were any longer *possible*

---

[46]Beecher, "Progress of Truth in the Church," *North American Review*, 135 (August 1882), 115, 116. In a similar vein, see also: Phillips Brooks, "The Seriousness of Life," *The Light of the World and Other Sermons* (New York: Dutton, 1899), pp. 73–88.

[47]W. K. Clifford, "Cosmic Emotion" (1877), *Lectures and Essays*, II, 253–85.

[48]See James, *Varieties of Religious Experience* (New York: Modern Library, 1929; 1902), pp. 475–516.

[49]Savage, "The Religion of a Rationalist," *Forum*, 2 (Jan. 1887), 460–69.

[50]Persons, *Free Religion: An American Faith* (Boston: Beacon, 1963; 1947), p. 57.

[51]O. B. Frothingham, *Recollections and Impressions, 1822–1890* (New York: Putnam's, 1891), pp. 142–45.

to describe the universe. Others chose to regard the mental revolution brought about by science as a unique opportunity to understand the universe and to fathom its meaning for the first time.

Among those who were confident that the universe *is* describable was Francis Ellingwood Abbot (1836–1903), the free religionist and would-be expounder of a new faith, who tried both to save and to advance religion by translating it from its outworn Christian idiom into the language of scientific philosophy. Abbot regarded science as "the intellectual mediator between the finite and the infinite," since it is man's best way of receiving the "divine revelation" of the system of nature.[52] He regarded nature as both an "intelligible" and "intelligent" order in which God is immanent. In studying nature in the various intelligible "relations" which constitute the natural order of things, we acquaint ourselves not merely with a limited range of predictable phenomena but with a vast system of meaning and purpose. Nature is not just a machine: it is a living organism, indeed a *person*. Thus, a full understanding of the universe involves the study of theology and morality as well as of science.[53] It is the noble task of philosophy, Abbot insisted, to bring together all the facts of science, and "to unite them in one harmonious, comprehensive, and trustworthy theory of the universe as a whole."[54] Strongly denouncing agnosticism, Abbot looked to nature in order to know God, who is both immanent ( "all is God," he said, and "God is all") and transcendent—an Unknown forever becoming known, thanks to the growth of man's scientific and philosophical imagination.

Abbot's "scientific theism," as he called it, reveals what Isaiah Berlin once described as the "hedgehog" mentality—the disposition to seek "a single central vision"—a "single, universal, organizing principle"—to which all things may be related and in terms of which they gain significance. (This in contrast to the mentality of the "fox," which pursues "many ends, often unrelated, and even contradictory." )[55] Abbot wanted not just Truth but Unity, a sense of the spiritual togetherness of things. The ground of "all Art, Science, Philosophy, Ethics, and Religion, in strict accordance with the Scientific method," he wrote in 1890, "is proved to lie in the immanent relational constitution of the Supreme Genus-in-itself, or Real Universe, and Absolute Divine Person. . . ."[56] The enthusiasm excited by apprehending this unity is not so much metaphysical as aesthetic: the cosmic beauty that was the achievement of the age of Dante and Aquinas may be recaptured in the age of Darwin. Science, having destroyed the coherence of the medieval

[52] F. E. Abbot, *Scientific Theism* (Boston: Little, Brown), p. 151.
[53] Ibid., pp. 1–56.
[54] Abbot, *The Way Out of Agnosticism* (Boston: Houghton, Mifflin, 1890), p. 5.
[55] Berlin, *The Hedgehog and the Fox* (New York: New American Library, 1957), pp. 7–8.
[56] *Way Out of Agnosticism*, pp. 74–75.

system, will replace it with an even more permanent and dazzling coherence in the nineteenth century. This quest for unity, an important feature of Victorian thinking,[57] is one of the things that accounts for Spencer's following—for many, beside Spencer himself, regarded him as the Aquinas of the modern age. Nineteenth-century thinkers longed for a universe that was not just intelligible, reassuring, and morally challenging, but symphonic as well.

In the United States Spencer had a following, although it is likely that, despite the promotional activities of his American publisher, E. L. Youmans, he was never as much in vogue as some historians have urged.[58] Abbot himself never attracted a following. In fact, Stow Persons has described his career as "one of the most colossal failures in American history."[59] If any synthesizer enjoyed a significant (though limited) following in America, it was probably John Fiske, whose language was intelligible to many of his generation, unlike Abbot's, and whose philosophical system, as we observed, was more accommodating to traditional Christian beliefs than was Spencer's. Although Fiske replaced the old, "anthropomorphic" theism with a depersonalized, "cosmic" theism,[60] his cosmic deity still had more solidity, personality, and humanity than Spencer's Unknowable or Abbot's Supreme Genus-in-itself. Fiske offered a cosmic unity that was—for all of its intellectual shortcomings—spiritually comforting and morally challenging to many. Although never the popular success he had once hoped to be, John Fiske managed, at least partially, to make up for in energy and high hopes what he lacked in critical intelligence and mass appeal. For Americans who wanted to educate themselves, Fiske helped make the new science intelligible;[61] moreover, he placed it within a reassuring philosophical and religious context that inspired confidence in the human prospect and made the universe seem friendly, ethically vital, and coherent.

\* \* \*

Ideas do not exist of themselves. They have to be thought; they are the creations of human minds. Agnosticism, positivism, naturalism: these are the products of human intelligence and probing. Seen in this light, it is clear that the Victorian crisis of faith was, in significant part, a creation of the Victorians themselves. Expecting to reconcile religion and science, and re-

---

[57] As an example, of course, one may note the fascination with Hegelian idealism in both Britain and the United States in the 1880's and 1890's.

[58] See, for example, Richard Hofstadter, *Social Darwinism in American Thought* (Boston: Beacon, 1955; 1944), pp. 31–50.

[59] *Free Religion*, p. 32.

[60] Fiske, *Idea of God as Affected by Modern Science*, pp. 81–96.

[61] On Fiske's popularity and the limits thereof, see Berman, *Fiske*, pp. 220–71.

joicing in the promise of a new, rational faith, the late Victorians helped create their own problems. They were confident that they could resolve what, in their own terms, was irreconcilable. They sought empirically to comprehend what Fiske called the Unseen World.

The Victorian crisis of faith marks the breakup of an intellectual system that had endured from the beginning of European civilization, a system of faith and reason in which the culture's central myths were shared and supported by the entire community, including its intellectual class. Revision of those myths began in the seventeenth and eighteenth centuries, and many were confident that western religion could, to use the term of a later day, be "demythologized," thereby bringing faith and reason into closer harmony. Those Victorian thinkers who sought an accommodation between science and faith, whether they were liberal Christians like Newman Smyth, philosophical system-builders like Fiske, or seekers like James, either did not know or came sadly to the conclusion that faith without its myth—faith abstracted and reduced to its "essence"—is both more vulnerable and less appealing to the imagination than faith ensconced in a system of unbroken myths. (This is not to make a modern case for Scriptural literalism, which, in a scientific age, can be maintained only by tenaciously denying most of modern culture.) The Victorians of the late nineteenth century replaced the medieval alliance of faith and reason with a combination of sentimentalism and intellectualism, producing a statement of belief which was tenuously established, floridly expressed, elaborately vague. Such faith could perhaps reassure those who articulated it, but it would attract few converts. By the twentieth century it was evident that the old system had been wrecked. People would still believe, worship, and hunger for things spiritual. Theology—even some very good theology—would still be written. But there would no longer be intellectual consensus in western culture, there would no longer be a common metaphysic and a shared mythos. The educated class, traditionally the custodians of culture, would cease to function as a class, and certainly could no longer be counted on to support the faith of the common people. If, as some contend, ours is a secular society, it is secular not in the sense that we lack a concern for things of the spirit, but in the sense that we no longer have a common language for speaking of such things. In this sense, the Victorian crisis of faith, whatever else it meant, marked the end of the Christian era in western culture.

In the United States, where intellectual life and popular culture have been less distinct than elsewhere, where democracy has had its impact on thought as well as on society, and where the relation between the sacred and the secular had become blurred, the effect of the Victorian crisis of faith was distinctive. To be sure, the common intellectual language of the shared myths were gone. But this loss—dramatized in the Scopes Trial of 1925—

was counterbalanced by the persistence of the civil religion in which all Americans participated, the continued growth of organized religion as churches competed like businesses to reach new members, and the rise of a pseudo-intellectual religiousness in which sentimentalism and popular philosophy combined to produce an inspirational literature designed for a middle-brow culture.[62] The Victorian concerns that we have examined—the quest for unity, comfort, inspiration—remain prominent in the history of twentieth-century popular culture. They can be found in the cult of positive thinking, the promise of peace of mind, the search for new harmony through a variety of mental disciplines and occult nostrums—all designed to restore to life some of that cosmic purpose and moral urgency that have been lost. Although we may scorn these modern efforts to redeem us, we can still appreciate the human needs they try to serve. And we must conclude that the American intellectuals of the later Victorian age sensed the general directions in which their culture was moving, and anticipated many of its deepest problems. Lacking their self-confidence and hopefulness, we are nevertheless still Victorians in our moral searching and our cosmic homesickness.

[62]This theme is developed in Donald B. Meyer, *The Positive Thinkers* (Garden City, N.Y.: Doubleday, 1965).

# The World of the Victorian Reformers

# THE VICTORIAN CONNECTION

*DAVID D. HALL*

THE BOUNDARIES OF AMERICAN INTELLECTUAL HISTORY HAVE NEVER CORRE-
sponded to our boundaries as a nation. In the seventeenth century,
American Puritanism ebbed and flowed in rhythm with its English counterpart, and in the eighteenth, a figure such as Franklin derived his rhetoric
from the European Enlightenment.[1] Early in the nineteenth century the
evangelical movement in Britain and America became the basis of a transatlantic network or "connection," across which flowed ideas of immense
significance for the course of antebellum reform.[2] The history of this
transatlantic connection is well known. Less well studied, and certainly less
appreciated, is the history of another network which came into being at the
middle of the nineteenth century. This was the Victorian connection, and its
emergence explains the agenda and style of an important group of
American intellectuals.

The "Victorian connection" was a distinct version of nineteenth-century
Anglo-American culture, involving a limited but influential group of
persons. I use the expression to denote those intellectuals who shared a
worldview which affirmed the validity of final truth, but located this truth
elsewhere than in Christian revelation. The nineteenth century remained a
time of belief for millions, including probably most of those defined as Victorians in the introductory essay to this collection. By contrast, the intellectuals who participated in the Victorian connection had all experienced
a loss of faith. While some settled comfortably into agnosticism, for most
the transition from faith to doubt left a residue of uneasiness, and a major
problem for the group became the definition of a realm of "Truth" more
permanent than the transient assertions of Christianity.[3] Equally important

[1]See Peter Gay, "The American Enlightenment," in C. Vann Woodward, ed., *The Comparative Approach to American History* (New York: Basic Books, 1968), pp. 34–36.
[2]See, e.g., Frank Thistlethwaite, *The Anglo-American Connection in the Early Nineteenth
Century* (Philadelphia: Univ. of Pennsylvania Press, 1959); Charles I. Foster, *An Errand of
Mercy: The Evangelical United Front, 1790–1837* (Chapel Hill: Univ. of North Carolina Press,
1950).
[3]John Stuart Mill approved Carlyle's description of the times as "destitute of faith, but
terrified at skepticism." Mill, *On Liberty,* ed. Currin V. Shields (New York: Liberal Arts
Press, 1956), p. 27.

to the group was the problem of reconciling democracy and authority. Liberalism seemed the answer to this problem, a liberalism which preferred democracy to any aristocratic system, but which also insisted on leadership by a moral and intellectual elite.

Thus defined, the Victorian connection is essentially equivalent to what we are accustomed to describe as the "Genteel Tradition" or the "Mug-wump" mind.[4] I prefer the term Victorian connection because most descriptions of the Genteel Tradition fail to note its derivative and international character, while most accounts of the Mugwumps do not locate them firmly in the context of nineteenth-century liberalism. The Mugwumps are merely our national version of that liberalism for which John Stuart Mill was the great advocate. Similarly, the Genteel Tradition is a domestic expression of the idea of culture as taught by Arnold, Mill, and other mid-century English Victorians.[5] From this perspective the social role of the Victorian intellectuals can be correctly recognized as that of an avantgarde. Conceiving of themselves as the "vanguard,"[6] and laying claim to cultural authority which others by tradition possessed, they were leaders in shaping a new cultural system in which the university replaced the church and the serious writer found means of reaching a wide audience. Innovative in their thinking, the members of the Victorian connection formed a bridge between the world of the past and the world of the modern.

* * *

The Victorian connection came into being over a period of two decades, from the mid-1840's to the mid-1860's. To fix upon any single date as the starting point would be misleading, for it was by a process of evolution that the connection disengaged itself from certain antecedents. These include evangelicalism, as Noel Annan has shown in his biography of Leslie Stephen and elsewhere.[7] Among the Americans, "Puritan" ancestry is frequent,[8]

[4]Deriving as they do from hostile critics, both of these terms, and especially the former, imply characteristics which bear little if any relationship to the real nature of Victorianism.

[5]See Raymond Williams, *Culture and Society, 1780-1950* (New York: Columbia Univ. Press, 1958).

[6]George Eliot to John Chapman, 1852, quoted in Gordon Haight, *George Eliot & John Chapman* (New Haven: Yale Univ. Press, 1940), p. 60.

[7]Noel Annan, *Leslie Stephen, His Thought and Character in Relation to His Time* (London: MacGibbon & Kee, 1951); Annan, "The Intellectual Aristocracy," in J. H. Plumb, ed., *Studies in Social History: A Tribute to G. M. Trevelyan* (London: Longmans, Green, 1955), pp. 241-87.

[8]According to the editors of Norton's letters, "John Norton lived in his descendant Charles Norton growing up in Cambridge in the years 1830 to 1845. The strong moral purpose, the concern with things of the spirit, the scholarly bent of mind, the grave devotion to a worthy aim in life were tendencies . . . unconsciously directing the boy's career. . . ." *Letters of Charles Eliot Norton,* ed. Sara Norton and M. A. DeWolfe Howe (London: Constable, 1913), I, pp. 12-13.

while among the English an equivalent background in nonconformity turns up again and again. Specific denominations seem to matter less than the general fact (noted by Annan) that the members of the connection arrived at their style of high seriousness by inheritance. The religious background of the movement also made itself felt in a theory of value and an ethic of service. Things spiritual ranked higher than things material, and it was the duty of the civilized man to preserve this hierarchy. The line of descent from evangelicalism is apparent in a lecture George William Curtis gave in Boston in 1855. "His subject," reported Charles Eliot Norton, "was 'Success,'—false and true success." Curtis claimed that "no earthly standard would measure a true success, and that all prosperity and fame and worldly splendour might be but the accompaniments of a failure in attaining the real objects of life." Norton applauded the role Curtis was playing: "A man who goes from town to town . . . with such a protest against a prevailing and fatal error may be considered as one of the best of modern missionaries."[9] In this regard all these secular intellectuals were "modern missionaries," carrying on into a new age an ethic derived from nonconformity and evangelicalism.

Apart from this tradition, the Victorian connection seems indebted to one particular religious denomination, the Unitarians. For many of the group, Unitarianism acted as a halfway house on the road away from orthodoxy to "free religion" and skepticism.[10] For others, Unitarianism provided an example of how to survive as an avantgarde surrounded by a hostile culture. Lacking access to most official agencies of culture, Unitarians in Britain and America had developed informal means of keeping in touch and influencing public opinion. An important step was the creation of periodicals. Another, as confidence accumulated, was the establishment of educational institutions, notably University College, London, in 1828. By no means were all British (or American) Unitarians interested in social reform. But to the extent that members of the denomination opposed the landholding aristocracy and the cultural alliance of church and state, the group prepared the way for the Victorian connection.[11]

The relationship of John Stuart Mill to Unitarianism suggests some of these functions. From his father, a former clergyman, Mill learned to regard organized religion as an obstacle to reform. Yet he and others of the Philosophical Radicals felt comfortable in the presence of Unitarians. In

[9] Ibid., I, p. 118.
[10] Ibid., I, p. 195.
[11] R. K. Webb, *Harriet Martineau, A Radical Victorian* (New York: Columbia Univ. Press, 1960), pp. 65–72, 88; and on the Anglo-American community of Unitarians, pp. 138–142. During Martineau's travels through America, "Where there was a Unitarian minister, he was her natural host, and where there was none he was missed."

the 1820's evidence accrued of a "growing rapprochement" between the two groups. An important go-between was the Unitarian minister William J. Fox, who wrote both for the *Westminster Review* and a British Unitarian periodical, the *Monthly Repository*. The web of Fox's personal connections stretched to include Harriet Martineau and Harriet Taylor among the Unitarians, and Mill and John Roebuck among the Radicals. All these friends he brought together for dinner at the Taylors' in the summer of 1830, an event from which sprang Mill's enduring association with Mrs. Taylor.[12]

Such personal consequences aside, the ease of Mill's relationship with the more advanced Unitarians indicates the making of a connection which was neither Unitarian nor Radical. During the 1840's, the outlines of this new connection grew clearer during the interchange between Ralph Waldo Emerson and certain Englishmen sympathetic to his work.[13] As Emerson became known in England, the response to him was almost entirely one of abuse and ridicule. The few critics who spoke differently—Carlyle and Richard Moncton Milne—were themselves outsiders.[14] When invitations reached Emerson in the mid-forties to make a lecture tour of the country, they came from persons and groups similarly placed: the Yorkshire Union of Mechanics' Institutes, the publisher John Chapman.[15] Once Emerson arrived in England, he discovered for himself that he was "preached against every Sunday by the Church of England . . . and the Examiner newspaper denounced in the newspapers for letting in such a wolf into the English fold." But the penny newspapers were sympathetic, and Emerson found an audience for his lectures among "the best of the people, (—hitherto, never the proper aristocracy, which is a stratum of society quite out of sight & out of mind here on all ordinary occasions,)—the merchant the manufacturers the scholars the thinkers—. . . ." It was precisely among the former two of these groups that Unitarianism and middle-class radicalism flourished in England.[16]

[12] Michael St. John Packe, *The Life of John Stuart Mill* (New York: Capricorn Books, 1970), pp. 110–28.

[13] The full story of Emerson's role in creating the Victorian connection would have to include the friendships he formed in the 1830's with Carlyle, Martineau, John Sterling, and Alexander Ireland.

[14] [Richard Moncton Milne], "American Philosophy—Emerson's Works," *Westminster Review*, 33 (1839–40), pp. 345–72. Milne befriended numerous Americans and became a superlative broker of the period's liberal avantgarde. Pro-Northern during the Civil War, he had earlier assisted Clough. James Pope-Hennesy, *Moncton Milne* (New York: Farrar, Straus & Cudahy, 1955); Lionel Trilling, "Profession: Man of the World," *A Gathering of Fugitives* (Boston: Beacon, 1956), pp. 107–16.

[15] Ralph L. Rusk, ed., *The Letters of Ralph Waldo Emerson* (New York: Columbia Univ. Press, 1939), III, pp. 366n–367n, 407; Haight, *George Eliot & John Chapman*, p. 8.

[16] *Letters of Ralph Waldo Emerson*, III, p. 444; William J. Sowder, *Emerson's Impact on the British Isles and Canada* (Charlottesville: Univ. Press of Virginia, 1966), p. 22; Earle Morse Wilbur, *A History of Unitarianism* (Cambridge: Harvard Univ. Press, 1945–52), II, p. 368.

In the end, however, Emerson's immediate contribution to the making of
the Victorian connection lay in the effect he had upon those "scholars" and
"thinkers" he detected in his audience. Shortly before leaving America he
received a letter from a tutor at Oxford, a young man who introduced
himself as an admirer. "Your name is not a thing unknown to us," wrote
Arthur Hugh Clough. "I do not say it would be a passport in a society
fenced about by Church Articles. But amongst the juniors there are many
that have read and studied your books, and not a few that have largely
learnt from them and would gladly welcome their author." Following up
these words, Clough gave Emerson warm welcome when the two met in
1848. The friendship between them reached a climax in their dialogue at the
moment of Emerson's departure for home.

> *Clough:* "What shall we do without you? Think where we are. Carlyle has led us
> all out into the desert, and he has left us there."
> *Emerson:* "Clough, I consecrate you Bishop of all England. It shall be your part
> to go up and down through the desert to find out these wanderers and to lead them
> into the promised land."[17]

There is much to be learned about the genesis of the Victorian connection
from this exchange. Emerson and Carlyle have torn down the sheltering
walls of belief. A crisis of faith develops. And the question of vocation is
posed: what role is there for the person swept by doubt but wishing to teach
the truth? "Action will furnish belief,—but will that belief be the true
one?"[18] Clough himself could not reconcile his radical views on religion
and politics with an academic position "fenced about by Church Articles."
Resigning his tutorship, he found new friends and, eventually, a new
vocation among Unitarians.[19] In 1852 he came to Boston, and although
failing to secure an appointment at Harvard, quickly established himself as
a member of the literary community. Through Clough this community
learned of other young writers in England, Matthew Arnold among them.[20]
But the greatest interest was in Clough himself. What has been said of him
recently, that "conveniently circumscribed in one person, he offers much
that we increasingly recognize as central to an understanding of Victorian
conflicts and difficulties," sums up the reaction among his American

[17] *The Correspondence of Arthur Hugh Clough,* ed. Frederick Mulhauser (Oxford: The
Clarendon Press, 1957), I, p. 186; Edward Everett Hale, *James Russell Lowell and His Friends*
(Boston: Houghton, Mifflin, 1899), pp. 136–37.
[18] Clough, "Amours de Voyage," Canto V, l. 220.
[19] ". . . The Unitarian connections he began to form at this period played a major role
thereafter in his life, for it was through them directly or indirectly that he met his wife, secured
the Principalship of University Hall, met Emerson, and emigrated to the United States."
Evelyn B. Greenberger, *A. H. Clough* (Cambridge: Harvard Univ. Press, 1971), p. 102.
[20] [A. H. Clough], "Recent English Poetry," *North American Review,* 77 (July, 1853), pp. 1–
30.

friends. The allure of Clough was as a representative man, for the crisis of faith he felt so intensely was felt also by the intellectuals of Concord-Cambridge-Boston. From his spiritual journey through the wilderness they all hoped to learn a middle way between doubt and affirmation. In this regard Clough was prototypical, while in the transatlantic breadth of his friendships he exemplifies the making of the Victorian connection.[21]

Born amidst the waning of Christian belief, the Victorian connection grew to maturity in the 1850's and early 1860's under the stimulus of liberalism. The liberalism of the Victorians owed much to the program of the Philosophical Radicals. But the mood of Victorian liberalism was tempered by awareness of the dangers inherent in democracy, and by a preference for experience over any doctrinaire scheme.[22] In John Stuart Mill, who drew sustenance from both Bentham and Coleridge, many Victorians found the balance they desired. The widening of enthusiasm for Mill in the 1850's is apparent in his election in 1857 as a corresponding member of the American Association for the Advancement of Science; in Frederick Law Olmsted's dedication of *The Cotton Kingdom* (1861) to him; in the swelling of his communications with Americans, including Chauncey Wright and Norton; and in the number of young men who avowed him their "prophet." The founding of the *Nation* by E. L. Godkin in 1865 and the naming of John Morley as editor of the *Fortnightly Review* in 1867 mark the point at which disciples of Mill gained the means of teaching liberalism to a wide audience.[23]

Specific connections between English and American liberals are many. Continuing a tradition, a number of Englishmen visited America in the 1850's and 1860's in order to judge for themselves the success of the American experiment. Invariably the liberal-minded among these visitors became friends with a particular set of Americans, the same Cambridge-Boston group to which Clough had been attracted. Godkin, who stayed to become founding editor of the *Nation,* rapidly made friends with Lowell, Norton, and the Jameses; in New York he came to know Olmsted, George Ripley, and George William Curtis. Goldwin Smith, who came in 1864, was enthusiastically greeted by Norton, who later described him as "a liberal by nature and by conviction, in religion and in politics," and as having "fairly thought his way out of social and political feudalism, and out of that state

[21] *Victorian Studies,* 17 (1973), p. 105; Charles Eliot Norton, "Arthur Hugh Clough," *Atlantic Monthly,* 9 (1862), pp. 462–69. Portions of Norton's essay are reprinted in Michael Thorpe, ed., *Clough: The Critical Heritage* (New York: Barnes & Noble, 1972), along with Emerson's essay of 1849 on Clough and key portions of other comments by Americans.

[22] Edward Alexander, *Matthew Arnold and John Stuart Mill* (New York: Columbia Univ. Press, 1965), p. 8.

[23] *The Later Letters of John Stuart Mill, 1849–1873,* ed. Francis Mineka and Dwight Lindley (Toronto: Univ. of Toronto Press, 1972), passim; Rollo Ogden, *Life and Letters of Edwin Lawrence Godkin* (New York: Macmillan, 1917), I, p. 11; Leslie Stephen, *Life of Henry Fawcett* (London: Smith, Elder, 1885), pp. 97, 102.

church which is its religious complement." A year earlier, in 1863, Norton was welcoming Leslie Stephen, and in 1867 it was Morley's turn to meet the Americans, Godkin and Norton among them, who shared his politics.[24] Like so many other liberals, Morley had first thought of entering the ministry. Turning skeptic, he learned to condemn (in true Mill fashion) sectarianism. Morley found in Mill's empiricism a convincing method for discovering truth; *On Liberty* he regarded as a ringing "protest against mechanism and uniformity." In a real sense Morley remained the liberal in search of truth, for he never fully gave himself to any system. He stands with Clough as a representative kind of Victorian, representative in the way he thought and in the span of his connections.[25]

This account of the rise of the Victorian connection cannot be concluded without giving due attention to Charles Eliot Norton. Quite possibly Norton was the most important link in this transatlantic network. From his family he inherited ties to Unitarians in both countries. Passing quietly into agnosticism, he befriended many others who had to travel the same road. Having shared with Lowell the editorship of the *North American Review,* Norton saw the need for another kind of periodical to teach liberalism, and his support enabled the *Nation* to be founded. The list of achievements is long, and there is a serious point behind William James's irritation: "The way that man gets his name stuck to every greatness is fabulous—Dante, Goethe, Carlyle, Ruskin, Fitzgerald, Chauncey Wright, and now Lowell. His name will dominate all the literary history of this epoch. 100 years hence, the *Revue des deux mondes* will publish an article entitled, 'La Vie de l'esprit aux Etats-Unis vers la fin du XIX$^{me}$ siècle; étude sur Charles Norton.' "[26] What is true of Norton is essentially true of all who participated in the Victorian connection. He belonged to a community which was neither British nor American, a community of the "best men" (as Mill called them) sharing common goals as reformers.

All too often Norton is described by historians as a mainstay of the cultural establishment. This mistake in judgment extends to others of his circle, who in retrospect are credited with a hegemony actually enjoyed by others at the time. The very reason for being of the Victorian connection was to afford relief to an avantgarde isolated in the midst of Anglo-American culture. These secular intellectuals despised demagogues, hot-gospellers, aristocrats, and entrepreneurs. Those groups hated them in return, and since cultural power lay predominantly with the evangelicals

[24]Ogden, *Life and Letters,* I, pp. 165–66, 303; [Charles Eliot Norton], "Goldwin Smith," *North American Review,* 99 (1864), p. 538.
[25]Edward Alexander, *John Morley* (New York: Twayne Publishers, 1972), p. 22; *Victorian Studies,* 13 (1969), p. 105.
[26]Ralph Barton Perry, *The Thought and Character of William James* (Boston: Little, Brown, 1935), I, p. 419.

and the entrepreneurs, making a living and being heard were not always easy matters for many in the Victorian connection. William Dean Howells could not accept a story from Mark Twain for the *Atlantic* in 1874 because of the reprisals it would bring; ". . . a little fable like yours," Howells explained, "would not leave [the magazine] a single Presbyterian, Baptist, Unitarian, Episcopalian, Methodist or Millerite *paying* subscriber—all the hot-heads would stick to it, and abuse it in the denominational newspapers."[27] For us today the denominational newspaper scarcely exists, but on the map of nineteenth-century culture it loomed large enough to frighten those who were skeptics and liberals. For us the *Atlantic Monthly* is *the* literary magazine of America in the second half of the nineteenth century; for the Victorians, it flew bravely the flag of humanism, which made it immediately the target of the great denominations. This was the context in which a group of intellectuals emerged as a connection and in which they shaped their agenda of reform.

* * *

John Stuart Mill believed that the regeneration of mankind would be accomplished by the power of the mind to distinguish truth from falsehood. Hence the imperative of free inquiry, of speculation and argument without restraint, for free inquiry would ensure that reform eventually occurred, that man would gain emancipation from all false and restrictive systems, whether moral or social. Mill was angered by the fact that in English society, organized religion opposed this freedom of inquiry. He had the sense of powerful opponents in the way of reform, opponents made yet more powerful by the liaison between the hierarchy of the Church of England, "seeking control over every department of human conduct," and the aristocracy. In *On Liberty* he described the churches as "engines of moral repression," and complained that the evangelical revival was, for those "narrow and uncultivated minds" attracted to it, "at least as much the revival of bigotry." Truth was indeed embattled, yet Mill based his politics on the assumption that it would prevail over dogma and superstition.[28]

To fears about the stifling effects of religion, Mill added in the 1830's a similar concern about democracy. Earlier, like other Benthamites, he had urged abolition of the aristocracy, holding up democratic America as an example for England to imitate. Then he read Tocqueville, and was "star-

[27] *Mark Twain-Howells Letters,* ed. Henry Nash Smith and William Gibson (Cambridge: Harvard Univ. Press, 1960), I, p. 24. Having committed himself to publishing Clough's "Amours de Voyage" in the *Atlantic Monthly,* Lowell wrote to Clough of his fears about the reaction: "Already the so-called religious newspapers . . . are out upon us charging us with all kinds of impieties and infidelities." *Correspondence of Arthur Hugh Clough,* II, pp. 480–81. The response of the British religious press to Emerson is traced in Sowder, *Emerson's Impact,* pp. 8–9.

[28] Mill, *On Liberty,* pp. 17, 38; *Autobiography* (London: Oxford Univ. Press, 1931), p. 137.

tled by the revelation of the possibility of a tyranny more efficient than that of any despot."[29] Awakened to the possibilities of the tyranny of the majority, Mill came to see public opinion as the greatest threat to truth and free inquiry. "At present," he declared in *On Liberty*, "individuals are lost in the crowd. In politics it is almost a triviality to say that public opinion now rules the world. The only power deserving the name is that of masses. . . . Their thinking is done for them by men much like themselves, addressing them or speaking in their name, on the spur of the moment, through the newspapers." The antidote to this condition of "mediocrity" was a political system in which power rested with the "few" who were trained to use their minds and had the courage to stand apart from the masses. A democrat in principle, Mill spoke increasingly after 1840 in favor of elitist rule.[30]

Mill shared these reactions with his fellow Victorians. Carlyle and Emerson were already forecasting the unwelcome consequences of democracy, while warning against the materialism and competitive spirit which infected contemporary man. These lines of cultural criticism converged upon the Victorians who came of age in the 1850's—Arnold and Ruskin in England, Olmsted and Norton in America. Like Mill before him, Norton condemned "feudalism" in society and "superstition" in religion. Urging "free thought" as the means of overcoming "the bonds of ancient error," he looked forward to replacing arbitrary, traditional "authority" with the authority of liberal inquiry.[31] Yet Norton also rejected populistic democracy, and he saw mirrored in Renaissance church architecture the rise of a blighting individualism. As competition increased, as "the spirit that seeks gain at any cost" prevailed, standards of quality had declined. The task which Norton set himself was to check this decline by reasserting culture over materialism.[32] Similarly, Olmsted complained of "the excessive materialism of purpose in which we are, as a people, so cursedly absorbed. . . ." Did democracy, he wondered, contain any "means of counteracting" its destruction of the "simple and sensible?"[33] In the *Nation* this analysis of the American condition was commonplace. "The *malaise* from which the country suffers," a writer declared in 1866, ". . . is the want of a greater diffusion of that highest culture which makes 'capable and cultivated human beings,' the object of which is not to make better miners or

[29]Emery Neff, *Carlyle and Mill, An Introduction to Victorian Thought* (New York: Columbia Univ. Press, 1926), p. 270.

[30]Mill, *On Liberty*, p. 80.

[31]*Letters of Charles Eliot Norton*, I, p. 160.

[32]Charles Eliot Norton, *Historical Studies of Church-Building in the Middle Ages* (New York: Harper's, 1880), pp. 178, 285.

[33]Laura Wood Roper, *FLO, A Biography of Frederick Law Olmsted* (Baltimore: Johns Hopkins Univ. Press, 1973), p. 93.

surgeons or pleaders, but to widen the range of our intellectual vision, elevate and purify our tastes." The same fear of democratic mediocrity lay behind Thomas Wentworth Higginson's essay, "A Plea for Culture," where, having insisted on the higher value of things spiritual, he called for a strengthening of "culture" as a "counterpoise to mere wealth."[34]

But how to carry out this program? The agenda of reform ran to many items. In politics, Mill urged proportional representation as the cure for the loss of independence and individuality. Such a scheme, he believed, would permit universal suffrage but in a way that ensured expression of every point of view.[35] Other suggestions included imposition of an educational qualification for the franchise, limits on the amount of money a candidate for office could spend on an election, and replacement of political patronage with a system of competitive examinations for filling state offices. On both sides of the Atlantic, civil service reform became a major demand of the liberals, merging with their general interest in placing public administration upon a scientific basis.[36] Outside the area of politics, reform proposals were less specific. It was necessary to detach higher education from the control of religious sects; equally essential was the development of a press which encouraged independence, quality, and free inquiry. Olmsted urged the creation of "public parks and gardens, galleries of art and instruction in art, music, athletic sports and healthful recreations" as "means of cultivating taste." His own varied services, not only as landscape architect but also (for example) as a trustee of the Metropolitan Museum of Art, typify the efforts of the Victorian intellectuals to establish a wide array of cultural agencies—city parks, art museums, orchestras, libraries.[37] If a single word can sum up the purpose of these agencies, that word is "discipline." Viewing the problem of their times as "the lack of *habits* of discipline," the Victorian connection sought to impose upon society an ethic of respect for quality, an ethic of deference to "the best."[38]

---

[34]*Nation*, 4 (1867), p. 276; Higginson, "A Plea for Culture," *Atlantic Monthly*, 19 (1867), pp. 29–37.

[35]Mill, *Autobiography*, pp. 219–20.

[36]The history of the American Social Science Association, a society generally paralleling the interests of the National Association for the Promotion of Social Science in England, is told in L. L. and Jessie Bernard, *Origins of American Sociology* (New York: Crowell, 1943), pt. 8.

[37]Roper, *FLO*, p. 93. Speaking of the design of two government buildings, the *Nation* argued that "both these buildings ought not to be simply great piles of masonry . . . but real works of art; not only the embodiment of the highest taste and cultivation of the country, but good enough to exercise a powerful influence hereafter upon the aesthetic education of the people." *Nation*, 4 (1867), pp. 111–12.

[38]Ibid., III (1866), p. 16; Roper, *FLO*, p. 169. ". . . There are wanted, I do not say a class, but a great number of persons of the highest degree of cultivation which the accumulated acquisitions of the human race make it possible to give them. From such persons, in a community that knows no distinction of ranks, civilisation would rain down its influences upon the remainder of society. . . ." Mill to James Barnard, *Later Letters of John Stuart Mill*, #1662.

Victorians fell naturally into the role of educators. The intellectuals in the Victorian connection committed themselves to teaching the public at large in the confidence that they could reach the middle class and direct its energies into the right path. In making this commitment they turned away from the roles of isolated artist and solitary scholar. Art and scholarship had to serve the public; and although self-culture could be justified as the means of achieving individual perfection, it was laid aside by persons such as Norton in favor of more explicit public service.[39] To say that the Victorian connection believed in public service does not mean, however, that its members proposed to work through the state or institutions. According to Mill and Arnold, moral and social force sprang from truth, and truth could never fully coincide with or be embodied in any institution. Only by teaching truth directly would the reformer succeed. "We live in times," Mill wrote Norton in 1869, "when broad principles of justice, perseveringly proclaimed, end by carrying the world with them." Hence these intellectuals kept their distance from all political parties and the state. Not unlike the Puritan ministry, they assumed that the act of sincere speech or writing would secure them the authority needed to accomplish their agenda of reform.[40]

Yet in the real world the relationship between writers and readers was not so simple or direct. On the one hand the publishing revolution of the 1830's and '40's, by lowering the price of books, had brought them within the reach of an enormous audience.[41] Serious books for everyman and everywoman: this was the Victorians' hope, that the new economics of publishing would enable them to educate all who could read. On the other hand the type of book which people actually bought in huge quantities was fiction, and not good fiction either but what the Victorians considered to be trash. Newspapers showed the same development. As their price decreased and as circulation expanded, the contents deteriorated in quality. The *New York Ledger*, circulation of "nearly three hundred thousand copies," was described by Godkin in 1858 as "filled with tales of the 'Demon Cabman,' the 'Maiden's Revenge,' the 'Tyrant's Vault,' and a great variety of 'mysteries' and 'revelations'. . . ." His judgment was summary: "barring its general decency of language, [it] belongs to as low and coarse an order of literature as any publication in the world." Clearly the marketplace threatened to forestall any use of literacy as a means of imposing discipline.[42]

---

[39] *Letters of Charles Eliot Norton*, I, p. 385.

[40] *Later Letters of John Stuart Mill*, #1618; Mill, *Autobiography*, p. 137; Alexander, *Arnold and Mill*, p. 67.

[41] See Richard Altick, *The English Common Reader* (Chicago: Univ. of Chicago Press, 1957), chapter 12.

[42] Ogden, *Life and Letters*, p. 179.

These Victorian intellectuals refused to believe that nothing could be done. It was a fixed principle of liberalism that "in the middle of the nineteenth century, every treasure of literature" should be "as available to the son of the day-laborer as heretofore they have been to the millionaire." The corollary, introduced to reconcile liberal theory with day-laborer indifference to literary treasures, was that an appetite for trash could be seduced to feed upon higher things. Given the right encouragement, the marketplace could function as a ladder, leading the typical reader onward and upward. These assumptions inspired the Boston Public Library's policies of free circulation and the acquisition of popular fiction for the collection. The public library movement as a whole owed much to the Victorian connection, which saw the institution as a means both of improving public taste and of breaking class and sectarian control of literacy.[43] Another step was to intervene directly in the marketplace and make serious books available at attractive prices. Olmsted proposed such a scheme in 1864, envisaging "the wide and cheap distribution of good literature through the organization of an association of book-buyers . . . that would print or buy books in quantity . . . and sell and lend to local reading clubs throughout the country." In 1865 Mill arranged to have three of his books specially republished in "People's Editions," priced low enough, he hoped, "to find readers among the working class."[44] In the same tradition stand Charles Eliot Norton's *Heart of Oak* books and his cousin Charles William Eliot's five-foot shelf. At no point in time, however, did the marketplace lose its power to reduce mass literacy to the lowest level, and it was left to utopian writers such as Edward Bellamy to envisage a new cultural order in which serious literature was the *only* fare desired.[45]

Despite its troubling consequences, the widening literary marketplace enabled the Victorian connection to create its own set of journals. The more important of these in America were *Putnam's* (1853), the *Atlantic Monthly* (1857), the *Nation* (1865), and the *Galaxy* (1866); in England the list included the *Saturday Review* (1855) and the *Fortnightly* (1865). Simultaneously with the establishment of these journals, the profession of literary or "higher" journalism (as distinguished from ordinary commercial journalism) achieved a satisfactory level of security. Leslie Stephen, John Morley, Godkin, and (briefly) Henry Adams were to make their careers as journalists in a way that had not been possible twenty years earlier.[46] The

---

[43]*Nation,* 14 (1879), pp. 350–51; *Report of the Trustees of the Public Library of the City of Boston* (Boston: City Document No. 37, 1852), p. 17.

[44]Roper, *FLO,* 276; Mill, *Autobiography,* pp. 236–37.

[45]Edward Bellamy, *Looking Backward: 2000–1887* (New York: Modern Library, 1951), chapter 15.

[46]On this development in general, see John Gross, *The Rise and Fall of the Man of Letters* (New York: Macmillan, 1969).

new outlets for serious writing catered to precisely that group of intellectuals which felt uneasy with orthodox religion and conventional politics. Millite in spirit, these intellectuals turned to journalism in order to accomplish two related reforms. The first was to defeat sectarianism by declaring the truth. The second was to present "the best," whether in art, politics or literature, and thereby overcome the blight of mediocrity. The higher journalism of these Victorians was synonymous, therefore, with their goal of imparting discipline. The very title of the *Nation* indicates the ambition to supply the missing center of American culture, to become that "authoritative circle . . . whose decision settles the fate of a book, a singer, an orator, or a work of art."[47]

The intellectuals who shared this ambition knew that cultural authority lay primarily with the churches in the 1850's. In pleading for their own independence, in declaring themselves the arbiters of artistic taste and political judgment, the secular Victorians were acting to seize this authority for themselves. Apart from establishing journals which were under their own control, they also proposed to refashion the university into an instrument for training the right sort of leaders. In England, reform of the university meant disengaging it from three influences: the aristocracy, the Church, and industrialism.[48] In America, religious orthodoxy (and attendant attitudes in philosophy and psychology) was the chief threat to independence. Charles William Eliot, having shocked "orthodox sensibilities . . . by some of his appointments," came under sharp attack in the religious press. In response Eliot proposed that Harvard be "reverent yet free," a formula which the founders of Johns Hopkins also found convenient for warding off criticism.[49] At Yale the struggle was sharper within the college, for officially it remained orthodox. Yet William Graham Sumner succeeded in winning recognition of the autonomy of the social sciences. On the whole, these later Victorians carried through the substitution of instruction in the humanities for instruction in that peculiar synthesis of religion, morality, and philosophy which had once crowned the college curriculum. And by encouraging the rise of the social sciences, they helped legitimize their own existence as secular intellectuals.

It is important for an understanding of our cultural history that the members of the Victorian connection be recognized as reformers who

---

[47]Christopher Kent, "Higher Journalism and the Mid-Victorian Clerisy," *Victorian Studies*, 13 (December 1969), pp. 181–98; Richard Grant White, "Why We Have No Saturday Reviews," *The Galaxy*, 2 (1866), p. 541.

[48]See Sheldon Rothblatt, *The Revolution of the Dons* (London: Faber and Faber, 1968).

[49]Ogden, *Life and Letters*, I, p. 294; Hugh Hawkins, *Between Harvard and America: The Educational Leadership of Charles W. Eliot* (New York: Oxford Univ. Press, 1971), chap. 4; Hawkins, *Pioneer: A History of the Johns Hopkins University* (Ithaca: Cornell Univ. Press, 1960), pp. 68–72.

transformed the structure of cultural authority. When the group came into being at the middle of the nineteenth century, it held itself apart from the traditional forms of authority—organized religion, the press, and the university as then constituted. These intellectuals did not begin with cultural hegemony and live in quiet desperation watching it decline.[50] They began as rebels, and slowly made themselves an influence, in the process destroying for good the dominance of Protestant sectarianism. But these Victorians were a most conservative sort of revolutionary. Against property they had no complaint at all, and because their essential concern was with its moral uses, they remained indifferent, even hostile, to the movement for social justice.[51] Their activity as educators flowed from a sense of their own firm social placement in the middle class. What an English historian has said of English nineteenth-century intellectuals applies fully to the Victorian connection: it "was neither rootless nor rebellious; at its center, it was stable and assured, with enough property to buy leisure and independence and with sufficient association with government to keep it in touch with the conduct of national affairs. It had its own sense of 'cousinhood,' and was as distinguished by good manners as by the weight of ideas. . . ."[52]

The special position of these Victorians as reformers is clearly indicated in their cultural politics. They wanted intellectual inquiry to go forward, they demanded independence from sectarianism. Yet they also wanted discipline, and they sought to create true centers of cultural authority. The dilemma was felt by John Morley as editor of the *Fortnightly;* was the magazine to be a "marketplace of ideas, or offer authoritative guidance?" The dilemma runs through the social thought of Mill, who was at once a democrat and a cultural elitist. As for Clough, "his radicalism was of a fundamentally qualified kind, balancing itself . . . against an ingrained respect for traditional social order."[53] It should not surprise us, then, that Charles Eliot Norton opposed erecting a statue of Bacchante in the courtyard of the Boston Public Library. Joyous female nudity clashed with the imperative to teach restraining discipline, and Norton the liberal reformer, Norton the agnostic, passed easily into being Norton the censor. We remember him for his censorship; should we not also remember him for leading us into modernity?

[50]As is implied in Stow Persons, *The Decline of American Gentility* (New York: Columbia Univ. Press, 1973).

[51]The thinking of Henry Fawcett is typical. Hostile to all proposals to limit the working day, he insisted that "Poverty and its attendant evils may be diminished, but diminished only by judicious measures, by looking beyond the momentary need, and especially by raising the moral standard of the poor themselves. Whoever professes to raise the position of a class without elevating its character is a charlatan." Stephens, *Life of Fawcett*, p. 152.

[52]Asa Briggs, *The Age of Improvement* (New York: McKay, 1959), p. 410, based on Annan's essay cited in footnote 7.

[53]Kent, "Higher Journalism," p. 193; *Victorian Studies,* 17 (1973), p. 106.

# A NEW LOOK AT THE GILDED AGE: POLITICS IN A CULTURAL CONTEXT

## GEOFFREY BLODGETT

HISTORIANS OF THE LATE NINETEENTH-CENTURY AMERICAN SCENE HAVE LONG gone without an adequate conceptual label for that era. In the absence of a better name, the phrase "Gilded Age" has stamped the decades following the Civil War. This term, lifted from the title of the novel by Mark Twain and Charles Dudley Warner published in 1873, came to apply vaguely to the entire period from the presidency of Ulysses Grant to that of William Mc-Kinley.[1] The implicit stigma in the phrase, with its overtone of cheap, pretentious fakery, made it seem to later generations a convenient device for summary dismissal of the politics and culture of those years. It facilitated a swift mental passage from the grandeur of the Civil War to the excitement of the Progressive Era. The age thus remained for many a vast gray zone of American history, monotonous and inconclusive, an era of evasion, avoidance, and postponement, glazed over with a mix of flamboyant rhetoric and sterile purposes.

In a paper delivered at the 1974 annual meeting of the Organization of American Historians, Vincent DeSantis, a leading scholar in the field, concluded a survey of recent trends in the writing of Gilded Age political history

Originally published as "A New Look at the American Gilded Age," *Historical Reflections/ Réflexions Historiques*, 1 (Winter 1974), 231–244. Reprinted by permission of the publisher.

[1]Samuel Langhorne Clemens and Charles Dudley Warner, *The Gilded Age: A Tale of Today* (Hartford: American Publishing Co., 1873). The novel's protagonist, Colonel Beriah Sellers, a grandiloquent, visionary speculator, captured the era's mercenary traits for many readers. The figure of Senator Silas Ratcliffe in Henry Adams' novel, *Democracy* (New York: Holt, 1880), did the same for the politics of the age. Another contemporary critic, Edwin L. Godkin, offered the term "Chromo-Civilization" to sum up American culture in 1874. Twentieth-century historians have suggested rival titles for the period. See especially Lewis Mumford, *The Brown Decades* (New York: Dover, 1955), originally published in 1931; Ray Ginger, *Age of Excess* (New York: Macmillan, 1965); and Howard Mumford Jones, *The Age of Energy* (New York: Viking Press, 1970).

by noting the durability of these inherited stereotypes. A Rip Van Winkle waking from a long nap, he remarked, would not find the latest overviews of the Gilded Age much different from those written twenty or even forty years ago. The caustic judgment on the era's politics has survived the historiographical combat of recent decades with remarkable resilience.[2] If historiography involves the study of succeeding victories by the present over the past, the Gilded Age might be likened to some twilight postwar Gettysburg, where interested students go to poke about and argue over wrong maneuvers. Historians keep winning the same old battles.

The aim here is to suggest some reasons for the tenacity of this older estimate; to isolate the promising newness in the era's treatment by winnowing away more hoary themes; and to suggest what opportunities might be pursued to keep the Rip Van Winkles among us from resuming their naps quite so tranquilly next time round.

The theme provoking the longest yawns is the notion that, either by myopia or purposeful calculation, the public leaders of the Gilded Age avoided the "real issues" of their time—that theirs was a politics of circumlocution and botched chances. The charge has been applied to professional politicians and reformers alike. It is possible to question the validity of the charge without fabricating fresh apologies for the age. When one tries to stack up the "real issues" avoided by its contemporaries against the supposedly unreal issues they endlessly debated, one concludes that underlying the indictment is a profound impatience with the Gilded Age for having not yet discovered the Welfare State. The "real issues" presumed to have dominated the era were, first, the economic maladjustments of an unmanaged economy, and, secondly, the social injustice imposed on its victims through the complacency or irresponsibility of its elected leadership. But what has been maddening to many historians is that neither the people in charge of the political system nor their most prominent and prestigious critics said much about these seemingly urgent issues until the 1890's. What is missing from the era's established vocabulary is the twentieth-century language of public compensation for private suffering—the redress of grievances, the prevention or mitigation of the human costs of fast economic change, the location of the causes of inequality in the social environment rather than in personal frailties, the idea of the federal government functioning in the name of equality as a countervailing force against aggrandizing entrepreneurs.

[2]Vincent P. DeSantis, "The Political Life of the Gilded Age: An Overview of its Recent Literature," paper delivered in Denver, April 20, 1974. Another recent historiographical survey of the period is Walter T. K. Nugent, "Politics From Reconstruction to 1900," in William H. Cartwright and Richard L. Watson, Jr., eds., *The Reinterpretation of American History and Culture* (Washington: National Council for the Social Studies, 1973), pp. 377–99.

Owing to the absence of this ethic of redress and all its corollaries, the age has come down to us not merely as an empty failure, but as the spawning bed for the major problems to be coped with by twentieth-century liberals. Against this background the genteel reformism of the age sounds like a polite apology offered across the generations for the bad manners of people like Roscoe Conkling and Jay Gould. The reformers are assigned complicity in the tactics of postponement by the apparent superficiality of their reforms.

The progressive-liberal interpretation of the age, originating in the revolt against nineteenth-century intellectual and political formalism which got under way in the 1890's, reached mature expression in Beard, Parrington, and Josephson. It may well be receding at last. But it has shown impressive staying power. It received fresh expression in John Sproat's *The Best Men* (1968) and in John Dobson's *Politics in the Gilded Age* (1972).[3] Sproat's comprehensive and lively critique of the reform mentality frees the rest of us from ever again having to prove that the Mugwumps were not New Dealers. With scholarly care and liberal gusto, he performs a job similar to that which Parrington did on the seventeenth-century New England Puritans, and leaves the Mugwumps in a historiographical stance comparable to that of the Puritans before Perry Miller went to work restoring their credibility over a generation ago. Dobson's book, a briefer study concentrating on the 1884 campaign, joins the search for relevance which lured many academics in the late 1960's. He leaves his reader with a distinct impression that the politicians and reformers of the Gilded Age left a bit to be desired as models for current civic activism.[4]

The durability of the progressive-liberal interpretation of the Gilded Age is testimony to the visceral emotions still engaging liberal historians who remain locked in combat with the era's leadership a century after the fact. A leading historian of the Age of Jackson recently confessed that if he were forced to a choice between the Jacksonian Democrats and the Whigs, he didn't know which party would have won his vote.[5] I daresay most liberal historians, if offered a similar choice in the Gilded Age, would have no such difficulty. They would enthusiastically vote "No!"

[3]The full citations are John G. Sproat, *"The Best Men": Liberal Reformers in the Gilded Age* (New York: Oxford Univ. Press, 1968), and John M. Dobson, *Politics in the Gilded Age: A New Perspective on Reform* (New York: Praeger, 1972).

[4]My coupling of Sproat's and Dobson's studies may obscure important differences between them. See Sproat's criticism of Dobson's presentmindedness in John G. Sproat, " 'Old Ideals' and 'New Realities' in the Gilded Age." *Reviews in American History*, 1 (Dec. 1973), 565–67. The latest appraisals of Mugwump reformers, stressing their cosmopolitan professionalism, revise both Sproat and Dobson. See for example Gerald W. McFarland, *Mugwumps, Morals, and Politics, 1884–1920* (Amherst: Univ. of Massachusetts Press, 1975).

[5]Ronald P. Formisano made this informal comment at the Overview session on The Age of Jackson at the Denver meeting of the Organization of American Historians, April 19, 1974.

If one tries to conjure up a surrealistic impression of the values which ought to have bloomed but for the misplaced priorities of the era's politicos, a bright liberal vision emerges of a world that might have been. It is reminiscent of the Popular Front imagery of the 1930's, but rather more folksy, more bucolic: a sort of national Grange picnic, a rival gathering to Parrington's Great Barbecue, thrown by the Patrons of Husbandry for the Knights of Labor, and presided over by Henry Demarest Lloyd. John Peter Altgeld and Henry George are the main speakers, and a young Jane Addams moves among the elm-shadowed tables offering quiet words of hope. The meal, featuring corn-on-the-cob, is a good one, which is fortunate, because the price of corn has been slowly rising. It is a noble, pleasant dream, and it would be nice to buy a ticket.

But those who thrash about in the past in search of things that might have been, had the age been wiser or kinder, reveal more of their talent for idealism than their capacity for analysis. By the same token, liberal historians who belabor the age for its false issues and suggest more proper goals for it to have strived for run the risk of stumbling on the familiar fallacies of presentism. They are about as shrewd as those radical historians who bewail the New Deal's failure to launch more daring forms of collectivism, or to integrate the races, during the Great Depression. The question which these sorts of presentist judgments raise is whether the public leaders who might pass muster by such criteria could possibly have been elected to office by their contemporaries.[6]

A recent study by James Mohr, *The Radical Republicans and Reform in New York During Reconstruction,* offers a note of caution on this point which is applicable to the politics of the Gilded Age as a whole. He reminds us that there were limits to what was possible in the postwar years when it came to redressing grievances—limits imposed on politicians not only by the courts or wealthy party patrons, but by the most thoroughly democratized electorate in the western world. When New York's Radical Republicans tried reform at home, they were promptly punished.[7] LaWanda Cox's review of Mohr's book includes a summary comment worth quoting for its broader relevance:

> Not the Republican politician but the voting public failed reform in the early years of the Gilded Age. Civic improvement did not win the anticipated votes from New York City's Democratic faithful, and Republican

[6]The point is explored in detail in Jerold S. Auerbach, "New Deal, Old Deal, or Raw Deal: Some Thoughts on New Left Historiography," *Journal of Southern History,* 35 (Feb. 1969), 18–30.

[7]James C. Mohr, *The Radical Republicans in New York During Reconstruction* (Ithaca: Cornell Univ. Press, 1973).

party support for equal suffrage brought political disaster. The hopeful union of idealism and practical politics within the state Republican party could not be consummated in the face of public repudiation at the polls.[8]

In the state of Massachusetts, perhaps the most advanced state in the Union in the realm of labor reform, legislative leaders were unable to muster popular support for comprehensive factory reform until the end of the 1880's.[9] From these examples, which could be multiplied, one of two conclusions follow. Either the *people* did not know what the "real issues" were, or the whole idea of "real issues" versus "false issues" is intellectually bankrupt. Twentieth-century liberal historians have scored enough posthumous victories over the Gilded Agers. It is high time we suspended our own democratic priorities and looked more carefully at theirs.

Fortunately the new close work is well under way. The missionary appeals of Lee Benson, Samuel P. Hays, and others have combined with the computer and the diligence of quantitative historians to generate a startling revision of assumptions about electoral behavior in the late nineteenth century. The quantifiers have permanently altered our perceptions of the political landscape of the Gilded Age and charted fresh road maps for the rest of us to travel by. The major finding of Paul Kleppner, Richard Jensen, Samuel McSeveney, and other scholars of like persuasion is that the mass of American voters, from the 1870's down through the early 1890's, from New England and New York across the Middle West, were prompted in their voting behavior primarily by ethno-cultural values, mostly religious and sectarian in their roots.[10] This finding is not only important in itself; it confirms a sense that despite frequent provocations to the contrary, class-consciousness and economic radicalism were shallow and ephemeral characteristics in the electorate. It also reinforces an awareness of decentralization and pervasive localism in the political horizons of most voters. This latter theme may be more widely agreed upon than any other emerging from the fresh scholarship of the past decade. By its very nature it renders generalizations about the operations of national politics more hazardous than ever before.

How the discoveries of Kleppner, Jensen, and McSeveney relate for instance to the perpetual congressional dance around the protective tariff is a

---

[8]*Journal of American History,* 60 (March 1974), 1136.

[9]Geoffrey Blodgett, *The Gentle Reformers: Massachusetts Democrats in the Cleveland Era* (Cambridge: Harvard Univ. Press, 1966), pp. 128–38.

[10]Paul Kleppner, *The Cross of Culture: A Social Analysis of Midwestern Politics, 1850–1900* (New York: Free Press, 1970); Richard J. Jensen, *The Winning of the Midwest: Social and Political Conflict, 1888–1896* (Chicago: Univ. of Chicago Press, 1971); and Samuel McSeveney, *The Politics of Depression: Political Behavior in the Northeast, 1893–1896* (New York: Oxford Univ. Press, 1972).

puzzle which neither they nor anyone else has yet entirely solved. The easy answer, that the tariff debates of the 1880's were a ritualistic exercise in rhetorical irrelevance, will no longer suffice. The more serious answer, proposed by H. Wayne Morgan and Lewis Gould among others, that tariff debate and other congressional approaches to decision-making, however inconclusive, were slowly forging a national political consciousness among localized Americans, remains to be integrated with the conclusions of the quantifiers about the situation at the grass roots.[11]

We are learning more about the structure of national political institutions which mediated between the two tiers of consciousness. The most influential studies—by David Rothman on the United States Senate and Robert Marcus on the presidential nominating apparatus of the G.O.P.—reveal both a high degree of professional partisanship (which may or may not have intensified as the years passed, depending on what particular evidence is under scrutiny), and a structure of party organization which remained far more dense and constraining on the turf of state and local politics than at the national tier.[12] To borrow the terminology of Samuel P. Hays in the most searching of his many important essays on the social structure of American politics, "community" loyalties prevailed over emerging "society" interests throughout the era.[13] The political scientist Walter Dean Burnham has gone so far as to suggest that after Reconstruction the major national parties became bulwarks of localist resistance to centralizing alterations in the political structure demanded by cosmopolitan elites.[14] The warfare between politically and geographically diffuse elite groups on the one hand and rooted local politicians on the other is yet another fertile new theme to emerge from recent studies.

[11]H. Wayne Morgan, *From Hayes to McKinley: National Party Politics, 1877–1896* (Syracuse: Syracuse Univ. Press, 1969), pp. 120–21, 165–70; Lewis L. Gould, "The Republican Search for a National Majority," in H. Wayne Morgan, ed., *The Gilded Age,* (Syracuse: Univ. Press, rev. ed., 1970), pp. 176–78.

[12]David J. Rothman, *Politics and Power: The United States Senate, 1869–1901* (Cambridge: Harvard Univ. Press, 1966); Robert D. Marcus, *Grand Old Party: Political Structure in the Gilded Age, 1880–1896* (New York: Oxford Univ. Press, 1971). Rothman's findings on the changing intensity of Senatorial partisanship were challenged in William G. Shade, Stanley D. Hopper, David Jacobson, and Stephen E. Moiles, "Partisanship in the United States Senate: 1869–1901," *Journal of Interdisciplinary History,* 4 (Autumn 1973), 185–205. The authors of this critique, a computer-armed strike force, modestly conclude: "Since there are significant differences in the types of evidence used by Rothman and those presented here, it cannot be said that this article represents a definitive refutation of Rothman."

[13]Samuel P. Hays, "Political Parties and the Community-Society Continuum," in William N. Chambers and Walter Dean Burnham, eds., *The American Party Systems: Stages of Political Development* (New York: Oxford Univ. Press, 1967), pp. 152–81.

[14]Burnham, "Party Systems and the Political Process," ibid., pp. 277–307. See especially p. 284.

Against the backdrop of this combat, it is clear that the partisan rhetoric of professional politicians was not merely theatrical entertainment designed to distract and disorient; it was the language which connected politicians to the most carefully organized and politically active grass-roots electorate in American history. Professor Burnham's broad-gauged analysis of changing patterns in voter participation from the 1870's down to the present provokes sobering reflections on the long-term costs involved in the grass-roots drought which hit this political system of the Gilded Age after the depression of the 1890's.[15] A recurring paradox emerges from all this. Decisive changes in the tight political system of the 1880's, whether achieved as acts of conscious reform to loosen the grip of local partisan leadership, or as a result of critical elections which finally broke the twenty-year competitive two-party deadlock in the 1890's, occurred at the expense of organized mass democracy rather than because of it.

Conventional narratives about the political excitement of the 1890's and the origins of Progressivism are already beginning to change under the impact of the new political history. Narrative accounts of the Gilded Age are undergoing similar amendment and adaptation, though at a somewhat slower pace. The rate of historiographical change ought not to be impeded by mutual disparagement of rival methodologies. Spokesmen for the quantitative and behavioral approach often season their analyses with appeals for less attention to isolated episodes, colorful incidents, idiosyncratic personalities, and other staples of impressionistic story-telling. They argue that these traditional preoccupations have obscured for too long underlying patterns of behavioral reality now being uncovered by the new methods. Historians who cling to a stubborn faith in the art of narrative synthesis need not be put off by this charge. Narrative impressionism will survive and continue to command an audience among those interested in durable issues of motivation and causation and in the unique particularity of how things happened. The insights of the quantifiers and behaviorists should be cheerfully exploited where their findings deepen understanding of these classic concerns.

Meanwhile, taking a cue from Howard Mumford Jones' reminder that the Gilded Age "did not exist as an imperfect prophecy of twentieth-century America [but] lived in its own right,"[16] historians can strive to free themselves definitively from the dead hand of progressive-liberal presentism. Efforts at suspended disbelief are worth pursuing as one tries to climb inside

---

[15]Walter Dean Burnham, "The Changing Shape of the American Political Universe," *American Political Science Review,* 59 (March 1965), 7–28. Philip Converse, "Change in the American Electorate," in Angus Campbell and Philip Converse, eds., *The Human Meaning of Social Change* (New York: Russell Sage Foundation, 1972), raises important questions about the assumptions supporting Burnham's analysis but leaves its architecture mainly intact.

[16]Jones, *The Age of Energy,* p. 16.

the minds of those strange Victorian Americans and look out at the world through their eyes. This will entail taking the rhetoric of the age seriously as clues to its perceptions—not viewing the rhetoric as a smokescreen to be cleared away, but as a filter through which men and women tried to comprehend what was happening to them and what was threatening them. In any given era a society seeks its own equilibrium, its own special cluster of inhibitions, anxieties, and urgencies, its own sense of what is possible and what is appropriate. In searching out the terms of equilibrium for the Gilded Age, we should bear in mind that people act on memory more often than on prophecy. The age is best understood not as a dark prelude to Progressivism but rather as a somber sequel to the Civil War. George Fredrickson's *The Inner Civil War* rivals Robert Wiebe's *The Search for Order* as the most important book of the past decade for understanding the Gilded Age.[17] Both studies illuminate the postwar era's quest for stability and equilibrium beyond the turbulence of war and reconstruction. And as Morton Keller pointed out some years ago, the great political fact of late nineteenth-century America was a direct consequence of the war—the gray triumph of organizational loyalty over the politics of ardent social purpose.[18] The war's concussive impact not only helped fix the partisan loyalties of the American majority for a long generation, but blunted its desire for headlong ideological strife under national leadership.

The crucial arena for choice for or against significant political change was by no means confined to Washington. Given the vitality of local politics, the resiliency in the police power of state and city governments, and prevailing constitutional assumptions about the authority of the federal government to intervene in private disputes between employer and employee, or producer and consumer, state and city governments continued well into the new century to affect the daily lives of the population more tangibly than initiatives from Washington. The monographic trend toward close studies of state and local political institutions, and group behavior within these structures, should be encouraged, however long it takes to change a single line in the standard textbooks. Seymour Mandelbaum's *Boss Tweed's New York,* treating the complex relations between urban localism, leadership legitimacy, communications technology, and the role of corruption in enforcing public decisions, is a model for the sort of history waiting to be written in urban politics.[19]

[17]George M. Fredrickson, *The Inner Civil War: Northern Intellectuals and the Crisis of the Union* (New York: Harper and Row, 1965); Robert H. Wiebe, *The Search For Order, 1877-1920* (New York: Hill and Wang, 1967).

[18]Morton Keller, "The Politicos Reconsidered," *Perspectives In American History,* 1 (1967), 401–408.

[19]Seymour J. Mandelbaum, *Boss Tweed's New York* (New York: John Wiley, 1965).

Among the multitude of national issues which have attracted long attention, at least two old chestnuts are worth re-examination. The first concerns
the familiar doctrine of *laissez-faire,* and the question of federal responsibility
for the oversight of national economic development. To economic specialists
of that day, conservative and radical alike, the overriding fact about the
American economy was its rising productivity. Whatever their differences in
attitude toward the problem of maldistribution, they were virtually unanimous in agreeing that expanding production was a Good Thing, and in the
best of all possible worlds ought not to be discouraged or curbed. The
politicians overwhelmingly agreed. With relatively little influential dissent,
the federal government tried to promote the goal of rising productivity
throughout the century. The particular set of tactics toward this end bore different labels, provoked hot debate, and varied from decade to decade, but the
goal endured. Twenty years ago David Potter touched briefly on this theme in
*People of Plenty,* showing how the government tried constantly to make the
potential abundance of the continent accessible to those who wanted to ex-
ploit it—through land laws, internal improvements, federal rail subsidies,
laws of incorporation, and protective tariffs.[20] One might add to this list an
earnest commitment to unrestricted immigration. In 1967 James Willard
Hurst elaborated this theme into a sophisticated essay in legal history,
demonstrating a continuous desire from the eighteenth century to the
twentieth to mobilize the law of the land behind a release of productive
energy.[21]

Hurst and Potter made a common point. What went by the name of
*laissez-faire* was less a negative limitation on the power of the state than it
was a widely agreed-upon set of tactics for promoting productivity in a hurry.
That was the tacit priority of the age, shared by the great bulk of its elected
politicians and most of their constituents, insofar as they understood what
was going on. In the American vernacular, *laissez-faire* was basically a policy
of promotional indulgence. The debates it provoked were mainly over degrees
and details of federal indulgence, not degrees and details of regulation.
Therefore it is hard to isolate any particular set of spokesmen for *laissez-faire*
and identify them as the villains in a Manichean melodrama between *laissez-
faire* and regulation. Far better to press Hurst's suggestions for legal history
into the realm of politics and see where they take us. The final chapter of his
*Law and the Conditions of Freedom* is a mine of incentives for fresh thoughts
about the political economy of the Gilded Age.

[20]David M. Potter, *People of Plenty: Economic Abundance and the American Character*
(Chicago: Univ. of Chicago Press, 1954), pp. 122–25.
[21]James Willard Hurst, *Law and the Conditions of Freedom in the Nineteenth-Century
United States* (Madison: Univ. of Wisconsin Press, 1967).

My second comment about national politics goes to another seemingly tired issue. Why, given all the other goals they might have chosen to improve the lot of their fellow man, did the genteel cosmopolitan reformers of the day concentrate so much fire on the narrow goal of civil service reform? Was this not an obvious misdirection of their talent and prestige? Were they not simply working off their frustration at being muscled from the halls of power themselves? Here I will enter a plea for the genteel reformers, and argue that their focus on the spoils system as the national political institution most in need of dismantling by the 1880's was absolutely correct. The operations of the spoils system compounded political localism and decentralization at a time when all the currents of economic and professional life were running the other way. It perpetuated a primitive, personalized politics, enforcing patterns of mutually demeaning dependence between politician and job-seeker which depressed the chances for longevity, experience, and technical competence in the clerical and administrative staffs of government at all levels. It devoured the time and energies of elected officials in endless gulps. The spoils system may have been the most enervating illness in American public life. Its reform was a precondition for the emergence of the bureaucratic ethic which Robert Wiebe sees as a major consequence of the search for order by the century's end.[22]

Because the Pendleton Act was cleverly drafted by the reformers to be slow and incremental in its impact, and thus more palatable to politicians, its consequences are often lost sight of. Wiebe, for example, dismisses it as a weak law of small significance.[23] We often read that only a tiny fraction of the civil service fell under its provisions at the outset of Grover Cleveland's first administration. What is less widely reported is that by the end of his second administration, a majority of the service was under the merit system. The long-time dean of administrative historians, Leonard D. White, concluded that the law had produced only minor improvements by 1900.[24] With all due respect I think he departed from his own evidence in reaching that conclusion. Another administrative historian, Paul Van Riper, was more perceptive in detecting the Pendleton Act's significance when he wrote:

> The economic reforms considered so essential by others would not have been possible except for civil service reform. A relatively stable and effective civil service [was] indispensable for the functioning of the modern

---

[22]Wiebe, *The Search For Order,* pp. 129–55, 160, 161.
[23]Ibid., p. 61.
[24]Leonard D. White, *The Republican Era: 1869–1901. A Study in Administrative History* (New York: Macmillan, 1958), pp. 386–96.

state. The civil service reformers diagnosed better than they knew or than others have usually given them credit. They did put first things first.[25]

If one accepts the argument that a major problem confronting national politicians in the 1880's was the lack of centralized facilities for systematic fact-gathering and the competent analysis and distribution of social informa-tion, then administrative reform was both a critical need of the age and one of its salient achievements.

One can broaden this point by casting the issue in terms of political modernization. Students of modernization theory see three important keys to the modernization of a political system: first, the rationalization of authority in a centralized power framework; secondly, the differentiation of political, legal, and administrative functions, separating administrative functions from partisan politics by the elaboration of bureaucracy; and thirdly, mass political participation by the population of the whole society.[26] In the 1870's there existed in the United States a radical imbalance among these three con-ditions. It had gone farther along the road toward mass participation than any other nation in the world. Yet on the first two counts, the centralization of authority and the differentiation of governmental functions, it remained in a relatively primitive condition, lagging well behind the nations of western Europe. Harold Hyman's new book on the constitutional impact of the Civil War underscores the consequences of this imbalance for the fate of Re-construction.[27] Throughout the Gilded Age the disparity between centralized federal responsibilities and centralized facilities to cope with them remained apparent. The nation's governing instruments often lacked both intrinsic coherence and the legitimacy of popular acceptance.

It was this situation, requiring (or enabling) politicians to behave in ways that violated accepted norms, which accounts for much of the contemporary rhetoric about "political demoralization" and "corruption" and the constant sputter of exchanges between "impractical theorists" and "corrupt politicians." Civil service reform did not completely solve the problem, of course. But meaningful change toward a more workable equilibrium between political responsibility and functional power in Washington did occur as a result of the administrative reforms of the 1880's, producing under Cleveland the outlines of what might be called the sanitary state.

[25]Paul P. Van Riper, *History of the United States Civil Service* (Evanston: Row, Peterson, 1958), pp. 83–84. For another assessment, see Ari Hoogenboom, "The Pendleton Act and the Civil Service," *American Historical Review,* 64 (Jan. 1959), 301–18.

[26]See for example, Samuel P. Huntington, *Political Order in Changing Societies* (New Haven: Yale Univ. Press, 1968), pp. 34, 93–139.

[27]Harold M. Hyman, *A More Perfect Union: The Impact of the Civil War and Reconstruc-tion on the Constitution* (New York: Knopf, 1973), pp. 282 ff.

To conclude this point, and tie it back to the ambiguities of national politics and civil service reform, and the Cleveland presidency, quotations from two letters written by Brooks Adams (perhaps the profoundest student of centralization the age produced) may be illuminating. In 1874, Adams wrote to Whitelaw Reid:

> The whole history of the past ten years has been the legitimate result of the unresisted growth of the centralizing element. Hence our very theories are now turning on ourselves and from a Federal Republic we are in the course of developing into a consolidated empire with a strong central government, with the states for provinces.
> That this result may be in the end inevitable is nothing to the purpose. It does not seem to me that we are ready yet. The means used to attain this end of subjugating the states are two: 1st, an army of log-rollers pensioned on the civil service, 2nd, the party system founded on the caucus which renders all organizations easy victims of the aforesaid log rollers.[28]

Like many other cosmopolitan elitists, Adams perceived a need for balance between ends and means in the administration of the new national state emerging from the war. The rationalization (or purification, as most reformers put it) of the means seemed urgently desirable. Ten years later Cleveland's candidacy for the presidency offered hope for progress on this front. For the thousands of lawyers, educators, publishers, journalists, and other urban professional men who joined the Mugwump movement of 1884, their bolt meant much more than a blind rush from James G. Blaine's dubious and expedient past. Brooks Adams, as a young Boston lawyer, was in the thick of the bolt. He wrote to Cleveland shortly before the election:

> From the first I have been one of your supporters because you seemed to me to represent the principles in which I believe more fully than any man now in public life.[29]

Ten years after that, Adams was writing his famous essay on the forces of concentration in history, *The Law of Civilization and Decay,* which signalled his intellectual journey down paths which completely detached him from the Mugwumps and from sympathy for Cleveland's public aims.[30] By 1896

---

[28]Brooks Adams to Whitelaw Reid, March 18, 1874, Whitelaw Reid Papers, Library of Congress.

[29]Brooks Adams to Grover Cleveland, Oct. 23, 1884, Grover Cleveland Papers, Library of Congress.

[30]Brooks Adams, *The Law of Civilization and Decay: An Essay on History* (New York: Macmillan, 1896). The 1943 edition, published by Alfred A. Knopf, includes an excellent introduction by Charles Beard.

Adams had aligned himself momentarily with the silverites and Populists, anticipating chaos as an alternative to centralization.

The events of the 1890's blew apart the alignment of principles and votes which produced the peculiar Cleveland Democratic coalition of the 1880's, propelling its group parts off on different tangents toward new political homes. Cleveland Democracy was an obvious casualty of the crack-up of the Gilded Age. But the failures that ended Cleveland's career under a cloud which shadows his reputation to this day should not obscure those earlier felt needs which had conspired to make him one of three men in American history (along with Andrew Jackson and Franklin Roosevelt) to attract more votes than his competitor in three straight presidential contests. How that happened remains another paradox worth probing. The answers lie not only in more strenuous analysis of voting returns and the structure of group behavior, but also in the realm of cultural and intellectual history. The most fertile recent suggestions may be found in Robert Kelley's foray in comparative intellectual history, *The Transatlantic Persuasion,* a book which places the phenomenon of Grover Cleveland in a context of cosmopolitan, international reform thought spanning the nineteenth century.[31]

Kelley's attempt to bridge the chasm between the history of ideas and the history of political behavior inspires a final suggestion for new work to be done. Now that the myth of Social Darwinism has been pretty well dissipated as a monolithic causal explanation for the quirks of the American mind in the Gilded Age, the interface between politics and culture requires more plausible interconnections. The job of synthesizing Robert Wiebe's brilliant insights about society and culture in the Gilded Age with the era's political arrangements remains.[32] For intellectual historians, the possibilities of synthesis may be discerned in Stow Persons' recent *The Decline of American Gentility* and John Higham's imaginative essay on "The Reorientation of American Culture in the 1890's."[33] For their part, political historians must reach out and meet the intellectual and cultural historians on common ground. We need to demolish the narrow and rigid boundaries of political history which confine it to the electoral behavior of the public and the political behavior of the elected. Only then can we include within its proper limits the full array of organizational, associational, and professional activity which flourished in baroque variety around the rim of the partisan electoral arena: not only the Grange and the Knights and the tariff leagues and civil service reform lob-

---

[31]Robert Kelley, *The Transatlantic Persuasion: The Liberal-Democratic Mind in the Age of Gladstone* (New York: Knopf, 1969), pp. 293–350.

[32]Wiebe devotes ten meager pages to the politics of the age in *The Search for Order.*

[33]Stow Persons, *The Decline of American Gentility* (New York: Columbia Univ. Press, 1973); John Higham, "The Reorientation of American Culture in the 1890's," in Higham, *Writing American History: Essays on Modern Scholarship* (Bloomington: Indiana Univ. Press, 1970), pp. 73–102.

bies, but the temperance unions, suffrage associations, fraternal orders, veterans' organizations, medical and bar associations, the new universities, the club network of the urban elites, the charities and churches and trade unions, the museums and historical societies and park associations. The list is endless, and it is heavy with political connections and significance. It is out of this broad associational matrix (to close on a note of anticipation of what lay ahead) that emerged the sophisticated interest group politics of the twentieth century replacing the mass political organizations of the Gilded Age.

Back in 1960 Bernard Bailyn wrote a little essay which criticized historians of American education for assuming that their subject was about schools, and could be confined to the study of formal institutions of classroom instruction. He suggested that in the future they pay less exclusive attention to how teachers taught and more attention to how people learned.[34] The essay had an impact. Educational history broke out of the schoolhouse to become the history of a whole society trying to organize and understand itself. The lesson should not be lost for political historians of the Gilded Age.

[34]Bernard Bailyn, *Education in the Forming of American Society: Needs and Opportunities for Study* (New York: Random House, 1960). See especially pp. 9–11.

# Victorian Morality in Institutions

# THAT GUILTY THIRD TIER: PROSTITUTION IN NINETEENTH-CENTURY AMERICAN THEATERS

### CLAUDIA D. JOHNSON

WHEN A NINETEENTH-CENTURY ACTRESS NAMED OLIVE LOGAN SPOKE OF "that dark, horrible, guilty 'third tier,' " she was referring to an upper row above the dress and family circles which was set aside for the sole use of prostitutes in American theaters. The third tier, or gallery as it was frequently called, struck the young actress as a "brutal exhibition of faces" at which she gazed from the stage "with some such feeling as one might have in looking over into pandemonium."[1] The playgoer, as well as the performer, could also observe in the top gallery "the hard-visaged, the ill-behaved, the boisterous, the indecent."[2] The custom of relegating prostitutes to a single gallery in the theater is rarely mentioned, much less discussed, now; but in the nineteenth century it was considered a matter of grave import to those who worked for the survival of the theater. Of all the accusations hurled at the theater by its enemies, the charge relating to the third tier was their strongest, least refuted argument. In its influence on American culture the third tier was much more than just a pivotal subject of discussion in the continual war between moralists and artists; it was a theatrical fact of life which probably shaped the American stage much more decidedly than historians have recognized. The assignment of prostitutes to one part of the theatrical house had a profound impact on theater design, on theatrical economics, and on the extent to which theater was accepted and supported in the nineteenth century.

To most of the early theater historians, the third tier seems to have been

[1] Olive Logan, *Before the Footlights and Behind the Stage* (Philadelphia: Parmelee and Co.), pp. 33–35.
[2] Thomas DeWitt Talmadge, *Sports That Kill* (New York: Funk and Wagnall, 1875), pp. 20–22.

regarded as a dark secret of the stage, better left unrecorded and undis-
cussed. It was, obviously, an embarrassment that one just did not talk
about. Eminent stage historians like Joseph N. Ireland, T. Allston Brown
and George C. D. Odell do not recognize those notable instances when the
Park and the Howard Athenaeum made headlines by closing the doors of
the third tier. Thus, "the gallery" becomes a dark side of America's theatrical history which receives only passing reference by modern scholars.

To learn about the third tier the modern student must consult the editorial pages of urban papers of the day and contemporary treatises attacking or defending the theater; a few theatrical memoirs are also useful.
William Dunlap, playwright, theater manager, and one of the first historians of the American stage, is another good contemporary source.
Fortunately Dunlap was not so reluctant as subsequent historians to discuss
this aspect of history. Furthermore Dunlap considered the presence of the
third tier sufficiently important to make it the subject of the conclusion to a
1797 account included in *The History of the American Theatre.* So it is to
Dunlap that students may go for a first-hand record of the early existence of
the third tier, written by a theater professional.[3]

This early historian records that the third tier was established in the
American theater as early as the mid-eighteenth century. In his words, it
was "a distinct portion of the proscenium" allocated to "those unfortunate
females who have been the victims of seduction." From the beginning it was
"a separate place," "set apart," which could "present to the gaze of the
matron and virgin the unabashed votaries of vice" and "tempt the yet
unsullied youth, by the example of the false face which depravity assumes
for the purpose of enticing to guilt." Its genesis, according to Dunlap, may
have been British; though unknown in eighteenth-century Continental
Europe, the third tier, which became so readily a part of the stage on this
continent, could also be found in England. Prostitutes displayed themselves
from a special portion of the house in the very beginnings of American
drama. Of the third tiers in the country's earliest theaters Dunlap wrote:
"It is to be lamented that when the people of Massachusetts introduced the
theater in their capital, having the experience of the world before them, they
had not set an example to their fellow citizens by purifying the dramatic establishment and abolishing this evil. They appear to have noticed it, but
instead of remedying, they, if possible, made it worse. . . . The new theater
of Philadelphia gave an opportunity for reform, as did that of New York;
but these opportunities were neglected."

Many first-hand references to the third tier in eighteenth-century America do no more than suggest its true nature. Bernard Hewitt translates a

[3]William Dunlap, *History of the American Theatre* (New York: J. and J. Harper, 1832), pp.
407–12.

1794 description of the Chestnut Theater in Philadelphia by a French traveler, Moreau de Saint-Méry, who noted, "Women as well as men sit in the pit, though not women of fashion. There are women also in the gallery and the Negroes have no other place."[4] Whether this meant that the women in the gallery (the cheapest part of the house) were prostitutes is left unsaid, but the fact that they were segregated on a tier with blacks suggests that the writer is speaking of the same women whom Dunlap describes as prostitutes. Hewitt also cites Washington Irving's Jonathan Oldstyle letters which note that the gallery is kept "in *excellent* order by the constables," but later recommends that the upper tier have "less grog and better constables." Again, there is no clear mention of the gallery's being given over to prostitutes and their customers, but, obviously, it was sufficiently rowdy to demand policing, which suggests that Irving left unsaid what Dunlap knew to be true, that the third tier was the domain of prostitutes.

By the nineteenth century the third tier had become an understood theatrical appendage. *Femmes du pavé* were welcomed into the gallery of New York's high-class Park Theater from the time of its opening in the late eighteenth century. Its lower-class counterpart, the Bowery, opened in 1826, reserving the gallery for the same clientele. By the 1830s and 1840s, the relinquishing of the third tier to prostitutes had become an established national tradition, not only in New York, but in most large cities, including Boston, Chicago, Philadelphia, St. Louis, Cincinnati, Mobile, and New Orleans, among others.[5]

The ritual of the third tier was apparently very simple: the entire inhabitants of houses of prostitution would customarily attend the theater in a body, entering the tier by a separate stairway an hour or two before the rest of the house was opened. Unlike the higher class prostitutes who sat throughout the theater and met customers there by pre-arrangement through such means as newspaper advertisements, the lower class prostitutes of the third tier made the initial contacts with their customers in the theater itself. Customers of long-standing took their places with the women in the third tier. Other men were introduced to these prostitutes when mutual friends took them up to the third tier from other parts of the house. A bar was located nearby to serve the upper tier, undoubtedly contributing to the rowdy behavior which was a constant disturbance to the rest of the house.[6] At times women would even leave the third tier and solicit cus-

[4] Barnard Hewitt, *Theatre USA, 1667–1957* (New York: McGraw-Hill, 1959), pp. 40, 59, 63.
[5] Dunlap, 407–12; John Murtagh and Sara Harris, *Cast the First Stone* (New York: McGraw-Hill, 1957), pp. 203–05.
[6] John J. Jennings, *Theatrical and Circus Life* (St. Louis, 1886), pp. 60–65; Meade Minnigerode, *The Fabulous Forties: 1840–1850; A Presentation of Private Life* (New York: G. P. Putnam's Sons, 1924), pp. 55, 151–56; William Everts, "The Theatre," *Problems of the City* (Chicago, 1866), pp. 19–43.

tomers in other parts of the house. In 1837 the Reverend Robert Turnbull was not nearly so indignant about the mere fact that prostitutes were allowed to use the theater as he was about their being allowed "to leave their appropriate place and invade the pit."[7]

The primary business of the gallery was not to watch the play but to make arrangements for the rest of the evening. Having met in the tier, the prostitutes and their customers might go directly to a house of prostitution. Others might lengthen the evening's activities, as did the higher class prostitutes whom John J. Jennings describes in St. Louis: they proceeded with their customers to a "quiet restaurant of the most questionable reputation and took one of the private supper-rooms, which are at the disposal of people whose visit to the establishment is not by any means for the sole purpose of drinking and eating, but has a broad and very unmistakeable suggestion of immorality in it."[8] John Murtagh and Sara Harris, writing on the history of New York prostitution, found that for many prostitutes the upper tier of the Bowery Theater was not just a meeting place, but a convenient spot for completion of their business: "They swarmed the galleries, using them not only for purposes of pickup, but also as places where their relations with unfinicky customers could be consummated."[9]

Even as the third tier flourished, campaigns to abolish it gathered great momentum, and the practice began to die out. The clergy and the press spoke frequently against the tier in the thirties and forties. Moreover, as early as 1837 Noah Ludlow made the revolutionary decision to close the third tier in the St. Louis theater which he managed and in all other cities, including Mobile and New Orleans, where his traveling company played. His description illustrates the degree to which the tier had become entrenched. It also shows that the decision to abandon the practice often called for a certain amount of courage on the part of the manager:

> On the opening of this house I made a beginning of a reform which I adhered to and carried forward in after years in all the theatres under my management. This was to refuse admission to any female to the performance who did not come attended by a gentleman, or some one having the appearance of a man of respectability, not even in the third tier; and women notoriously of the *pavé* were never, under any conditions, admitted. The result of these rigid measures was that the third tier in our theatres was as quiet and orderly as any portion of the house.
>
>                                    . . .
>
> I had a hard struggle for this scheme of reformation. There were several attempts made by lewd women and their bullies to pass door-keepers having ob-

[7] Robert Turnbull, *The Theatre* (Hartford, 1837), pp. 82–89.
[8] Jennings, 60–65.
[9] Murtagh, 203–05.

tained tickets by sending boys and servants for them under the names of respectable citizens. However, I foiled their stratagems through the vigilance of a private policeman, well acquainted with such kind of persons by sight, and who knew how to deal with them. From time to time, for some two or three years following my management in St. Louis and Mobile, and in subsequent years in New Orleans, I had sent to me through the post-office threatening missives, such as "cow-hidings," "fisticuffings," and "shooting" and the like, for refusing admission to these filles de joie; but I persisted in my course, and finally gained my point.[10]

An interesting episode in the closing of the third tier took place at the Park in 1842. Edmund Simpson, the manager, attempted to meet the objection of critics of theater immorality by producing a religious play, "The Israelites in Egypt, or the Passage of the Red Sea." As a letter-writer to the *New York Herald* in November of 1842 pointed out, however, the Park's continuation of the third tier made any other attempts at moral reform somewhat ludicrous: "Look at the inconsistency of the production of sacred drama in a temple devoted to the harlot." As a result, Simpson closed the third tier and was congratulated by the *Herald* for his courage in "purifying the third tier," by excluding "the frail women who frequented that quarter." Unfortunately, Simpson's courage failed; before the end of the play's eighteen-night run, the prostitutes were back in the Park's third tier.[11]

Another milestone in the third tier's closing was recorded by *The Spirit of the Times,* which lauded manager J. H. Hackett for closing the third tier when he reopened the Howard Athenaeum in 1846: "We understand that the great objectionable features of theatrical representation are to be excluded from the Athenaeum—the 'third row' and 'the bar' which have proved the ruin of so many young men."[12]

In 1857, however, a hostile observer noted that the third tier was still the "resort of lewd women" who went there "to attract attention" and continued to make the theater "the house of the harlot" where "she holds her court."[13] Even as late as 1875, Thomas DeWitt Talmadge insisted that prostitutes still sat in the third tier.[14] By the 1880s, however, writers sympathetic with as well as those antagonistic to the stage seem to have agreed that the third tiers of all legitimate theaters were finally closed.[15]

There is, then, no doubt that the appropriation of an upper tier for pros-

---

[10]Noah Ludlow, *Dramatic Life as I Found It* (St. Louis: G. I. Jones and Co., 1880), pp. 478–79.

[11]*New York Herald* (Nov. 1 and 2, 1842), 2; Minnigerode, 155, 156.

[12]*Spirit of the Times* (July 18, 1846), 2.

[13]David H. Agnew, *Theatrical Amusements* (Philadelphia, 1857), pp. 8, 20.

[14]Talmadge, 20–22, 39, 232.

[15]Logan, 542.

titutes was a reality of America's theatrical history, despite the inclination of many of the older writers to ignore it. Had the practice of reserving a tier for prostitutes been a short-lived, isolated instance, the subject would perhaps deserve no more than the passing reference which it has received. But such was not the case: records indicate that this peculiar relationship between the American theater and prostitution was widespread and covered a period of fifty years or more. Moreover, the relationship was not inconsequential; it had the most profound influence on every aspect of theatrical life. The third tier dictated the very design of the theater building, was at the foundation of theatrical economics, and was largely responsible for the reputation, and consequently the clientele, of the nineteenth-century theater.

Theaters in most American cities were designed expressly to house prostitutes in the third tier, but as quietly as possible. To this end they were built so that opening onto a side street was a separate stairway for the use of third-tier patrons only. Patrons of the rest of the house used a front entrance and central stairway. This arrangement was very like the separate balcony stairways in movie houses once designed for blacks in the segregated South. Dunlap writes that in Boston, "the Federal Street Theatre provided a separate entrance for those who came for the express purpose of alluring to vice. The boxes displayed the same row of miserable victims, decked in smiles and borrowed finery, and the entrance could only, by its separation from those appropriated to the residue of the audience, become a screen inviting to secret guilt." [16]

St. Louis theaters had a similar design: there were three tiers or galleries of seats and a parquet. The first tier was called the dress circle; the second, which included a bar, the family circle; and the third, the gallery. The entrance to the third tier was from the outside of the building by a "flight of winding stairs having no connection with the other entrances." [17] At a theater in New York, the separate stairway onto a different street was only later provided for prostitutes. This move was called "a laudable effort to reduce to less prominence this disgusting feature of the stage." The manager of this theater was less successful in erecting a partition to shut off the prostitutes from other patrons altogether: "He soon yielded to the dreadful necessity of the stage, and the protest of this class, and removed the partition." [18]

Another policy of the theater seems to have been intended to further the ends for which the separate stairway and partition were designed: public announcements indicate that the third tier was open to the public much earlier

[16] Dunlap, 407–12.
[17] Ludlow, 477.
[18] Everts, 42, 43.

in the evening (sometimes by as much as two hours) than other parts of the house.[19] One suggested explanation is that third-tier patrons were expected to be off the adjacent street and out of sight well before other "respectable" theatergoers arrived in front of the theater. Thus design and policy served to lay a thin veneer of respectability over the third tier.

It is impossible to make a valid study of the economics of theater management in America without taking the third tier into account. Many managers argued that profits from the third tier kept the theaters open. For example, one manager in answer to an inquiry declared that the theater's bar would never be closed because the third tier supported the theater and the bar supported the third tier.[20] To fill the third tier was almost a guarantee of a good house because the gallery held more people than any other tier. Ludlow, for example, describes his St. Louis theater as holding three hundred and fifty in the third tier.[21]

In the earlier part of the nineteenth century managers were content merely to make the third tier available for prostitutes in exchange for a good house. However, as the century wore on, in order to insure a good house, the third tier was open to prostitutes on many occasions even without the low price of the gallery ticket. When receipts were poor managers often became very aggressive and would send messengers to houses of prostitution with blocks of free gallery tickets in order to attract and secure both the women and their followers for the audience.[22] In 1866 William Everts reported: "In some instances in Eastern cities, in addition to free admissions, messengers have been sent to the haunts of vile women, to invite their attendance as the necessary attraction of a large and indispensable portion of the patrons of the stage."[23] If public pressure occasionally led managers to close the third tier, Olive Logan explains, profits usually fell off miserably and forced the managers to change their minds and redouble their solicitation of prostitutes.[24]

Some theatrical people, Logan among them, argued that despite initial losses that would be caused by the gallery's closing, the presence of the third-tier clientele kept away too many other patrons and hurt the life of the theater in the long run.[25] Dunlap had come to similar views long before: "the prohibition of the immoral display would remove a just stigma from the theatre, and would further the views of managers by increasing their

---

[19] John N. Ireland, *Records of the New York Stage From 1750 to 1860,* I (New York, 1866), p. 29. Playbills and theatrical advertisements indicate this practice.
[20] Everts, 81.
[21] Ludlow, 477.
[22] Logan, 510–40; Turnbull, 84.
[23] Everts, 81.
[24] Logan, 539, 541.
[25] Ibid.

receipts."[26] P. T. Barnum evinced this approach when he turned the prostitutes out of his theater and began appealing to family audiences with his "museums." Most managers, however, and some writers of the day believed that the closing of the third tier had broken many a theater. The Tremont Theater in Boston was a frequently cited example. Speaking of the gallery prostitutes, William Everts wrote: "The neglect of provision for this class would probably be fatal to the prosperity of any theatre. The experiment has been partially tried in different cities without success. In one instance, the night after their interdiction, scarcely fifty persons were present and the third tier was again opened as usual."[27]

Of at least equal importance to its influence on the theatrical economy was the contribution of the third tier to the continual warfare between friends and enemies of the theater and the subsequent influence on the theater's regular clientele and base of support.

The degree of public, especially clerical, condemnation against which the nineteenth-century theater had to struggle is hard to overstate. The American public were still very much heirs of the Puritans, who, of course, had been hostile to the theater as long ago as the time of Shakespeare. Religious awakenings had touched great numbers of people to whom Charles G. Finney and Lyman Beecher were heroes of tremendous stature. If the stage had not by tradition already been anathema for most Protestants, powerful segments of the clergy and their followers were prepared to educate the public. Albert Palmer estimated in 1895 that seven-tenths of the population in mid-nineteenth-century America had looked on stage attendance as a sin.[28] Typical attitudes of the day are reflected in statements from sermons and tracts. Thus, the Reverend Robert Hatfield wrote in 1866:

> Let me ask you, my young friend, justly proud of your sister, would you not rather follow her to her grave tonight, then to know that tomorrow she shall stand at the altar and pledge her faith, and trust her precious future to an actor?[29]

The Reverend Phineas Densmore Gurley believed that Lincoln's assassination by an actor was God's way of showing Americans the character and influence of the theater.[30] Talmadge expostulated on how many a man on the scaffold said in his dying speech: " 'The theatre has ruined me!' "[31]

The battle against the stage was waged from the pulpit and in news-

[26] Dunlap, 407–12.
[27] Everts, 42.
[28] Albert M. Palmer, "American Theatres," in Chauncey Depew, *1795–1895, One Hundred Years of American Commerce* (New York: Haynes Publishing Co., 1895), p. 165.
[29] Robert H. Hatfield, *The Theatre* (Chicago, 1866), pp. 19–38.
[30] Phineas D. Gurley, *The Voice of the Rod* (Washington, 1865), pp. 14–16.
[31] Talmadge, 232.

papers, periodicals, and tracts. Those who disapproved on principle argued that the theater was affiliated by its very nature with vice of every kind. The "gallery" was clear and irrefutable evidence, they contended, because without it the drama would disappear. Turnbull was convinced that the third tier continued to be open to prostitutes because "that class of persons know that it [the theater] is a favorite amusement of those who are most easily tempted to sin. Besides, they find there much in accordance with their habits and feelings."[32] Another minister believed: "The theatre has been a moral pest all of its life of two thousand, five hundred years . . . [It] has affinities with crime and destroys neighborhoods. . . . The private house is turned into a bagnio; the shop of honest trade into the faro saloon or barroom, and the playhouse stands as a spectacle of vice, supported by its congenial aids of rowdyism, gambling, drunkenness and prostitution. . . . The theatre leans upon them and supports them, and is supported by these places."[33]

The main danger of the tier, its enemies contended, was that it was not self-contained; it corrupted patrons in other parts of the house who had come, presumably, only to see the play. One of Turnbull's sad stories in proof was frequently told by others as well: A once-innocent young man is dying from pneumonia after having fallen in a canal while in pursuit of a prostitute named Emily. On his deathbed he tells the story of his ruin, which supposedly appeared in numerous newspapers: " 'It would tire you to relate how I was first enticed to go up stairs into the splendid saloon, then to the third tier where the prostitutes are allotted a place. One night, the most fascinating amongst them, Emily was her name, came up to me, and took my arm. I had not the power to resist the tempter, and was persuaded to accompany her to her brothel. . . .' "[34]

Although attackers of the theater often displayed ignorance and wild melodrama, the third tier's existence could not be denied and was not defended by theater supporters. It proved to be the theater's one truly vulnerable spot. Of course, whenever financial collapse followed the closing of a third tier, critics found "proof" that theaters and vice were inseparably linked. Friends of the theater, on the other hand, were encouraged by the closing of the third tiers and could, in the late 1800s, at last point to a dramatic establishment in the country free of any open, formal alliance with prostitution.

The highly influential clerical stand against the theater, based in large measure on its relationship with prostitutes, kept many would-be theatergoers away and prevented any broad-based support from developing.

[32]Turnbull, 82–87.
[33]Hatfield, 3, 19–20.
[34]Turnbull, 85–89.

Furthermore, many patrons were driven away by disagreeable first-hand experiences and by the location nearby of houses of prostitution. In fact, the theatrical district was often too dangerous for families or "ladies" to enter. The managers were caught in an almost impossible situation. They could, by continuing to keep the third tier open, find themselves condemned in the press and avoided by many "respectable" patrons, or they could close the tier and face sudden financial ruin.

A recognition of the influence of the "gallery" raises other literary and cultural questions not so readily reflected in nineteenth-century documents. The most important literary question is the extent to which the third tier may have directed the types of plays written for and performed on the American stage. Why American drama was so unmemorable in a period of literature called the American Renaissance continues to be an intriguing question. Is there a relationship between the third tier and the "family" stage entertainments and "leg shows" which followed in its demise? The existence of the tier also suggests socio-cultural investigations: what were the extra-financial motives behind this remarkable custom? What was the impact of the tier on other patrons in the theater—particularly the women and children? What was the relationship of the tier to acting companies?

The history of the third tier is paradigmatic of the cultural history of Victorian America. Two struggles are going on here: a secular art form is struggling for legitimacy against long-standing religious disapproval, while a stricter moral code is struggling against customary vice. It takes about half a century for the two struggles to be resolved. When they are, this manifests a change in the state of American public opinion. The theater has achieved respectability, but it has had to dissociate itself from prostitution. Certainly the third tier's extensive and lively history presents the social historian and critic of dramatic literature with an opportunity to arrive at a truer understanding of the full range of literature and life in nineteenth-century America.

# PATRONS, PRACTITIONERS, AND PATIENTS: THE VOLUNTARY HOSPITAL IN MID-VICTORIAN BOSTON

*MORRIS J. VOGEL*

THE HOSPITAL OF THE IMMEDIATE POST-CIVIL-WAR PERIOD DIFFERED LITTLE IN some respects from its colonial and early nineteenth-century predecessor. It treated the same socially marginal constituency that American hospitals had always served. Its patients were the poor and those without roots in the community; dependence as much as disease still distinguished them from the public at large. Yet in some other respects the hospital of this era displayed concerns that were typically Victorian—concerns that shaped the transition of the institution into the hospital as we know it.

The general hospital of the 1870's was likely to be a charity, linking the voluntary efforts of doctors and donors in providing free medical care for those without any suitable alternative. For a hospital to exist, doctors had to be willing to provide gratuitous medical service for the sick poor while feeling sufficiently remunerated that they eagerly sought hospital positions. Donors had to be willing to support an institution that they themselves were never likely to use.

Traditionally, Boston's physicians had provided free care for the sick poor who had sought them out. Self-consciously advancing their claim to be professionals rather than businessmen, medical practitioners recognized a responsibility not to refuse advice or treatment to those who could not pay.[1] But in the hospitals and dispensaries organized up to the very end of the nineteenth century, many physicians went well beyond their professional obligations and actively made themselves available to patients who could not,

---

[1] See, in this regard, the career of George Cheyne Shattuck (1813–93), Shattuck Papers, Massachusetts Historical Society.

and in most instances were forbidden to, pay any fee. Not only did doctors seek duties in such institutions, but often actually founded them, as in the case of inexpensively operated dispensaries, providing only outpatient care. In the case of hospitals, doctors shared leading roles in organizing them with those who provided financial backing.[2]

Hospital and dispensary staff members were part of the city's medical and social elite. They were close in social origins to the donors who supported Boston's voluntary Protestant hospitals, if not directly related to them.[3] This background was part of the reason for their hospital work. The gratuitous treatment they rendered hospital patients was in the same tradition of stewardship as the charitable donations that supported voluntary hospitals.

But free medical treatment was much more than a charitable obligation. As a further consequence of social position, hospital practitioners had professional qualifications and interests that set them apart from their less fortunate medical brethren. In a period when locally available medical training was not advanced, men who later became associated with the city's hospitals were more likely than others to have enjoyed a European medical education after initial training in Boston. Once established in Boston, these upper-class doctors were more likely to assume positions in medical school faculties. And, though conservatives of their own class and background sometimes opposed specialization and even certain imported innovations, young physicians returning from Europe in the second half of the nineteenth century embraced specialization and the increasing scientific content of medicine more readily than Boston doctors less privileged by birth and social standing.[4]

Hospital positions furnished these upper-class doctors with the clinics that were becoming increasingly necessary for medical school teaching. Teaching brought financial benefits, as former students referred difficult cases to former professors for paying consultations. A hospital position also enabled a medical man to see and treat numbers of special cases, comparatively rare in private practice, and so develop a reputation that would itself be remunerative. Thus, though hospital patients did not pay fees to hospital practitioners,

[2]Nathaniel I. Bowditch, *A History of the Massachusetts General Hospital* (Boston: The Bowditch Fund, 2nd ed., 1872), p. 3; "A Statement made by four physicians . . ." (Boston: 1869), in "Papers and Clippings" (hereafter P&C), a scrapbook kept by Dr. F. H. Brown about the Children's Hospital, 1869–79, in the Countway Library, Boston; For the Dispensary for Skin Diseases and the Dispensary for Diseases of the Nervous System, *Boston Medical and Surgical Journal,* 86 (1872), 81, 82; 87 (1872), 58; F. H. Brown, *Medical Register for the Cities of Boston, Cambridge, Charlestown, and Chelsea* (Boston: J. Wilson & Son, 1873), n.p.

[3]Morris J. Vogel, "Boston's Hospitals, 1870–1930: A Social History," (doctoral dissertation, Univ. of Chicago, 1974), pp. 147–50.

[4]James Clarke White, *Sketches from My Life, 1833–1913* (Cambridge: Riverside Press, 1914), pp. 267–71.

these men received what contemporaries referred to as "certain well-under-stood advantages."[5]

Hospital physicians earned their livelihoods in the care of well-to-do private patients who paid for the knowledge gained in hospital work. Private practice remained the norm. And because the nineteenth-century hospital was not the center of the doctor's work world, the few hours he put in there each day during his term of perhaps three months each year did not represent income lost.

Economic motives led nonelite doctors to complain about the abuse of charity they perceived in the medical care offered without fee in hospitals. They saw their natural clientele—the poor and working classes—drained off to the hospitals.[6] When the nature of the hospital patient population changed in the 1890's and in the first decade of the twentieth century, complaints about abuse came from a new quarter—from doctors who treated the well-to-do patients beginning to enter hospitals at the turn of the century.[7] These complaints were a significant force in leading the hospital away from its purely charitable organization. But until late in the nineteenth century, Boston's hospitals, whether municipally or voluntarily supported, were charities.

In part, the wealthy supported these institutions because of their connections with the physicians who staffed them. Amos Lawrence, the mercantile prince, underwrote the entire cost of a children's hospital under the charge of his son, Dr. William R. Lawrence.[8] The staffing of South Boston's Roman Catholic Carney Hospital by Back Bay physicians brought in financial contributions from their friends and families.[9]

In part, too, the wealthy supported these institutions because enlightened selfishness led them to share certain of the physicians' goals. The knowledge and experience doctors gained in treating the poor "raised the standard of medical attainments"; hospital and dispensary practice thus "proved a blessing to rich and poor alike."[10] The Children's Hospital appealed "to all those

[5]*Bost. Med. Surg. J.*, 107 (1882), 455. See also Henry J. Bigelow, "Fees in Hospitals," *Bost. Med. Surg. J.*, 120 (1889), 378. Bigelow noted: "It has been said, with truth, that these hospital offices would command a considerable premium in money from the best class of practitioners were they annually put up at auction." An Annual Report of the Boston Dispensary discussed why doctors served: "It is not to be supposed that the motives of the attending physicians have been wholly foreign from considerations of personal advantage. They have doubtless been actuated by the hope of professional improvement and the prospect of building up an honest fame, as well as by the desires of fulfilling the benevolent intentions of this charity." Quoted in *Bost. Med. Surg. J.*, 106 (1882), 137.

[6]*Boston Journal of Health*, 1 (March 1886), 100.

[7]*Bost. Med. Surg. J.*, 152 (1905), 295–320.

[8]Bowditch, *MGH History*, p. 415.

[9]Carney Hospital, *Annual Reports*, 1879–89.

[10]Boston Dispensary, *Annual Report*, quoted in *Bost. Med. Surg. J.*, 106 (1882), 137.

who have children of their own," reminding them that they had a "double interest" in the institution; "not only on account of the great benefit it will confer on its little inmates, but also because of the advantages it offers for the study of special diseases by which their own offspring may be afflicted."[11] The *Boston Evening Transcript* warned the fortunate that their own well-being depended on the continued well-being of hospitals:

> The aids which society distributes to the hospitals are amply restored by the hospitals to society. . . . Mainly in these institutions the experience and insight, the methods of observation and treatment, the scientific research, are evolved which become employed for the general health of the country. . . . If we could imagine the hospitals abolished, the general death rate in all private practice would be increased.[12]

However, the "double interest" remained a divided interest, for the more fortunate classes did not expect to make direct use of the general hospital in the 1870's. Home care remained the norm. Accident victims, for example, though they might be injured outside the home, were likely to be brought home and cared for there. Speaking in 1864 at the dedication of the Boston City Hospital, its president, Thomas C. Amory, Jr., acknowledged that it was unlikely that hospitalization would replace the ideal of home care. Amory gave an example of what he regarded as a futile attempt to remove the prejudice against hospital care:

> One of our former governors . . . meeting with an accident in the street from which he narrowly escaped with his life, insisted, in order to remove this prejudice, upon being carried to the [Massachusetts General] Hospital. His example may have had its effect. But we doubt if many of our own people, born in Boston, when tolerably comfortable at home, will go, when ill, among strangers to be cured.[13]

When Amory himself was run down by a streetcar in 1886, "a doctor was called and the injured gentleman was removed to his home in a carriage."[14]

The pattern of care obtaining at local railroad accidents is revealing.[15]

[11]Children's Hospital, *Appeal*, 1869, in P&C.

[12]*Boston Evening Transcript*, April 20, 1881.

[13]Boston, *Proceedings at the Dedication of the City Hospital*, (Boston: J. E. Farwell, 1865), p. 58.

[14]*Boston Evening Transcript*, June 10, 1886.

[15]Detailed sources exist for who used hospitals, but since there is no reliable census of accident and illness, it is difficult to deduce what proportion of any different category of sickness or injury was hospitalized and what was not. Catastrophes, like train wrecks, can provide a rough idea. The pattern derived, while inconclusive, is reaffirmed by an examination of actual hospital use in the period.

When a commuter train crashed near Roslindale in 1887, twenty-four passengers were killed and fourteen hospitalized. But most of the nearly one hundred victims were taken to their homes.

> The fact that the accident occurred in the midst of a settled suburban district, and that nobody upon the train was more than five miles away from home, made it possible to transport the dead and injured, so far as it was practicable under the circumstances, directly to their homes, and many were so taken.[16]

The severity of their injuries did not separate those hospitalized from those brought home. Only two of the six admitted to the Boston City Hospital were listed as seriously injured, and only one of eight at the Massachusetts General. Of the cases brought to their own homes, a doctor making fifty-five home visits the day after the wreck reported nine patients in dangerous condition.[17]

The hospital offered patients no medical advantages not available in the home; actually hospital treatment in the 1870's added the risks of sepsis or "hospitalism." The fact that the hospital offered no special medical benefits reinforced a resistance to hospitalization that stemmed from the role of the home as the traditional setting for those undergoing illness and from a negative image of the hospital. That image derived from the actual danger of hospitalism and the traditional identification of the hospital with the pesthole and almshouse. Thus even when home care was unavailable, hospital care was sometimes shunned.

The well-to-do might make use of a hospital in what were labeled peculiar circumstances. This category included individuals away from home because they were from out of town, and old people living alone. For these potential patients, limited separate facilities existed at both the Massachusetts General and Boston City Hospitals.[18]

Even the sick poor would avoid the hospital if possible. One of the stated advantages of a dispensary was that out-patient care sidestepped the "dread" which the prospect of hospitalization evoked among many of the poor.[19] The city's two diet kitchens, founded in the 1870's, supplied home meals for dis-

---

[16]*Boston Evening Transcript*, March 14, 1887.

[17]*Boston Evening Transcript*, March 14 and 17, 1887; *Bost. Med. Surg. J.*, 116 (1887), 268. Another "frightful disaster" with the same general pattern occurred with the wreck of an excursion train on the Old Colony Railroad, *Transcript*, October 9 and 10, 1878. There was a different pattern after a crash on the Eastern Railroad in Revere. A greater proportion of the injured were hospitalized; probably because an express Pullman was involved, many of the survivors were from out of town. *Transcript*, August 28, 1871.

[18]MGH, 60th *Annual Report*, 1873, p. 9; George H. M. Rowe (superintendent, B.C.H.) to John Pratt (superintendent, M.G.H.), March 7, 1894, in MGH archives, Phillips House file.

[19]*Bost. Med. Surg. J.*, 86 (1872), 81, 82.

pensary patients too sick or poor to secure their own food.[20] The truly unfortunate shared with that minority of the prosperous classes who used the institution the problem of an inadequate or nonexistant home. The Boston Lying-in Hospital received some of its cases from dispensary physicians "who suddenly found themselves called upon to attend some poor woman in quarters utterly unfit for such purposes."[21]

The hospital offered shelter and attention to the sick poor. It replaced comfortless homes "in close courts, narrow alleys, damp cellars or filthy apartments, which the sunshine never enters, nor fresh air purifies." It made up for the absence of "natural protectors" for those without families. It provided relief for "helpless people, who would suffer tenfold more from neglect and ill treatment than they now suffer from disease, were it not for the shelter and care of the hospitals."[22] Indeed the role of the hospital was defined in terms of the services it offered the sick and injured victims of a catalog of social ills.

The statistics of hospital use reflected these concerns. An analysis of nativity and occupation shows that patients treated at the Massachusetts General and Boston City Hospital in the 1870's were not a cross-section of the population.

Hospital annual reports listed the occupations of patients admitted; these occupations may be organized according to the socioeconomic classification in Stephan Thernstrom's *The Other Bostonians* and then compared with Thernstrom's observations about the occupational structure of the city.[23] Male patients at the city's two major hospitals were divided into four categories: white collar, skilled blue collar, semiskilled and service, and unskilled and menial. Such an analysis shows occupations with high socioeconomic status were under-represented among hospital patients in 1870 and 1880, while those with low status were over-represented.

At the Massachusetts General in 1870, 16.9 per cent of the classifiable male patients were in white collar occupations, while in 1880 that figure was 18.1 per cent. In the city population, 32 per cent of males were white collar in 1880. Skilled blue collar workers accounted for 41.9 per cent of Massa-

[20]North End Diet Kitchen founded 1874; South End Diet Kitchen a short time later. *Boston Evening Transcript,* October 20, 1874; November 9, 1875; December 2, 1878.

[21]Boston Lying-in Hospital, *Annual Report* for 1881, quoted in *Bost. Med. Surg. J.,* 106 (1882), 462.

[22]Children's Hospital, *Appeal,* 1869, in P&C; *Boston Evening Transcript,* October 28, 1876; April 1, 1881; November 17, 1883.

[23]Thernstrom does not classify census data for 1870 into these socioeconomic categories, so hospital figures for both 1870 and 1880 are compared to data for the general population derived from the 1880 census. Since Thernstrom finds very little change in the city's occupational structure from 1880 to 1920, this is not unreasonable. Stephan Thernstrom, *The Other Bostonians: Poverty and Progress in the American Metropolis, 1880–1970* (Cambridge: Harvard Univ. Press, 1973), pp. 50, 51, 289–302.

chusetts General patients in 1870 and 19.4 per cent in 1880, while they provided 36 per cent of the general male population in 1880. Among patients, 14.2 per cent and 11.1 per cent were in semi-skilled occupations in 1870 and 1880 respectively, while the city population contained 17 per cent in that category in 1880. The unskilled accounted for 26.9 per cent (1870) and 51.4 per cent (1880) of the patient population and 15 per cent of the city population in 1880.[24]

Much the same pattern prevailed at the Boston City Hospital. The largest single occupational category among patients was laborer, consisting of 524 of 1,419 men admitted in 1870/1871 and 792 of 2,696 in 1880/1881. Patients in white collar occupations totaled 8.2 per cent of the hospital's male admissions in 1870/1871 and 10.5 per cent in 1880/1881. Skilled blue collar workers accounted for 36.3 per cent of Boston City patients in 1870/1871 and 31.6 per cent in 1880/1881. Workers in semi-skilled and service occupations made up 11.8 per cent of City Hospital patients in 1870/1871 and 21.7 per cent in 1880/1881. As at the Massachusetts General, unskilled (including laborers) and menial workers—43.5 per cent and 36.1 per cent—were disproportionately over-represented.[25]

Unfortunately, the listing of many women patients as simply wives or widows, and the absence of a satisfactory analysis of the female occupational structure, makes a comparison of female patients with the general female population more difficult. But the fact that nearly half the female patients admitted to both hospitals in the 1870's were identified as domestics reinforces the conclusion based on male employment patterns that hospital patients were drawn disproportionately from among the lower classes.[26]

Though the absolute and relative numbers undergoing hospitalization continued to increase in the 1870's as they had since the city's first hospital opened in 1821, the hospital's constituency remained largely the same, with the greater number of patients coming from an expanded lower class. The continued use of the institution by the stricken and helpless poor served to associate it with the almshouse and reinforced the negative image of the hospital held by society at large. Its image as a refuge for the unfortunate was

[24]The category of skilled workers in both 1870 and 1880 consisted entirely of Massachusetts General patients listed as "mechanics." This is an ambiguous term and appears to have been applied differently in 1870 and 1880. The number of patients in this category fell from 291 in 1870 to 219 in 1880. Over the same years there was a large jump in laborers (the whole of the unskilled category) from 187 to 580. This suggests that mechanics were not all skilled workers in 1870 and that their 41.9 per cent of the male population over-represents skilled workers among the hospital's patients. At the same time, the figure of 26.9 per cent may undercount the proportion of hospital patients who were unskilled in 1870. The MGH admitted 780 males (85 unclassified, all minors) in 1870 and 1,363 (235 unclassified) in 1880. Computed from MGH, *Annual Reports.*
[25]Computed from BCH, *Annual Reports.*
[26]Computed from MGH and BCH, *Annual Reports.*

further heightened by the fact that its patients were not just poor but, after the beginning of large-scale immigration at mid-century, largely foreign born. The Massachusetts General trustees had at first resisted allowing the Irish to enter the hospital as patients, claiming that "the admission of such patients creates in the minds of our citizens a prejudice against the Hospital, making them unwilling to enter it,—and thus tends directly to lower the general standing and character of its inmates." Feeling "the excess of foreigners among the patients" to be a bane, they had advised the admitting physician to use "the utmost vigilence," but found that "some such admissions must unavoidably take place." Hospital rules directed that all cases of sudden accident were to be admitted, thus by-passing the screening procedure; a very large proportion of accident cases was Irish. In time, the Massachusetts General trustees, "moved by a sense of duty and humanity," opened their wards to the foreign-born.[27]

In 1865, the hospital accepted 628 foreign as against 571 native-born patients. In 1870, the totals showed 718 foreign and 584 Americans, and in 1875 the figures were 1,042 and 799 respectively. The Irish made up the largest segment of the foreign-born population, maintaining at least a majority throughout the 1870's, with those born in the Canadian provinces second.[28] From the opening of the Boston City Hospital in 1864, a majority of its patients was foreign born. In 1865, 647 of its patients were born abroad and 459 in the United States, and in 1870/1871, 1,635 were foreign and 761 native-born. The foreign-born numbered 2,187 and native Americans 993 in 1875/1876. Throughout the period, Irish patients alone outnumbered the native-born.[29]

Just as Irish immigrants tarnished the image of the general hospital, so did the kind of women it cared for taint the image of the lying-in hospital. Maternity care would be among the last reasons causing the comfortable classes to enter hospitals. In the late nineteenth century women still considered childbirth a natural function, something that could, and should, be performed

[27]MGH, "The Report of a [trustees'] Committee on the Financial Condition of the MGH, February 16, 1865." The trustees dated their financial difficulties from the change from "the industrious classes of our native population," many of whom had paid something toward their board, to the foreign-born, who dramatically increased the numbers treated free. The trustees' committee recommended carefully restricting the number of nonpaying patients (read foreign-born) and segregating them in a distinct section of the hospital, so that the institution could get back to serving "the classes for whose advantage it was established." The trustees rejected that suggestion, apparently because of the urging of the medical staff which feared that decreasing the numbers of the really poor would hurt medical education. MGH Trustees [printed letter], April 1, 1865, both in Countway Library; Bowditch, *MGH History,* p. 454.

[28]Computed from MGH, *Annual Reports.* In 1870, the United States Census listed 35.1 per cent of Boston's population as foreign born.

[29]Computed from BCH, *Annual Reports.*

in the simplest and poorest home.[30] The hospital offered no specialized medical paraphernalia or contrivances, but instead threatened contagion, puerperal fever, and high maternal mortality. Generally, only the most desperate women entered hospitals to have their children. And perhaps the major cause of this desperation was illegitimacy. Small lying-ins, often no more than a few rooms in a tenement or boarding house, kept by midwives or the unscrupulous and untrained, served those seeking "to hide their shame" or having absolutely no alternative. These lying-ins, and the baby farms that sometimes accompanied them, were seen as accessories to vice and degradation, and as adjucts to brothels. Lying-ins were the first hospitals needing licenses to operate in Massachusetts (1876), but the enforcement problems of the Boston Board of Health suggest that more lying-ins were operated without sanction of law than with it.[31]

Licensed and respectable lying-ins did exist, and did leave records, but their patients, too, were "unfortunate women." Cases included in the first volume of the maternity records of the New England Hospital for Women and Children, covering one-and-one-half years in the early 1870's, list 61 married and 57 unmarried mothers. Over 50 per cent of the more than 1,300 mothers delivered in the 1870's at the Boston Lying-in were unmarried. And at St. Mary's Lying-in Hospital, only 20 of 550 patients cared for in the decade from 1874 to 1884 were married.[32] The lying-in hospitals of the period reaffirmed the notion that hospitals were institutions especially for the poor and desperate, and the illegitimacy intimately associated with them added the stigma of immorality.

The hospital was perceived as the kind of place all but the desperate would want to avoid. Yet, although it dealt primarily with the poor, its very nature—the omnipresence of death within its walls—imbued its concerns with a powerful attraction. The community at large was curious as to what went on inside it. This desire to know was heightened by the relative newness of the institution; though its history could be traced back to antiquity, hospitals began to emerge in numbers in Boston and the rest of the nation only after the Civil War. Finally, the curiosity as to what went on within hospitals derived from the fact that even the fortunate individual could not be certain that he would not someday be hospitalized.

Horror was a common response to such a prospect. Joseph Chamberlin,

[30]Francis E. Kobrin, "The American Midwife Controversy: A Crisis of Professionalism," *Bulletin of the History of Medicine,* 40 (1966), 350–63.

[31]Boston, Board of Health, *Annual Report* for 1879, p. 20.

[32]New England Hospital for Women and Children, mss Maternity Records, vol. 1, in Countway Library; Computed from Boston Lying-in Hospital, *Annual Report* for 1930, p. 58; for St. Mary's, *Bost. Med. Surg. J.,* 110 (1884), 363, 364.

for many years the *Transcript's* "Listener,"[33] reacted strongly after visiting a hospitalized friend:

> If it should fall to the Listener's lot to be called upon to go in sickness to the very best of [hospitals], he would say, "Better a straw cot in an attic at home, with the clumsiest of unprofessional attendance, than the best private room in this place." . . . [T]here is something about the all-pervading presence of Sickness, with a large S, this atmosphere of death, either just expected or just escaped, and all of this amiable perfunctoriness of nursing and medical attendance, that is simply horrible. The hospital . . . gives one sickness to think about morning, noon and night.[34]

A visitor might be acutely discomforted by the unnatural concentration of disease and death. But for the patient the environment was threatening:

> The doctors visit you incessantly, and, in spite of their courtesy, you feel as if you were not exactly an ailing human being, but merely a "case" that was being read as one reads a novel which is interesting enough, no doubt, but which is expected to develop a much more interesting phase, to wit, the catastrophe, at almost any moment. And then the grim disquieting presence of all these people like you in the ward around you![35]

The hospital reaffirmed the patient's mortality, but denied his humanity.

Chamberlin told the story of a patient hospitalized for an operation. After surgery, she was put to bed. She lived through a night punctuated by the "wailing and crying" of fellow patients, the death "in dreadful agony" of a neighboring patient, and the quiet but quick, and therefore ghostly, movement of attendants. It was terrifying: "Why it was like being dead and conscious of it!" The next day was quiet, but "spent in anticipating the coming of such another night, was almost as terrible." This particular hospital stay was cut short when a physician inquired "whether I had not any friend to whom I could go," found she had and "made immediate arrangements to have me taken away." Clearly, this patient and many of her contemporaries shared Chamberlin's conclusion: "What a matter for infinite sorrow it is that there should be homes in the world so dismal, so unhealthy, so ill attended, that their inmates are better off in the public wards of the hospital, when they are sick, than they are at home."[36]

[33]Joseph Edgar Chamberlin, *The Boston Transcript: A History of its First Hundred Years* (Boston: Houghton Mifflin Co., 1930), p. 165.
[34]*Boston Evening Transcript,* February 24, 1888.
[35]Ibid.
[36]Ibid.

Because the hospital was a strange and frightening place, the public welcomed reassurance from the informed. This might take the form of a newspaper article giving the generic history of the hospital and thus implying that it was not simply a modern aberration but an old institution that had proved its value in the past.[37] Or it might take the form of a correspondent's story of a hospital visit or a patient's description of his hospital stay.

Chamberlin's story was idiosyncratic: more common in the Boston press were counterphobic presentations that were almost uniformly formulaic. These addressed fears based on ignorance and substituted for them informed chronicles which denied the presence of death, disease, and pain in the hospital. Insanity, for example, was not mentioned in an extensive account of an insane asylum, though beautiful flowers and homelike accommodations in cottages were.[38] The smallpox hospital emerged from another narrative as a delightful place, serving wonderful food and providing comfortable beds, while smallpox itself, it was concluded, much improved the system.[39] For those hospitals which depended on the beneficence of the public to operate, reassurances that all was well within served a double function in that they encouraged contributions as well as disarmed anxieties.

\* \* \*

Boston's City Hospital was supported as a municipal service, but the hospital tradition in Boston, as in the rest of the United States, had been set by the voluntary hospitals, with groups of private individuals undertaking the care of the sick poor as a public trust.[40] The Massachusetts General Hospital and Children's Hospital formed part of the complex of Boston's Protestant charities that owed their founding and existence, at least in part, to the religious doctrine of stewardship. Social and economic inequalities were legitimized by the notion that God meant for them to exist. But the elect, whose heavenly salvation was generally already demonstrated by their earthly riches, held their wealth only as God's trustees. With their wealth came the obligation to aid the less fortunate. The poor provided their economic betters the opportunity, the privilege actually, of spending God's wealth in a way that continually reemphasized their own chosen state.

The Children's Hospital was founded in 1869. It was intended for the poor, for "the little waifs who crowd our poorer streets." In its early years the institution stressed its spiritual role. Making their first annual report, the trustees

---

[37]E.g., a long feature article, "The Origin of Hospitals," ibid., July 13, 1886.

[38]Ibid., July 10, 1885. This account is of the McLean Asylum, a branch of the MGH.

[39]Ibid., November 29, 1881.

[40]Odin Anderson, *The Uneasy Equilibrium: Public and Private Financing of Health Services in the United States. 1875–1965* (New Haven: College and Univ. Press, 1968), p. 29.

stated that the institution would provide its patients "Christian nurture."[41] Sickness provided an opportunity for spiritual healing; the philosophy of the Children's Hospital reflected that of a local newspaper, which editorially downgraded the function of hospitals in furnishing medical treatment while commending them for giving patients the best gifts of all, "wrought through a ministry of sorrow."[42] The theological language in which all this was expressed was largely a carry-over from an earlier time; religious terminology provided a familiar and convenient vocabulary. Soon, society would no longer justify the hospital in traditional religious terms. One can already sense the beginning of a shift in the hospital's mission during Victorian times, from succoring the sick poor as its role in God's order, to denying that man had to accept God's diseases. Within a generation, this would give the hospital a drastically altered justification. But in the 1870's, these religious terms still symbolized real moral and social concerns.

The Children's Hospital defined its role in terms of the "moral benefit" it offered its patients. Socially, these benefits translated into a program of uplift and social control which it was hoped would help cope with the masses of threatening and increasingly alien poor crowding into the city. The trustees had expected that most of their patients would come from the poorest classes of the community. They found that many came "from the very lowest; from abodes of drunkeness, and vice in almost every form, where the most depressing and corrupting influences were acting both on the body and mind."[43] Hospitalization provided an opportunity to separate these children, at a most impressionable time in their lives, from corrupting influences that, if otherwise permitted to proceed unchecked, could perpetuate an impoverished and vicious class, permanently threatening society.

When a child entered, the hospital first decontaminated its new charge. "On their entrance they are immediately placed in a refreshing bath and clothed in the clean robes of the hospital." Uniform red flannel jackets replaced streetclothes.[44] The decontamination process went deeper; new influences were substituted for old in the hope that, in the few weeks it had, the institution could "help the child-soul to lift itself out of the mud in which it had been born, to assert its native purity in spite of unfortunate surroundings."[45]

Since treatment was not purely medical, the hospital did not restrict its

[41]Children's Hospital, 1st *Annual Report*, 1869, p. 10.
[42]*Boston Evening Transcript*, April 20, 1881.
[43]Children's Hospital, 3rd *Annual Report*, 1871, pp. 7, 8.
[44]Charlestown *Chronicle*, November 11, 1871; Boston *Post*, March 1, 1872; both in P&C.
[45]"The Children's Hospital: What 'Fireside' Thinks About It," *Boston Evening Transcript*, January 22, 1879.

practitioners to the medical profession. The entire Christian community was invited to participate in the healing process, to visit patients and encourage them "by word or counsel."[46] The hospital's first nurses were Episcopalian nuns. Their strength lay less in medical training than in the "Christian nurture" they provided patients. Sister Letitia was a model of this style of charity untainted by medical pretension. "Though enfeebled by disease of the lungs, which she knew must soon terminate her life, yet entirely forgetful of self," she continued nursing—all the while, of course, subjecting her charges to tuberculosis—until she died.[47]

The trustees wanted "to bring [their young patients] under the influence of order, purity and kindness." Among the means employed were tender nursing, books, pictures, "little works of art," and "the visits and attentions of the kind and cultivated."[48] Middle and upper-class children outside the hospital were encouraged to undertake the painting, as wall decorations, of inspirational mottos that would "cultivate the devotional feelings" of the little sufferers inside. The fortunate who supported the hospital were encouraged to visit the children in its wards at any time of the day, to speak with them, provide role models, and in general to furnish that cultivated influence which the children of the poor had missed.[49] At the same time, parents having children in the hospital were severely restricted in the hours they could see their own children. The original parents' visiting hour allowed one relative at a time between eleven and twelve o'clock on weekdays only, raising difficulties for working fathers (or mothers) who wished to visit. Later, parent visiting was further restricted to the hour between eleven and twelve on Monday, Wednesday, and Friday only.[50] The trustees hoped that this regimen would change the children by "quickening their intellects, refining their manners, and encouraging and softening their hearts."[51]

Supporters of the institution hoped that a different child would leave the hospital than had entered it.[52] Children would leave having been "carefully taught cleanliness of habit, purity of thought and word" and with as much at-

[46]Children's Hospital, 1st *Annual Report*, 1869, p. 13; 3rd *Annual Report*, 1871, pp. 8–10.
[47]Children's Hospital, 8th *Annual Report*, 1876, p. 8. It is perhaps unfair to draw so sharp a distinction between medicine and charity in this case. Koch's work was yet to come, and there was no hard medical knowledge of the transmission of tuberculosis.
[48]Children's Hospital, *Appeal*, 1869, in P&C; Children's Hospital, 1st *Annual Report*, 1869, p. 13.
[49]Children's Hospital, 3rd *Annual Report*, 1871, p. 10; 5th *Annual Report*, 1873, p. 9. Young readers of the *Christian Register* were invited to come with their mothers to visit "the dear little occupants." *Christian Register*, May 8, 1869, June 5, 1869; in P&C.
[50]Children's Hospital, 1st *Annual Report*, 1869, back cover; 15th *Annual Report*, 1883, p. 9.
[51]Children's Hospital, 1st *Annual Report*, 1869, p. 13.
[52]Boston *Post*, March 1, 1872, in P&C.

tention "paid to their moral training as can be found in any cultivated family," but the benefits of the hospital would not stop there:

> Think what a widespreading influence this becomes when the children return to their homes. . . . Even among the better class of poor people, the children soon notice the discomforts of careless, untidy habits, and are quick to compare such with the "so much better" at the hospital. In the joy of the child's homecoming, the parents are ready to gratify it by trying the new ways, and all unconsciously rise a little in the social scale by so doing.[53]

"In this wise," the hospital's founder wrote, the institution would "commence the education of the poorer classes."[54]

Even if the child did not go home and improve his family, he himself would be changed by the hospital in a way that would benefit society. The affluent and cultivated were told that they could not tell the difference between their own children and those within the hospital, even though the latter might be immigrant children from the North End. One visitor noted that "the faces of the children quickly lost the expression which we commonly meet in our little street Arabs, and become once more human and civilized."[55] Their hearts softened by kindness, mistrust and hostility evaporated from their faces and they no longer appeared as threatening as they had on the streets.

The hospital promised other far-reaching improvements. The health and strength gained during a hospital stay would not only aid the children, by enabling them to grow into "better men and women," but society as a whole—having escaped childhood invalidism, those healthier adults could support themselves. A promotional article mentioned the institution's success in educating its charges, even implying that it taught some how to read.[56] A hospital stay could help prepare a child for a socially desirable role in adult life.

These perceptions were colored, of course, by expectation. No doubt they express more than actually happened in the hospital in the way of having the children of the poor fulfill the fantasies of the rich. Further, these social expectations were less than the full rationale for the institution. The Children's Hospital was founded by physicians, in part for the sorts of professional reasons earlier suggested. At the same time, however, the founding physicians

---

[53]"Fireside," *Boston Evening Transcript,* January 22, 1879.

[54]*Bost. Med. Surg. J.,* 83 (1870), 140, 141, editorial; the hospital's founder doubled as the editor of the *Journal.*

[55]Boston *Sunday Times,* December 29, 1872, in P&C; letter to the editor, "My Visit to the Children's Hospital," by "A Lady," *Boston Evening Transcript,* February 22, 1875.

[56]Boston *Post,* March 1, 1872, in P&C; Children's Hospital, 7th *Annual Report,* 1875, p. 13.

were responsible for much of this socially-oriented promotional rhetoric. There is no reason to believe these doctors did not take their own language seriously. They were members of a social class as well as of a professional group, and shared the didactic concerns typical of Victorian culture.

The Massachusetts General Hospital, a secularly oriented Protestant hospital in the same sense as the Children's Hospital, also began with the mission of uplifting its patients. When founded, it had been intended for native American patients, and had offered to tide them over a bad time and send them on their way having meanwhile reinforced their view of a basically good society in which they could lead good lives.[57] But after the hospital had been overwhelmed by unappealing and apparently intractable and unimprovable adult immigrants, it gave up this aspect of its role. By the 1870's, its literature no longer expressed concern for the character of its patients, and the hospital continued to care for the sick poor with a diminished concern about what it was doing for its patients in a nonphysical sense. The hospital kept the support of its donors for a variety of reasons, the chief (probably) being an inertia in which benefactions served as a quiet reaffirmation of stewardship. An obligation to keep the hospital going because it served the needs of medical practitioners was recognized. Finally, the fact that the McLean Asylum for the Insane was a branch of Massachusetts General and served the upper classes in a very direct way maintained their interest in the corporation. Since the asylum generally met its operating expenses from patient revenues, the contributions it generated helped support the hospital.

Yet the loss of reforming zeal brought no relaxation of discipline within Massachusetts General; if anything, it reinforced it. The "influence of order" which pervaded the Children's Hospital furthered that institution's resocialization of its young patients. Order was a concern in Massachusetts General, too, but there it was a reflection of social reality, not part of a vision of social change. Many of the hospital's patients were not bedridden, but able to move around the wards and grounds, and expected to be able to leave the institution to walk about the city or enjoy the carriage rides into the countryside furnished by the Young Men's Christian Union. The hospital treated people new to urban life (through the 1870's the percentage of its patients born in Boston never approached 10 per cent) and to the demands of institutional living. To help maintain discipline, its grounds were surrounded by a high wall and an always guarded gate through which patients and visitors had to pass.[58] Patients needed signed passes to leave and re-enter the hospital,

[57]Drs. James Jackson and John C. Warren, "Circular Letter," [1810], in Bowditch, *MGH History*, pp. 3–9.

[58]Grace W. Myers, *History of the Massachusetts General Hospital: June, 1872 to December, 1900* (Boston: Griffith-Stillings Press, 1929), p. 12.

and visitors were carefully screened.[59] This discipline was maintained for internal reasons; rather than reform a patient who misbehaved, the hospital expelled him.[60]

In one sense, Massachusetts General helped keep order in the general community. Like other hospitals, it functioned as a guarantor of social stability, or as one supporter of the Children's Hospital put it, "There is a practical side to this charity, which may commend it to thoughtful men." Hospitals provided the working classes with evidence that the wealthy were aware of their responsibilities: "the only sure way to reconcile labor to capital is to show the laborer by actual deeds that the rich man regards himself as the steward of the Master."[61] Until workmen's compensation went into effect, corporations, especially railroads and street railways, underwrote free beds at the Massachusetts General to which they sent employees injured on the job. These accident-prone enterprises provided a paternalistic form of insurance, absolved themselves of responsibility to their injured employees, and attempted to defuse issues that might otherwise build up workers' grievances.[62]

Concern for social order was apparent in the community's support of hospitals in general. One observer noted that "the hospitals act as a kind of insurance system for the laboring classes. They take the risks incidental to their position the more cheerfully, because they know that if injured they are assured of a special provision for their need in our hospitals."[63] Similar reasoning was used to elicit support for the Children's Hospital. Were it not there, or were it unable to admit a suffering child, there would be no telling what even the most respectable worker, distraught over his inability to secure aid for his child, might do. "It is under such circumstances the iron enters a man's soul, and he is ready for a 'strike' or any other desperate remedy that promises better times and money with which to provide good nursing and delicacies for his suffering children." A mother, turned down when applying for admission for her sick child, might go "fiercely on her way, ripe for any evil deed. . . ." But assured that the hospital would care for their sick children, the poor would respond with gratitude rather than violence.[64]

Beside acting as a guarantor of social stability, the hospital was perceived

---

[59]Dr. D. B. St. John Roosa described the visitors lining up at the gate for the twice weekly visiting hour at the New York Hospital, and how visitors were searched before entering. *The Old Hospital and Other Papers,* (New York: W. Wood & Co., 2nd ed., 1889), p. 12.

[60]E.g., MGH Trustees mss Records, August 3, 1877, in MGH archives.

[61]"Fireside," *Boston Evening Transcript,* January 22, 1879.

[62]MGH, *Annual Reports,* 1870–1910.

[63]*Boston Evening Transcript,* April 20, 1881.

[64]Children's Hospital, 7th *Annual Report,* 1875, p. 7; *Boston Evening Transcript,* January 22, 1879; a letter from a grateful parent, *Transcript,* February 29, 1874.

by some as contributing to community prosperity, both through the more tractable labor force it ensured and through the fact that the health of the population was directly translatable into material wealth. In encouraging support for the city's voluntary hospitals, the *Transcript* editorially assured "those who look into the matter [that they would] see that our hospitals are among the very bases of national health and prosperity, and the working of these institutions is, therefore, a matter of general interest and public importance."[65] The hospital thus served much the same function as the public school, to which it was sometimes likened by those arguing that the institution served the entire community and those needing it should use it as a guaranteed right with any cost borne by the community. But of course only a minority fully appreciated all the functions of a hospital; Boston's City Registrar complained that too many of those "by mere fortuitous circumstance different situated" had yet to learn that "the material condition of the whole community is involved in this subject."[66]

Though hospital treatment of the poor protected the established order and added to the wealth of the community, the people for whom it was intended were made to feel recipients of charity and reminded repeatedly that they were enjoying a privilege and their gratitude was expected in return. This attitude was embodied in law. In one case, a man treated gratuitously sued the Massachusetts General Hospital claiming his broken leg was set improperly. The courts held that even if he had been treated incompetently and negligently, he was not entitled to recover because the institution was a charity.[67] In another case, a woman charity patient operated on at the Free Hospital for Women sued, claiming her operation was not successful. During the course of protracted litigation, "A Friend to our Charities" wrote the *Transcript* complaining that such hospital malpractice suits arose because "there are some patients so wholly devoid of ordinary gratitude for favors to which they had not a shadow of a claim, as to make their benefactors suffer by reason of their very kindness." When a verdict for the hospital was finally returned, the *Transcript's* headline, "A Victory for Charity," translated the jury's decision into a reaffirmation of the status of the hospital, though only meaning to imply that money given hospitals would not be drained by lawsuits.[68]

[65]Registrar's Report of the City of Boston, quoted in *Bost. Med. Surg. J.*, 85 (1871), 83; *Boston Evening Transcript*, April 20, 1881.
[66]Letter to the editor, *Boston Evening Transcript*, February 29, 1888; Registrar's Report, in *Bost. Med. Surg. J.*, 85 (1871), 84.
[67]McDonald vs. MGH, 120 Mass. 432, in E. B. Callander, "Torts of Hospitals," *American Law Review*, 15 (1881), 640; *Boston Evening Transcript*, July 12, 1875.
[68]Stogdale vs. Baker, reported in *Boston Evening Transcript*, November 21, 1885, December 12, 1887, January 5, 1888.

It is from this background that the modern hospital emerged. Changes in social attitudes and medical practice—products of social change and scientific progress—have reshaped the institution. But the hospital that was transformed by these forces was itself a shaping force, a product of its own past. It has influenced medical organization and the kind of medical care available. The hospital now cares for patients of all classes, but it is not a classless institution. The hospital allows physicians to practice the best medicine available, but its clinical setting sometimes discourages the human component of caring. And while government financing and third party payment have redistributed the burden of hospital support throughout society, the institution has often remained unresponsive to the mass of its patients. Finally, the hospital has not evolved toward any foreordained perfection. It is no more the ideal form of medical organization today than it was of social consideration for the poor in the second half of the nineteenth century.

# The Decline of American Victorianism

# IMMORAL FICTION IN THE LATE VICTORIAN LIBRARY

*DEE GARRISON*

ONE OF THE MOST IMPORTANT SOCIAL CHANGES IN THE LATE VICTORIAN AGE, perhaps the furthest reaching of all in its revolutionary implications, was the triumph of mass culture. Blithely ignoring the warnings of their betters against the evils of reading "salacious" fiction, the American masses, with unrepenting self-indulgence, consumed the "volumes of trash poured forth daily, weekly and monthly" in the form of imaginative literature.[1] Above all it was the American woman who found in light reading a temporary escape from her isolation and discontent. By the last quarter of the nineteenth century, the shelves of the American public library began to reflect the influence of the new mass readership upon literary standards. Codified in fiction-fantasy, the alteration of fundamental values expressed in best-selling novels aroused the indignation of those Americans who resisted the value change.

Significantly, the objection to deviation in literary standards, as reflected by the public librarian's preoccupation with "the fiction question," was placed largely on moral grounds. Although present, aesthetic complaints were minor matters compared to the moral ire of those who sought to shape mass reading taste. It was the moral boundary which the late nine-teenth century perceived to be most seriously threatened, and library censorship of fiction was part of the institutional reaction which authorities erected to resist or channel rapid change of values.[2] Perhaps conservative

---

[1]U.S. Bureau of Education, *Public Libraries in the United States of America: Their History, Condition and Management,* Special Report, Part 1 (Washington: GPO, 1876), p. 393.

[2]See John Tomsich, *A Genteel Endeavor: American Culture and Politics in the Gilded Age* (Stanford: Stanford Univ. Press, 1971), pp. 121–22. I am also indebted to a discussion with Robert Wiebe. Jack P. Gibbs, "Conceptions of Deviant Behavior: The Old and the New," *Pacific Sociological Review,* 9 (Spring, 1966), pp. 9–15, considers problems in deviance theory, and Joseph R. Gusfield, "Moral Passage: The Symbolic Process in Public Designations of Deviance," *Social Problems,* 15 (Fall, 1967), pp. 175–88, questions the general concept of "social control" as it has been used by some recent historians and argues instead that the designation of deviance is a tactic used by groups who seek to maintain cultural dominance.

Victorians recognized that deviance in moral theory was a good index of
radicalism in general. The person who questioned ethical standards was also
likely to entertain heretical views regarding the efficacy of prayer, the concept of private property, and the benevolence of political parties.

Guided as they were by the standards of literary conservatism, public librarians made a bold attempt in 1881 to define the best-selling fiction that
offended genteel sensibilities. In that year the American Library Association Cooperation Committee sent a questionnaire to seventy major public
libraries to determine if they had ever held, or had later withdrawn, the
works of certain authors. The list was limited to those "whose works are
sometimes excluded from public libraries by reason of sensational or immoral qualities."[3] As might have been expected the librarians did not entirely agree on the objectionable authors, but the list does give a good indication of the suspect fiction which because of its popular appeal was most
troublesome to the public librarian—the genteel guardian of the period.[4]

An analysis of the major themes in these widely-read but "injurious"
books provides clues to the genteel conscience and to mass thought as well.
It is in popular fiction, Arthur Lovejoy has argued, that the tendencies of an
age may appear most directly. Writers of genius "are for all time. . . . But in
the sensitive, responsive souls of less creative power, current ideals record
themselves with clearness."[5] Yet there is serious disagreement among
scholars as to how accurately popular fiction reflects the reader's
curiosities, values, and views in the context of the characters to which he responds. Is mass culture the "number two brain in the withering tail of the
dinosaur? Or the antennae of the race?"[6] Does widespread fantasy which

[3] A.L.A. Cooperation Committee, "Report on Exclusion," *Library Journal*, 7 (1882), p. 28.

[4] This analysis of the belief of American librarians in their role as guardians of the public morality rests upon a larger study of the socio-economic backgrounds and social and literary
ideals of 36 library leaders in the period from 1876 to 1900. Esther J. Carrier, *Fiction in Public
Libraries, 1876-1900* (New York: Scarecrow Press, 1965), is a summation of library literature
on the "fiction question." For typical comments addressed to the masses by literary conservatives, see: Noah Porter, *Books and Reading or What Shall I Read and How Shall I Read It?*
(New York: Scribner's, 1882), and William Atkinson, *On the Right Use of Books* (Boston:
Roberts Bros., 1880). For bibliographical aids to the library guides most often recommended
by librarians, see: William E. Foster, "Books and Articles on Reading," in *Libraries and
Readers* (New York: Putnam's, 1877); Augusta H. Leypoldt and George Iles, eds., *List of
Books for Girls and Women and Their Clubs* (Boston: A.L.A., 1895). Richard A. Altick, *The
English Common Reader, A Social History of the Mass Reading Public, 1800-1900* (Chicago:
Univ. of Chicago Press, 1957), p. 139, notes the same attempt to control mass reading occur-
ring in England where "literally thousands of chatty homilies" were printed between 1850 and
1900.

[5] Arthur Lovejoy, *Great Chain of Being: A Study of the History of an Idea* (Cambridge: Harvard Univ. Press, 1936), p. 20.

[6] David Madden, "The Necessity for an Aesthetics of Popular Culture," *Journal of Popular
Culture,* 7 (Summer, 1973), p. 2.

violates established standards precede value change, as Weinstein and Platt contend,[7] or does such fantasy-making more often tend to be antirevolutionary because it permits vicarious discharge of conflict? These are extraordinarily complex questions and the historian who puzzles over popular culture must be exceedingly cautious in his imputations of collective behavior. Certainly any analysis of popular fiction which does not mesh with extensive outside historical evidence of a more traditional nature can be justly criticized as "presentism" or as a fallacious jump from information about the limited book-reading public to inferences about the "collective mind" or the "average American." However, when fiction is both "immoral" and immensely popular we can be certain that it does catch cultural reverberations which are disturbing to the group which designates it as deviant. Because there is abundant outside evidence of a questioning of the traditional role of women during this time, we can safely assume that many readers of this fiction were responding to its themes not with confusion and anger, but with excitement and interest. Above all, an understanding of the themes of *immoral* fiction gives insight into the troubled concern of the time with intellectual and ethical problems. Amid the whirl of social change in the late nineteenth century, the small literary flurry over book selection in the public library serves to dramatize not only aesthetic problems but important questions of morality and religion that perplexed the age.

\* \* \*

Sixteen questionable authors were listed by the librarians' committee.[8] Ten of these can be generally classified as domestic novelists, writing chiefly for women and about feminine experience: Ann Sophia Stephens (1813–1886), Mrs. E.D.E.N. Southworth (1819–1899), Mary Jane Holmes (1828–1907), Caroline Lee Hentz (1800–1856), Augusta Jane Evans Wilson (1835–1909), Jessie Fothergill (1851–1891), Rhoda Broughton (1840–1920), Florence Marryat (1837–1899), Helen Mathers (1853–1920), and Mrs. For-

---

[7] Fred Weinstein and Gerald M. Platt, *The Wish to Be Free: Society, Psyche and Value Change* (Los Angeles: Univ. of California Press, 1969). For another approach to fantasy as an indicator of value changes, see Neil J. Smelser, *Social Change in the Industrial Revolution* (Chicago: Univ. of Chicago Press, 1959), and Edward J. Tiryakian, "A Model of Societal Change and Its Lead Indicators," in Samuel Z. Klausner, ed., *The Study of Total Societies* (New York: Praeger, 1967), pp. 69–98.

[8] Actually, a total of twenty-eight questionable authors were listed; but nine of these will be excluded from consideration in this study becuse they wrote primarily for children. Three other authors—Edmund Yates, E. L. Bulwer and Wilkie Collins—also will not be considered because the reaction to the published list revealed that most librarians did not concur with the committee's inclusion of these men among the objectionable.

rester (1850–1896?). Mary Elizabeth Braddon (1837–1915) and Ellen Price Wood (1814–1887) represent the school of domestic criminals in their tales of outwardly ordinary women who commit adultery, bigamy, and murder. A little less oriented toward feminine readers are George Alfred Lawrence (1827–1876) and Ouida (1840–1908) with their muscular heroes and wild, sensuous women. William Harrison Ainsworth (1805–1882) and G.W.M. Reynolds (1814–1879) wrote the "Newgate Novel" with its complicated action, violence and unabashed emphasis on sex. Eleven of the sixteen authors were British; all were popular in the United States. Despite misgivings, most large American public libraries did stock "immoral" novels to meet the demands of the public.

Common to all these best-sellers is a rejection of traditional authority, particularly in domestic life, in religious faith, and among class-ordered mankind. The rebellion is sometimes blatant and crude, more often subtle and half-hidden by platitudes. Indeed, it is the imbedding of covert anti-masculinity within a strongly conventional framework which may be the crucial factor in the popularity of these works with women readers; feminine protest is made more acceptable when served in a traditional setting. These authors strike out at the clergy, the pompous rich, the penal system. Receiving the most vigorous blows is the marriage system itself, as its faults are perceived through the eyes of women. And throughout most of these books is one dominating theme—how strong woman decisively conquers and slyly manipulates weak man.[9]

"Women *must* marry—it is their vocation!" exclaimed the simpering Miss Alton as she plotted an alliance with the repugnant but wealthy Lord Clayton.[10] Even so self-sufficient and lively a young woman as Nell Adair had to agree that a spinster was a poor and powerless creature. "No wonder men call themselves lords of creation!" Nell mused. "It is not for what they

[9]There has been little of serious study given to these sixteen authors. Most commentators, however, have seen the domestic and sensational popular fiction of this time as basically conservative. Representative of this view are Frank Luther Mott, *Golden Multitudes: The Story of Best Sellers in the United States* (New York: Macmillan, 1947); James Hart, *The Popular Book* (New York: Oxford Univ. Press, 1950); Fred Lewis Pattee, *The Feminine Fifties* (New York: Appleton-Century, 1940); Clifton Joseph Furness, ed., *The Genteel Female* (New York: Knopf, 1931); and Herbert Ross Brown, *The Sentimental Novel in America, 1789–1860* (Durham: Duke Univ. Press, 1940). A few writers have emphasized the revolt against male supremacy; these are Beatrice Hofstadter, "Popular Culture and the Romantic Heroine," *American Scholar*, 30 (Winter, 1960–61), pp. 98–116; and Helen Waite Papashvily, *All the Happy Endings* (New York: Harper, 1956). Also see Elaine Showalter's unpublished paper presented at the Victorian Studies Conference, 1975, entitled "Family Secrets: Domestic Subversion in the Novels of the 1860's." Robert Reigel, *American Feminists* (Lawrence: Univ. of Kansas Press, 1963), comments that these domestic novelists would not have openly admitted their revolt. It seems to me that anyone reading these novels could not help but see that the heroine triumphs again and again.

[10]Mrs. Forrester (Mrs. Colonel Bridges), *Fair Women* (New York: Worthington, 1881), p. 77.

are, but for what they give, that they are of so much importance; all good things come to a woman through a plain gold circlet, apparently!"[11] Most fictional heroines acknowledged that even an unloved husband, assuming that he was at least not cruel, was preferable to none at all. The overriding interest of the unmarried girl was to trap a husband and the main concern of the married woman was to be content with the man she had—or failing that, to escape into fictional dreams of domestic bliss or wild abandonment.

The domestic novelists of immoral fiction met their woman reader's needs; their work was a kind of strategy manual for prospective brides and unhappy wives. In their novels the male figure is frequently either stupid, wholly submissive to feminine whims, or in some way an emotional cripple. Those male figures who show spunk and strength are finally brought to heel by the more dominant female. Nor do women fail to recognize the true meaning of their performance. It may be a man's world but the fictional heroine in these novels knows she is the real ruler on the throne, her realm gained and held by the tender mechanisms of "weakness" or "love." So far there is nothing really new in woman's reaction to her ancient state of "powerlessness"; manipulation of the male toward female-selected goals is an old and honored preoccupation.[12] What is *new* about the morally objectionable popular authors of this period is their much more open discussion of the female's plight: the necessity of selling one's life to the best bidder in exchange for security, the indignity and injustice of such a system, and the wearisome isolation of the woman within her home. New, too, is the bold heroine, with more energy than virtue, who scoffs at convention and wins a worthy husband despite her uncommon approach.

Rhoda Broughton's outspoken Belinda is such a heroine—full-bodied, intelligent and caustic. Belinda and her sister Sarah cavort through Europe "chaperoned" by a bright-eyed grandmother who harbors memories of an exciting past beneath her ruffled cap. Granny always lets the girls go where they want, so long as they do not ask her to accompany them. Frivolous Sarah takes full advantage of the situation but Belinda is too proud to copy her sister's light coquetries and masks her tumultuous inner passion with a "cold hard voice and a chill set face." Yet young David Rivers finally succumbs to her will and proposes to her, after Belinda has lured him into going alone with her into a romantic spot in the forest. Rivers is aware that Belinda's outward conformity to Victorian propriety is but a cover for her eager sexuality. He would not mind if a woman treated him like a dog in public, he tells her, "if she were—if she were—as I would have her when we

---

[11]Helen B. Mathers (Mrs. Helen B. Reeves), *Coming Thro' The Rye* (New York: Macmillan, 1898), p. 209. The first edition was published in 1875.
[12]See Ronald V. Sampson, *The Psychology of Power* (New York: Pantheon, 1966), pp. 92–102.

were alone." But Rivers forsakes Belinda because he feels he is too poor to support a wife.

Our heroine finally enters a loveless marriage with a flat-footed, aged pedant from Oxford. "It is a mere matter of business," she explains to her husband. "You want a secretary, housekeeper, nurse for your mother; I want a home of my own, and a guide, philosopher and friend." In less than a week her marriage goes sour.

> Belinda had been married three days . . . recollecting how many lumps of sugar he likes, as she has already discovered that he has no objection to repeating. . . . Nor is it less monstrous to be warming his overcoat, and cutting his newspapers, and ordering his dinner with that nice attention to digestibility and economy which she finds to be expected of her. They have been enormously long, these three days.[13]

Her life becomes that of a sullen coolie in harness as she responds to her hated husband's calls—to the "voice she had given the right to command Belinda; to chide Belinda; immeasurably worst of all, to *caress* Belinda."[14]

When Rivers reappears upon the scene, now a rich man, Belinda responds to his longing for her with only the barest twinge of conscience. She feels more anger than shame. Indeed, what is sin? she rebelliously questions. "Is it to fulfill with nice scrupulosity every tasteless or even nauseous duty of a most dreary life? To sing as she walks her treadmill? To forego her own hot bright youth. . . . To be a secretary without pay, a drudge without wage?" After pages more of maneuver, yearning, and husband's cruelty, Belinda and Rivers, in one "drunk, oblivious moment," embrace with "loud blood dinning in their ears and hammering their temples."[15] Belinda decides to risk ultimate disgrace and run away with Rivers. Happily this is unnecessary as her husband falls dead on the last page of the book. When she finds his body, Belinda is apparently overcome by sheer delight and falls in a faint—thus succumbing to a feminine stratagem which she has heretofore scorned in women. The book ends on a note of high glee, with illegal love triumphant.

More respectable than Belinda, but just as unconventional in thought, is Jessie Fothergill's heroine, May Wedderburn, who at age seventeen manages to escape her dull existence as the daughter of an English clergyman. Living alone in Germany while she studies for a singing career, she falls in love with a mysterious gentleman named Eugene whose eyes shock "with a kind of tameless freedom in their glance."[16] May moves into

[13]Rhoda Broughton, *Belinda* (London: Bently, 1883), Vol. II, p. 109. There is a story that the author's father, a minister, had strictly forbidden her to read her own novels.
[14]Ibid., p. 114.
[15]Ibid., p. 141.
[16]Jessie Fothergill, *The First Violin* (New York: Grosset and Dunlap, n.d.), p. 29; first published in 1878.

Eugene's hotel where she has a room so conveniently situated that she can spy on him through his window. Obviously sensual and competent in love, May is continually washed with "wave after wave of wild emotion," especially when brushing against Eugene as they pass each other on the stairs. The author often emphasizes May's passionate nature: "sometimes a subdued fire glowed in her eyes and compressed her lips, which removed her altogether from the category of spiritless beauties."[17]

Eugene is finally won over by his apparent weakness for the female form draped in clinging wet clothes. After some maneuvering on her part, he rescues her from drowning and carries her home in his arms. Trembling in his embrace, May thinks, "In the midst of the torpor that was stealing over me there shot every now and then a shiver of ecstasy so keen as to almost terrify me."[18] May—bohemian, talented, irreligious, and "that most dreadful of all abnormal growths, a woman with a will of her own"—does have some qualms about her adjustment to married life.

> Should I not be shocking him by coarse, gross notions as to the needlessness of this or that fine point of conduct? by my ill defined ideas as to a code of honor— my slovenly ways of looking at questions?[19]

The reader, though, feels little doubt that May's steel center will ever collapse or that she will allow herself to remain in any situation which she does not control. Eugene, of thin ankles and worshipping heart, is no match for dauntless May.

Whereas Belinda and May verily throb with sexual energy, the incredibly popular heroine Edna Earl seems to be free of all drives except the urge to dominate her world. In St. Elmo Murray she finds a worthy opponent in the battle of the sexes. Edna, an orphan, has been taken into St. Elmo's home by his wealthy mother. With unremitting application, Edna tackles the whole of knowledge, learning along the way Sanskrit, Chaldee, Arabic, Cufic, Greek, and Latin. Edna did not approve of bluestockings or of pushy women who wanted the vote. Nonetheless she was ". . . obstinately wedded to the unpardonable heresy, that, in the nineteenth century, it was a woman's privilege to be as learned as Cuvier, or Sir William Hamilton, or Humboldt. . . ."[20]

[17] Ibid., p. 153.
[18] Ibid., p. 171.
[19] Ibid., p. 360.
[20] Augusta Jane Wilson, *St. Elmo* (New York: Carlton, 1866) p. 235. Within four months after publication the book had been read by one million people. Total sales place it securely within the ten most popular books ever published in America. Even in 1949 there were four editions printed. For further discussion of the author and her work, see: William Perry Fidler, *Augusta Evans Wilson, 1835-1909* (Birmingham: Univ. of Alabama Press, 1951); Ernest Elmo Calkins, "St. Elmo, or Named for a Best Seller," *Saturday Review of Literature,* 21 (1939), pp. 3-4; and Hofstadter, Papashvily, Mott, Hart, and Brown.

Edna and her learning have provided wits with numerous opportunities for ridicule, for, as one commented, she could not bring home a cow from pasture without a dozen classical allusions to fit the occasion. Words like epoptae, chrysolegent, lotophagi, places like Alfrasib and Demophaon, references to "Meleschott's dictum" and the "incipent Isotta Negarole" abound in her communication with others. Even when crying into her pillow she speaks in grandly structured sentences: "Commit me rather to the horny but outstretched hands, the brawny arms, the untutored minds, the simple but kindly-throbbing hearts of the proletaire!" she weeps.[21] It is easy to laugh at Edna's high-blown language, less easy to be amused at the woman reader's pathetic hunger for status through knowledge reflected in the popularity of *St. Elmo*.[22] Edna, who eventually becomes a famous author, understands her public's longing for education.

The major theme of *St. Elmo*, however, is the reduction of the strong and sinful hero to a blob of jelly by the indomitable Edna. St. Elmo admits to having killed his best friend in a duel and to having jilted his fiancée at the altar. The shock had caused that unfortunate bride-to-be to have a hemorrhage of the lungs on the church steps and she had died two months later; thus St. Elmo was responsible for two deaths. The effects of these happenings, said St. Elmo, had warped his nature and deformed his soul. He entered a life of wandering and hatred: "I drank, gambled, and my midnight carousals would sicken your soul, were I to paint all their hideousness."[23] Edna is unbending; St. Elmo must become purified if he is ever to be worthy of her love. She defers marriage to him until she has won fame and fortune on her own and he has become a spineless ghost of himself—a mild-mannered minister, inferior to her even in his religious potency. Thus did Edna, and her readers, realize their dream—a marriage in which the real psychological and intellectual power is firmly held by the wife.

Sometimes the hero of domestic fiction is not merely subjected to female domination but is literally destroyed by his love for the heroine. This fate awaits Paul Vasher in the very popular *Coming Thro' The Rye*, perhaps because the heroine, Nell Adair, had very early in her childhood rejected male supremacy.[24] Nell decisively repudiates a decorative femininity and glories in her delight at feeling "more than half a boy." She even resents her restrictive clothing.

[21] Ibid., p. 120.

[22] See the author's many asides on the subject as when Edna, speaking of her readers, muses, "If there should accidentally be an allusion to classical or scientific literature, which they do not understand at the first, hasty, novel-reading glance, will they inform themselves, and . . . then thank me for the hint . . .?", p. 519.

[23] Ibid., p. 314.

[24] Her earliest memories center upon her hatred of her cruel and domineering father. Donald Meyers, *The Positive Thinkers* (New York: Doubleday, 1965), has noted the hostility toward father in many popular novels of the day; often he is dead.

> How cumbrous, and useless, and ridiculous they are; how my gowns, petticoats, crinolines, ribbons, ties, cloaks, hats, bonnets, gloves, tapes, hooks, eyes, buttons, and the hundred and one et ceteras that make up a girl's costume, chafe and irritate me! What would I not give to be able to leave them all in a heap and steal . . . Jack's cool, comfortable, easy grey garments?[25]

Her heart abounds in joy when she dons knickerbockers for the first time to play a game of cricket. Nell is as emotionally rugged as any man. Tears are to her a cowardly refuge for suffering women. She would "far rather storm" through a crisis than simply weep and bear the pain.

Unable to locate a man who shares her advanced views, Nell drifts into a betrothal with Paul who is heavily traditional in his ideas about female passivity: "Paul Vasher is like the rest of his sex, who value their privileges too highly to permit women to encroach the merest jot upon them, and would build so prickly a wall of propriety around us, that we shall not be able to climb up and see what is going on on the other side."[26] The conflicting views of Nell and Paul provide the author with numerous opportunities to discuss the relation of the sexes. Invariably Nell begins a debate:

> "The Man should always rule," says Paul, in his masterful way; "and you may say what you like, Nell, but you would love to be ruled, you would like to be kept in order."
> "No, no," I say gravely . . . "a man grows tired of treating his mistress or wife like a goddess or baby; he wants more solid stuff to live on, and the one everlasting dish palls them. If she will look the knowledge in the face that such is the case, and putting sentiment on one side enter heartily into his ambitions and aims, and hopes, and amusements, she becomes not only the beloved woman, but the bright, pleasant comrade, who is bound to him by fifty ties of mutual interest and support; they are equals, and he considers her as capable of giving advice as taking it."[27]

Despite the running battle which he fights with Nell, it is clear that even strait-laced Paul prefers a girl with spunk. But Paul, who mistakenly believes that Nell has wed another man, is tricked into marriage to a stock villainess. Realizing his error, Paul offers to leave his wife and run away with Nell but Nell refuses to endure such disgrace. Broken and tortured, Paul ages thirty years in two years time and finally escapes to a merciful death on the Sudan battlefield. Nell elects to remain a spinster, supremely confident of her ability to function independently of men.

Unlike the heroines above, who were not physical beauties, Rachael Norreys combines all the characteristics of beauty, will, intelligence, and

[25] Mathers, p. 51.
[26] Ibid., p. 258.
[27] Ibid., p. 158.

passion. Rachael had eloped when she was sixteen but her father had found the errant couple before the marriage was consummated. When her husband, Raymond, after an absence of five years, returns to claim his bride, Rachael finds that she is not ready to settle down to domestic isolation. But the celibacy which she imposes on herself and her husband is not easy for either of them to endure. Her sensuality is the one force that:

> ... could subdue her pride. ... No one could help seeing it who saw anything. It flashes out of her liquid eyes; it hung upon her ripe, tremulous mouth; it made itself known in the sensitiveness of her nervous little hand; in the sudden flushing of her cheek—the low, impassioned accents of her voice. Yes, she could love, and she *should* love![28]

When Raymond unjustly accuses her of having a man in her bedroom she is too proud even to explain the truth to him. She moves out of their home in a rage. "With fire flashing from her irradiated eyes, with her delicate nostrils distended,"[29] she determines never to return. Even when Raymond begs her forgiveness, she refuses to submit or to allow him to "lay his feet upon her neck." Only many months later, when he is near death (and has also, incidentally, inherited a baronetcy and rich estates) does Rachael accept his apology and return as his wife. Raymond has presumedly learned a life-long lesson: "However unpleasant they may be at times, it is your stormy women, after all, that can love the best, although they may be the most dangerous when crossed."[30]

The preoccupation with man-handling and man-trapping which is characteristic of domestic fiction is particularly blatant in *Fair Women*—a tale of matchmaking in high society. Rich Lord Clayton makes the point clear in his assessment of marriage: "Why the devil should I bind myself to one woman, of whom I should get heartily sick in a month, when I can indulge myself with all the pleasing varieties of the sex at half the cost? ... Of *course* you can buy them—it only depends on whether you're willing or able to pay the price."[31] Miss Alton realizes that Clayton is malicious and cruel, and yet she imagines that she can use his money to escape him: "If you lived in the country and were to be bored with him all day long, it would be the most awful thing conceivable; but you know that fashionable wives are not much troubled with their husband's company, and can always get away from it." The less fortunate middle-class woman reader who was also caught in an unhappy marriage must have been glad to see that Miss Alton's freedom, once she became Mrs. Clayton, was as severely limited as

[28]Florence Marryat (Mrs. Florence (Marryat) Church Lean), *Woman Against Woman* (New York: Scribner, Welford, 1869), p. 164.

[29]Ibid., p. 301.

[30]Ibid., p. 254.

[31]Forrester, p. 60.

her own. However, bold Mrs. Clayton's married life is enriched by a love affair with a handsome colonel who begs her to run away with him. Lord Clayton's behavior drives her to heretical thoughts: "We hear sometimes of women leaving their husbands, and then the world cries them down, and they never dare show their faces in society again. If people could know [one-half] of what a wife may suffer, I wonder if they would be so harsh?"[32]

It is what an unhappy wife suffers that these novels present in rich detail. The morally suspect authors could not always defy convention and allow a runaway wife to live in full contentment forever. Therefore they often killed off the husband in one way or another—in Lord Clayton's case, with cholera—before they could assure lasting joy to the rebellious heroine. But even the unhappy runaway has been given more than enough reason to escape the repression and isolation of a loveless marriage.[33] The reader is strongly encouraged to sympathize with the wife rather than with the betrayed husband. Interesting too is that the husband's sins are not the obviously distressing ones of adultery, desertion, drunkenness, or physical cruelty, from which most states provided legal escape via divorce, but are instead the core traits of his tyrant personality—intolerance, stupidity, and insensitivity. In essence the morally questionable authors effectively argued that difficult divorce and intolerance of the divorced woman kept many wives in painful life-long servitude. And in these books the innate strength of the heroine is constantly stressed. Either she escapes from the chains placed on her by an unhappy marriage or she successfully enslaves her compliant husband.

The six domestic novelists discussed above made their women daring and unconventional; in other equally popular forms of domestic fiction, the heroine's steel fist is concealed in a prim silken glove. The writing of E.D.E.N. Southworth, Mary Jane Holmes, Ann Sophia Stephens, and Caroline Lee Hentz is of low quality; the characters are often wooden and the involved plots move along only by ridiculous coincidence and unbelievable incidents. Each novelist, however, had an easy flowing style and all but Mrs. Southworth displayed a real talent for writing fast-moving dialogue. But if their faults of expression are many, their real forte is the intuitive understanding with which they catch and communicate the rebellious hearts of their feminine characters. In 1872 the Boston Public Library reported that the books of Southworth, Hentz, and Holmes were called for more than any other volumes held. Holmes sold a total of two million books and Hentz sales exceed ninety-three thousand in one three-year period.

[32] Ibid., p. 123.
[33] See, for example, the portrayal of runaway wives in the characters of Adelaide, May's sister, in Fothergill's *The First Violin*, Mrs. Craven in Marryat's *Woman Against Woman*, Rebecca in G. A. Lawrence's *Guy Livingstone*, and Mrs. Leicester in Stephen's *Fashion and Famine*.

Southworth sold more books than any female author in American history. Even in 1936, eighty-four years after her first best-seller, one publisher still printed 27 Southworth novels. Only in the 1940's did her work generally drop out of print. Stephens is best known for *Maleska,* the highly popular first Beadle novel. *Maleska* alone probably sold over 300,000 copies. The remarkable similarity of the lives of these four best-selling authors can be used to question the charges so often brought against them by later critics that they were sympathetic supporters of the traditional concept of woman's place and nature. Southworth and Hentz suffered gravely in deeply unsatisfying marriages, and each of the four women very early surpassed her husband in energy, intellect, and achievement. They all struggled desperately to succeed in the male world of action and were all personally incensed by the restrictions imposed on them by the operating assumption of male supremacy.[34]

Linda Walton, the most popular creation of Caroline Hentz, exemplifies the heroine of mighty, though hidden, strength. In the ultimate rebellion, Linda refuses to marry Roger, the husband selected for her by her father. She runs away with Mr. McLeod, a local schoolteacher who has offered to help her escape. When McLeod begins to hint at their destination as "a secluded place," Linda realizes she has misplaced her confidence. To escape his embrace she dives from the boat and is picked up on shore by Tuscarora, a noble savage. It is her amazing good luck that he speaks perfect English. For several adventurous years Linda prowls the wilderness with her brave (and apparently celibate) Indian protector at her side. By remarkable coincidence she meets Roger, who by now has forsaken earthly love and has dedicated his life to missionary work among the heathen Indians. Now free to leave her exciting exile, Linda returns to her first love, a young steamboat pilot. Amid sunlight and music, we leave her supremely happy.[35]

To understand the deeper implications of Linda's popularity with female readers, it is useful to compare Linda with Edith Lyle, Mary Jane Holmes' well known heroine. Fifteen-year-old Edith had been brought to the United States from England by her mother who hoped to make a brilliant match for her daughter with a wealthy man. Edith upset her mother's plans by a secret marriage to a poor carpenter who was almost immediately killed in an accident. Disgraced and pregnant, Edith is returned to England by her disappointed and domineering mother. After the loss of her child, Edith en-

[34]See: Papashvily; Rhoda Ellison, "Mrs. Hentz and the Green-Eyed Monster," *American Literature,* 22 (1950), pp. 345–50; Madeline B. Stern, "Ann S. Stephens, Author of the first Beadle Novel, 1860," *New York Public Library: Bulletin 64* (1960), pp. 302–22; Regis Louise Boyle, *Mrs. E.D.E.N. Southworth, Novelist* (Washington, D.C.: Catholic Univ. of America Press, 1939).

[35]Caroline Lee Hentz, *Linda, or the Young Pilot of the Belle Creole: A Tale of Southern Life* (Philadelphia: A. Hart, 1854).

ters into a long state of depression and illness. Eventually finding a job as companion to a spinster, Edith meets a wealthy American widower who proposes marriage. Her suitor "felt a thrill of exultant pride as he saw her in his fancy at the head of his table and moving through his handsome rooms, herself the handsomest appendage there."[36] Edith, however, refuses to "sell herself for a name and a home," for she believes:

> He does not love me, but he admires my face and form, and would no doubt be very kind and careful of me, just as he would be kind and careful of a favorite horse . . . he would hang on me jewels rare, and silks and laces and satins. . . .[37]

Only after he has convinced her of his appreciation of her individuality will she marry him and return to his wealthy estates in America. A major crisis occurs when her aristocratic-minded husband discovers that she has been the wife of a lowly carpenter. His devastation is greeted by her with magnificent disdain. Chastened by the withdrawal of her approval, he eventually adjusts to the knowledge that he must accept her as used merchandise and he becomes more devoted to her than ever.

In both style and plot these two novels are literary rubbish. Of course, it was not any artistic merit that gave them their wide popularity, but the forces of psychological attraction. Both Linda and Edith are placed in sharp conflict with the authority which attempts to force them into traditional feminine passivity. Each girl escapes successfully from psychic oppression and feels the confidence proceeding from proven self-sufficiency. In contrast to the strong heroines, their male lovers are pitifully ineffectual and compliant. In a society which bolstered the social and legal authority of the male, some women readers could find confirmation of their own value in the pages of popular domestic novels like these. The long-lashed heroines, despite their glossy curls and physical fragility, were clearly women in revolt, feeling, establishing, and maintaining a strident female protest in the fantasized world of "immoral" fiction.

Mrs. Southworth's extremely popular creations, Capitola and Ishmael, also illustrate the message which these domestic novelists were disseminating about the relationship of men and women. Capitola, a foretaste of the New Woman, was vigorous, daring, and radiant. This adventuress, sometimes disguised as a boy, fought duels, outwitted villains, scoffed at ministerial sanctimony, and once even "put her thumb to the side of her nose, and whirled her fingers into a semi-circle, in a gesture more expressive than elegant."[38] Ishmael is, on the other hand, so saintly and sub-

---

[36] Mary Jane Holmes, *Edith Lyle* (New York: Carleton, 1876), p. 75.

[37] Ibid., p. 76.

[38] Mrs. E.D.E.N. Southworth, *The Hidden Hand* (Chicago: Donahue, n.d.), p. 122. The book was first published in the New York Ledger in 1859. Mott estimates that *The Hidden Hand* and *Ishmael* sold over two million copies apiece.

servient to woman's will that Mrs. Southworth felt compelled to assure her public that his exalted character was real: "Reader! I am not fooling you with a fictitious character here."[39] In his first law case he defended the rights of a deserted wife and worked his whole life "to modify those cruel laws which . . . made woman, despite her understanding intellect, an idiot, and despite her loving nature a chattel—in the law."[40] Ishmael finds his place with the feminine gender—at their feet.

Mrs. Ann Stephens, the last of the morally suspect writers of domestic fiction, does not so often portray the subtly rebellious heroines found in the books of Southworth, Hentz, and Holmes. Perhaps her greatest appeal lay in the sheer excitement of her feminine characters' lives—set in rapidly growing cities, with thrilling glimpses of poverty, crime, luxury, and sin.[41] But Mrs. Stephens made Maleska, the famous Indian heroine with whom Beadle began his dime-novel series, into a woman whose heart beat at one with her lighter-hued sisters. Although Maleska's "sentiments were correct in principle and full of simplicity," she, too, toiled all her life,

. . . . in piling up soft couches for those she loved, and taking the cold stones for herself. It was her woman's destiny, not the more certain because of her savage origin. Civilization does not always reverse this mournful picture of womanly self-abnegation.[42]

Mrs. Stephens, the other domestic novelists, and their millions of women readers had each in her own way learned to resent the "mournful" feminine passivity induced by cultural presentiment. To their tremendous audience these ten novelists spoke of the pressing concerns of a woman's daily life, of how to assert individuality, of how to win a man as trophy and then how to cut him down to manageable size. Feminine discontent, vaguely defined but deeply felt, permeates the domestic fiction judged "immoral" by leading librarians and literary conservatives. Indeed, the Victorian librarians judged it rightly, for it does reflect the unsettling cultural shift in the nineteenth century from an idolatry of women to a more realistic consideration of feminine needs and abilities.

Startling as it was, the work of these ten novelists was not considered so shocking as was the writing of the six remaining authors judged questionable by the American Library Association in 1881. Whereas the writing of the popular domestic novelists was apt to be sneered at as the "pablum" of the uncultivated masses, the work of the "sensational school" was

[39] Southworth, *Ishmael* (New York: Fenne, 1904), was first published in 1863.
[40] Ibid., p. 471.
[41] See Ann Stephens, *Fashion and Famine* (New York: Bruce and Bros., 1854), for an example of this setting.
[42] Cited in Papashvily, p. 144.

condemned with real horror by persons of genteel literary taste.[43] The single common element in the works of Ainsworth, Reynolds, Braddon, and Wood—the use of the criminal as an important character—does not preclude a wide variation in their treatment of the fallen man or woman. Ainsworth and Reynolds tended to low-life settings; Braddon and Wood used a middle- or upper-class background. The genteel objection to these books was that they brought to their readers a dangerous familiarity with vice. The extraordinary popularity of the humanized criminal made the "Newgate Novels" of Ainsworth and Reynolds the most fearful.[44]

The strain of the sensuous in *Jack Sheppard* and *Robert McNaire* is undeniably startling. Pain and sexual passion are fully experienced and described with gusto.[45] Feminine beauty is portrayed with considerable physical detail. McNaire's paramour, Maria, wore "a morning wrapper, which was as yet open at the breast; and her young and beautiful bosom, which the garment only half-concealed, heaved with frequent signs."[46] "Voluptuous" is one of Reynolds' favorite words. The criminal heroes are made to seem dashing, acceptable, and even admirable. Daring deeds of murder, robbery, and extortion are described with a light-hearted suspension of morality, and the reader is often impressed with the criminal's virtuous traits.

Ainsworth and Reynolds turned genteel ethics upside down. In their books women are loose *and* lovely and while the hero and heroine do not always escape punishment they have a wonderful run for their money first and really *enjoy* themselves, free of the reproaches of a tortured conscience. The aristocracy and clergy are repeatedly lashed; the vices of the wealthy are contrasted with the restricted lives of the poor who cannot afford sensual indulgence.[47] Despite incredible coincidence, involved action, and flighty dialogue, the story moves along in pizzicato style and the criminal characters are usually convincing persons, with real human mixtures of virtue and vice. Beginning in the 1830's in England, Ainsworth and Reynolds drew heavy ire

---

[43]The term "sensation novel" was first given to a certain class of popular novels by literary critics in the 1860's. The term was applied to those novels which contained something abnormal and unnatural, inserted into the story for its own sake to extract the greatest possible thrill. Often this thrill was to shock morality and custom.

[44]Keith Hollingsworth, *The Newgate Novel, 1830–1847* (Detroit: Wayne Univ. Press, 1963); Margaret Dalziel, *Popular Fiction 100 Years Ago* (London: Cohen and West, 1957); S. M. Ellis, *William Ainsworth Harrison and His Friends* (London: n.p., 1911); Malcom Elwin, *Victorian Wallflowers* (London: Jonathan Cape, 1934); and Louis James, *Fiction for the Working Man, 1830–1850* (London: Oxford Univ. Press, 1963).

[45]William Ainsworth, *Jack Sheppard* (New York: Colyer, 1839); George W. M. Reynolds, *Robert McNaire in England* (London: Willoughby, n.d.). Possible sadism and pornography in fiction seems to be a perennial problem, being even now the chief concern of those who seek to protect public morality.

[46]Reynolds, p. 38.

[47]When his indignation with social injustice grew too great, Reynolds would produce dietary tables of workhouse meals or diagrams to show the excess of wealthy men.

from those of discriminating literary taste but the appeal of their books continued high in the United States until the end of the century.[48]

Following the example set by Ainsworth and Reynolds, Mary Braddon and Mrs. Henry Wood also had a large public following in the United States. Their immensely successful books, *Lady Audley's Secret* and *East Lynne,* were sprinkled with murders (real and attempted), bigamy, adultery, insanity, endless complications, and painful predicaments.[49] In their books the rigid conduct expected of proper Victorian heroes and heroines decidedly gives way to a wider freedom. Young maidens cavort with married men and wives solemnly plot their husbands' betrayal or, sometimes, death. It is all great fun for everyone involved and when retribution comes it is given brief treatment by the authors. Often insanity is offered as explanation for the heroine's general infamy. Underlying these action-packed tales one finds a most tolerant attitude toward human frailty, an engaging undertone of malice toward the petty arrogance of the rich, and a cynical portrayal of feminine character against the background of a world which is generally indifferent to justice.

Similarly, the novels of G. A. Lawrence and those of Ouida—who is the best of a large group of inferior imitators of Lawrence—displayed a strong sympathy for actions which greatly violated the prim moral codes of the Victorian world. The principal source of Lawrence's popularity was his portrayal of the superhuman hero. Guy Livingstone, his best-known creation, is a gigantic patrician of unparalleled strength, passion, and lust for general risk-taking. This superb male animal was also cynical (especially about the purity of women) and strictly amoral. Unhampered by any religious injunctions, contemptuous of parental and societal controls, Guy forces his will upon the world and upon the women who love him—amidst a constant round of hunting, warring, and revelry. Guy attracts and enjoys women with all the "confidence of one who knew his subject well."[50]

---

[48] In 1879 Frederick Perkins, the librarian of the San Francisco Public Library, removed *Jack Sheppard* and a set of the works of Reynolds from circulation on moral grounds. When attacked in 1885 by a liberal-minded reporter for his action, Perkins insisted that it "is no more right that this library should circulate dirty books than that the Lincoln School . . . should instruct in criminal practices, . . . obscene language and vulgar habits." Frederick Perkins, "Free Libraries and Unclean Books," *Library Journal,* 10 (1885), p. 397.

[49] Mary Braddon, *Lady Audley's Secret* (Leipzig: Tauchnitz, 1862); Mrs. Henry Wood, *East Lynne* (London: Bently, 1863). In 1900 Mrs. Wood's sales were advertised as over two and one-half million copies. *East Lynne* was produced as a movie in 1931. Hart lists *Lady Audley's Secret* as the book most widely read in America in 1862; Mott places sales as at least 300,000 between 1862 and 1869.

[50] G. A. Lawrence, *Guy Livingstone* (New York: Stokes, 1928), p. 24, was first published in 1857 in London. See Gordon H. Fleming, *George Alfred Lawrence and the Victorian Sensational Novel* (Tucson: Univ. of Arizona Press, 1952).

Guy's female counterpart is Flora Dorillon, a *femme fatale* par excellence. Needless to say, Flora is beautiful. But what attracts Guy to her is her "daring disregard of opinions, conventionalities, and more sacred things yet, which carried him on straight to the accomplishment of his thought and purpose."[51] In a scene highly unusual by Victorian standards for its suggestive eroticism free of moral judgment, the reader sees the unmarried couple off to bed and the narrator, watching them go, comments: "I know men who would have given five years of life for the whisper that glided into his ear . . . ten for the Parthian glance that shot its arrow home."[52]

Ten years after *Guy Livingstone's* publication, Ouida began to write her florid novels. In her heyday, "she was considered an apostle of insidious immorality. . . . She was smutty and 'not nice'; therefore everybody read her."[53] Bertie Cecil, the Life Guardsman in *Under Two Flags,* is a hard, masculine, unintellectual Lawrentian superman, adored by women. Although aristocratic Bertie's goings-on and the incidents that lead him to a long exile in Africa, all told in purple prose, appear truly absurd to the modern reader, it is in her depiction of the *gamine,* Cigarette, that Ouida exceeds her natural literary limitations and creates an original and enchanting heroine. This little creature is a camp-follower and mascot of the Foreign Legion. Reared in a barracks-room, Cigarette can toss off brandies and shoot from a gallop as well as the toughest Legionnaire. In admiration, Ouida pauses to ponder Cigarette's future death:

> Well, she will die, I dare say, some bright day or another, at the head of a regiment, with some desperate battle turned by the valour of her charge. . . . That is what Cigarette hoped for—why not? There will always be a million of commonplace women ready to keep up the decorous traditions of their sex, and sit in safety over their needles by the sides of their hearths. One little lioness here and there in a generation cannot do overmuch harm.[54]

But this sun-browned girl is not entirely unsexed. She has had:

> . . . a thousand lovers, from handsome marquesses of the Guides to tawny black-brown scoundrels in the Zouaves, and she had never loved anything, except the roll of the *pas de change,* and the sight of her own, arch, defiant face, with its scarlet lips and its short, jetty hair, when she saw it by chance in some burnished cuirass, that served her for a mirror.[55]

[51] Lawrence, p. 94.
[52] Ibid., p. 353.
[53] Elwin, p. 298; See also: Eileen Bigland, *Ouida: The Passionate Victorian* (London: Jarrolds, 1950); Elizabeth Lee, *Ouida: A Memoir* (London: Fisher Unwin, 1914); and Monica Stirling, *The Fine and the Wicked: The Life and Times of Ouida* (London: Gollancz, 1958).
[54] Ouida (Louise de la Ramée), *Under Two Flags* (New York: Stein and Day, 1956), p. 314. Mott believes Ouida was more widely read in the United States than either Braddon or Wood.
[55] Ibid., p. 182.

Long accustomed to demure and spotless damsels for the most part, the reading public of the late nineteenth century must have found Cigarette and Lawrentian heroines like Flora extraordinary beings deliciously designed to shock the stolid bourgeoisie.

Clearly, the major themes of these "immoral" bestsellers are in opposition to convention. Most prevalent is the depiction of a new heroine— sensual, active, defiant. Parental authority is repeatedly denied and is openly resented. The major characters, if they are not overtly antireligious, are at least rebelliously critical of clerical pomposity. There is also a sympathetic presentation of the inner conflicts of the sinner, whether his sins be actual crimes or simply revolts against sexual and religious mores. Emphasis is placed upon the responsibility of the social structure itself for the miseries of the world, rather than upon the individual's deliberate and willful choice. In short, the traditional procedures and idolatries of society are unquestionably under pressure. The lines of battle are drawn in the pages of these subtly revolutionary, sensibility-jolting, extremely popular novels.

The great majority of the readers of these novels were women. Here, in the domestic and sensational novels which they consumed by the tens of millions, they could read of the wildly independent heroine putting the lie to the premise of masculine superiority and gaily negating societal controls. In these pages emancipated women rule over slavish men and new answers to the question of the place and meaning of sex are devised. A new consciousness of thwarted sensuality emerges. Desire becomes alluring and women not so pure, sex not so degrading, as literary idealists would have them believe. And all about them, toward the end of the century, women readers could find abundant signs that men, too, were impatient with the narrowness of life and wished for new ideas and modes of behavior.

In effect, a demand for greater individual autonomy, triggered by previous changes in religious and political authority relationships, was being expanded in the late nineteenth century to include a liberalization of controls over sexual and familial norms. Specifically, as women's older role-performance became increasingly archaic under changing historical circumstances, a disturbing demand for change surfaced in many forms—one form was "immoral" fiction-fantasy. The longer-term process of structural and cultural change is related to the shorter-term process of the library's institutional effort to channel and slow the suspect novel's desacralization of the *status quo*. The new moral order which gradually emerged was more differentiated than the old. As a sociologist could remark by 1908, "Virtue no longer consists of literal obedience to arbitrary standards set by community or church but rather in conduct consistent with a growing personality."[56] Today the trend toward personal standards of morality is so well established that it would be difficult for most present-day readers to understand what the late nineteenth-century librarian's fuss was all about. The difference lies in the high degree of Victorian opposition to sensual stimulation and challenge to patriarchal authority.

The advent of mass culture worked to negate the ancient presumptions which enclosed the individual in community structures and standards maintained, at least in principle, from the top. No matter how well-stocked its rooms, the public library could not attract the public without providing the reading which reflected mass concerns. By 1900 public library leaders had all but given up an attempt to discredit best-selling fiction. When the mass literary movement aided the nineteenth century trend toward individualized morality which women novel readers strengthened, the decline of library paternalism became a sign of the times.

[56]Cited in David Kennedy, *Birth Control in America: The Career of Margaret Sanger* (New Haven: Yale Univ. Press, 1970), p. 68. See his excellent chapter on "The Nineteenth Century Heritage" for a summary of value shifts in the late nineteenth century. William Wasserstrom, *Heiress of All the Ages: Sex and Sentiment in the Genteel Tradition* (Minneapolis: Univ. of Minnesota Press, 1959), pp. 3-38, concentrates his attention upon high literature of the post-Civil War era and finds traces of the New Woman heroine as early as the 1850's. Shortly before the Civil War, he believes, the genteel code was challenged, "first in the popular literature of the times," and then, after the war, "serious literature, too, more and more openly reasserted half-forgotten values." (p. 21).

# THE ASSAULT ON VICTORIANISM IN THE TWENTIETH CENTURY

*STANLEY COBEN*

VICTORIAN CULTURE STILL FLOURISHES IN MANY NOOKS AND CRANNIES OF the United States, modified only slightly, though significantly, since the late nineteenth century. On medium-sized farms and in towns that serve them commercially, in cities which lie just out of the suburban commuter's reach, the essence of Victorianism still thrives. It also pervades places where more far-reaching influence is exercised: in prestigious metropolitan clubs, conservative private boarding schools and suburban country clubs, and in the executive dining rooms of Pittsburgh steel companies, for example. This is not to suggest that Victorian ideas and values have disappeared elsewhere. Even the most liberated member of a California commune and the coolest pimp or pusher in a central city ghetto subconsciously hold Victorian precepts to some extent, no matter how vehemently they consciously reject those doctrines. Victorian values implicit in messages from parents, ministers, more acculturated friends and relatives, the mass media, and even teachers have reached them all. The basic elements of a culture are transmitted early in an individual's development, and efforts to change these ordinarily are resisted steadfastly. Furthermore, not all of Victorianism offends contemporary tastes. Values associated with traditional Victorian family roles, for example, retain wide appeal. Nevertheless, unmistakable shifts in the place of crucial Victorian values in American life, and in their nature, have occurred during the twentieth century. Probably the most important aspect of those changes is a loss of confidence in the civilization's conceptual bases. Even the most dedicated twentieth-century adherents of Victorianism suffer from a progressive decrease in certainty—more obvious in each succeeding generation—that *their* ideas and values are indisputably true.

Twice in the twentieth century, culminating in the 1920's and 1960's, discontent with the prevailing culture became so intense and widespread that strong, organized movements and dense networks of rebellious individuals developed with the intention of instituting drastic change. Dissident intellectuals, blacks and other minority ethnic groups, radical feminists, and disgruntled youths led the way in each period when rebellion flowered. Their revolts were handicapped by failure within each dissenting group to agree on ideology or objectives, and therefore on specific solutions for their complaints; they suffered also from near-total absence of cooperation among the groups and from counterattack by those satisfied with the status quo. Nevertheless efforts to effect change, most obvious during the two periods of upheaval, have carried Americans a considerable distance from the era when Victorianism could be said to enjoy cultural hegemony. This essay will be concerned largely with the revolt which culminated in the 1920's against a culture still appropriately called Victorian.

* * *

Confidence in Victorianism eroded primarily as a result of continuous attacks on its conceptual foundations by academic and literary intellectuals—attacks which reached full force in the 1920's. This insidious criticism of the Victorian ethos diminished the conviction with which its formidable superstructure of institutions and behavior patterns had been defended, leaving them more vulnerable to onslaughts by minority groups.

Intellectual critics of the traditional cultural synthesis, fairly isolated during the 1890's,[1] two decades later were part of a rapidly growing subculture of alienated intellectuals—which could aptly be called an "intelligentsia." Henry May has described comprehensively the early stages of this development. A sizable group of intellectuals initiated what May refers to as "the beginning of cultural revolution" in the period just before World War I. He asserts: "We can see the massive walls of nineteenth century America still intact, and then turn our spotlight on many different kinds of people cheerfully laying dynamite in the hidden cracks."[2] During the 1920's, those walls crumbled noticeably, though they continued to exist. May's metaphor of dynamite, implying potential explosions, however, does not quite fit the intellectuals' effort. Their accomplishment resembled more closely the role of termites which irreversibly weaken a structure which then suffers irresistible pressure.

Social scientists proved most effective at undermining crucial Victorian doctrines after World War I. Franz Boas and his Columbia University students in anthropology affected the beliefs of both their fellow scholars

[1] The loosening of Victorianism in the 1890's, without severe damage to its central value patterns, is described in a cogent and intellectually stimulating essay by John Higham, "The Reorientation of American Culture in the 1890's," in John Weiss, ed., *The Origins of American Consciousness* (Detroit: Wayne Univ. Press, 1965), 25–48.

[2] Henry F. May, *The End of American Innocence* (New York: Knopf, 1959), x–xi.

and the public more profoundly than did any other group among academic intellectuals.[3] Boas' classes exuded an atmosphere of cultural relativism, and while the master tried to maintain at least a superficial neutrality when discussing various cultures, his students almost all tended to make invidious comparisons between middle-class Western civilization and the more coherent of technologically primitive cultures, which, according to their accounts, filled most human needs more satisfactorily. The least attractive of these cultures—such as the fiercely competitive Dobu and Kwakiutl described in Ruth Benedict's *Patterns of Culture*—seemed travesties upon or exaggerations of Western civilization's least lovely characteristics. Benedict's preference for the cooperative spirit and communal life she had observed among the Zuñi was apparent. Although *Patterns of Culture* was published in 1934, Benedict carried out most of her field work in 1923; a series of articles and addresses to professional organizations beginning in 1928 acquainted scholars with her message. Thus, during the 1920's, Benedict's critique of the Victorian culture she detested[4] enjoyed a place in the wave of intellectual dissent. Most of her ideas already were shared by many other anthropologists, and by other social scientists, as well.[5]

Almost every major theme in the literature of complaint published during the 1920's appeared in two volumes by Mead. She returned from trips to two primitive societies in the South Pacific with comparative evidence that Victorian culture crippled Americans emotionally. Her famous dissertation on the adolescence of Samoan girls, *Coming of Age in Samoa*, established the virtual absence of adolescent tempest among Samoans and related this to the freedom—particularly sexual freedom—granted Samoan boys and girls. Throughout the volume, but consistently in her two concluding chapters, Mead compared aspects of Samoan culture to American middle-class counterparts, almost without exception to the latter's disadvantage.

Samoans, Mead maintained, lived happier lives; they felt more connected and useful to their society. Their early pleasurable sexual experiences led to

[3]The most thorough studies of the Boas school's role in shifts in attitudes toward race among social scientists have been carried out by George W. Stocking, especially in his *Race, Culture and Evolution: Essays in the History of Anthropology* (New York: Free Press, 1968), and his "American Social Scientists and Race Theory: 1890–1915," unpublished Ph.D. dissertation, Univ. of Pennsylvania, 1960.

[4]Before entering the anthropological profession, Benedict was preparing a volume dealing with the terrible obstacles Western civilization placed before talented women who insisted upon careers beyond the roles of wife and mother. See her "Mary Wollstonecraft, Rebel," and notes for a biographical essay on Margaret Fuller in the Papers of Ruth Benedict, Vassar College.

[5]Benedict, "Psychological Types in the Cultures of the Southwest," *Proceedings, Twenty-Third Annual Congress of Americanists* (1928), 572–81; "The Science of Custom," *Century Magazine*, 117 (1929), 641–49; *Patterns of Culture* (Boston: Houghton Mifflin, 1934), 128, 133, 140, 152, 158; Margaret Mead, ed., *An Anthropologist at Work: Writings of Ruth Benedict*, 211–12; Eric R. Wolf, *Anthropology* (Englewood Cliffs: Prentice-Hall, 1964), 42.

more stable marriages. They suffered little from the neuroses so common among middle-class Americans. Fundamental to this apparently superior Samoan way of life was a family structure in which many people shared equally in the nurturing of children, a system almost diametrically opposed to the tight-knit Victorian family unit. The most hostile critic of Victorianism could not intentionally have drawn the lines of battle more clearly, or at a more crucial point: What are the rewards to Americans, Mead inquired, "of the tiny, ingrown, biological family opposing its closed circle of affection to a forbidding world, of the strong ties between parents and children. . . ?" Seemingly disdainful of the peculiar Victorian "character" forged in these units, Mead discovered few advantages: "Specialization of affection, it is true, but at the price of many individuals' preserving through life the attitudes of dependent children. . . . Perhaps these are too heavy prices to pay. . . ." Thus Mead's "scientific" study not only discerned a contradiction at the heart of Victorian culture, which she claimed crippled the children it supposedly nourished to strong adulthood; but it also described a model suggesting improvements which could change the entire society.[6]

In 1928, as *Coming of Age in Samoa* moved onto the best-seller lists, Mead traveled to New Guinea to expand her research into alternative modes of raising children. *Growing Up in New Guinea* gave more attention to the prices paid by males in the United States. The least attractive part of Manus culture resembled conditions in America. Children never taught to feel themselves a part of adult life resented participation in that life with "ferocious inferiority" when it suddenly was thrust upon them, regarding it as something akin to slavery.

On the other hand, boys in New Guinea benefitted from close association with their fathers. This relationship, though as inferiors, protected these boys from the attitude, common in America, that work such as child-rearing and educational, contemplative, and artistic pursuits, all associated with women as parents or teachers, were not proper roles for males. Unlike the United States, where fathers were practically strangers to their families, sons of successful fathers in New Guinea absorbed skills, techniques, and self-assurance, facilitating their absorption into satisfying roles once they overcame their early inclinations toward rebellion.[7]

Such damaging indictments by cultural anthropologists dealing with the family, work, and the excessive strength of materialistic values in America were summarized most cogently for intellectuals by Edward Sapir, long considered the most brilliant among Boas' many generations of students.

[6] Margaret Mead, *Coming of Age in Samoa* (New York: William Morrow, 1928) 158–60, 206–09, 212–14.
[7] Mead, *Growing Up in New Guinea* (New York: William Morrow, 1930), 158–73.

Sapir's supreme exposition of this critique, "Culture, Genuine and Spurious," appearing in the *American Journal of Sociology* in 1924, spread among other social scientists' arguments already familiar to anthropologists.[8]

Those American Indian tribes whose cultural cohesion had not been destroyed by white intruders, Sapir declared in this article, usually remained "inherently harmonious, balanced, self-satisfactory. . . , the expression of a richly varied and yet somehow unified and consistent attitude toward life." He compared these "genuine" Indian cultures favorably to the "spurious" American civilization, with its spiritually unrewarding work for most people ("a desert patch of economic effort in the whole of life") and its education that too often bore no relationship to the rest of students' lives.[9]

An aura of despair hung over a large portion of works derived from the most innovative sociological research undertaken during the 1920's. The chief theme of studies conducted at the University of Chicago's Department of Sociology—the first real school of sociology—became the social disorganization rampant in the city. Rapid change of many kinds, the Chicago sociologists discovered, weakened traditional social controls, broke down feelings of community and group solidarity, and fragmented society. Evidence of social disintegration—crime, divorce, mental illness, social deviancy, and race and ethnic conflict—were subjected to intensive investigation. Poverty, graphically described in the monographs emanating from this research, accompanied the fragmentation as either cause or effect within ethnic and racial ghettos, and among individuals described by the sociologists as "marginal."[10] A similar pattern in rural areas was discovered in research conducted by the Institute for Research in the Social Sciences founded by sociologist Howard W. Odum at the University of North Carolina during the twenties.[11]

This unhappy vision, which also served as a denunciation of American Victorian culture, pervaded the single most influential book by social scientists published during the 1920's: Robert and Helen Lynd's *Middletown*. The clearest statement of the book's purpose appeared in its

[8] Edward Sapir, "Culture, Genuine and Spurious," *American Journal of Sociology*, 29 (1924), 401–29. Sapir widened his audience further by publishing somewhat different versions of the essay in the literary journals *The Dial*, 67 (1919), 233–36, and *The Dalhousie Review*, 2 (1922), 165–78.

[9] Sapir, "Culture, Genuine and Spurious," 408, 409, 411, 413–14.

[10] On the Chicago school of sociology, the most relevant works are the essays by James F. Short, Jr., Harvey W. Zorbaugh, Ellsworth Faris, and W. I. Thomas, in Short, ed., *The Social Fabric of the Metropolis: Contributions of the Chicago School of Urban Sociology* (Chicago: Univ. of Chicago Press, 1971); Thomas V. Smith and Leonard D. White, eds., *Chicago, An Experiment in Social Science Research* (New York: Greenwood, 1929); and Robert Farris, *Chicago Sociology, 1920–1930* (San Francisco: Chandler, 1967).

[11] See Rupert Vance's perceptive essay on Odum in the *International Encyclopedia of the Social Sciences* (New York: Crowell, 1968), 11, 270–71.

foreword, written by anthropologist Clark Wissler. The volume, he explained, was a pioneer effort "to study ourselves as through the eye of an outsider" by dealing with "a sample American community as an anthropologist does a primitive tribe." [12] The Lynds subtitled their book "A Study in American Culture," intending it as a general statement about American civilization.

The Lynds' "sample" city, Muncie, Indiana, seemed like a stopping point along the way to Dante's Inferno. The great majority of inhabitants, defined by the authors as "The Working Class"—over 70 percent of Middletown's population—earned less per family than the U.S. Bureau of Labor Statistics estimated as necessary for mere survival. Furthermore, interviews with businessmen and workers proved that the latter had good reason to fear both periodic unemployment in the present, and the probable permanent loss of their jobs in the future as soon as their physical capabilities began to decrease.

Among many symptoms of a society unable to satisfy its members' needs was the divorce rate. This had increased from nine divorces for each hundred marriage licenses issued (not all used, of course) in 1889, to forty-two for each hundred in 1924, and the rate appeared to be still rising. Among possible causes of this massacre of marriages, the Lynds found a near total absence of what they termed "companionship" between husbands and wives of all classes. Interviewed privately, however, married men and women in Middletown demonstrated a desperate desire for this companionship. Yet not a single woman of either business or working class mentioned spending more time with her husband among the things she would like to do if given an extra hour in the day.[13] Conversations with businessmen also disclosed deep dissatisfaction. "One after another of these fellows appears," the Lynds declared, "each hungry for companionship, but knowing no one else in the city who speaks his language." Awareness of failure as a parent also was expressed frequently. Typical examples included: "I'm a rotten dad. . . . I'm so busy I don't see much of them and I don't know how to chum up with them when I do." A malaise which they found difficult to define troubled a large but uncounted proportion of the more sensitive or perceptive businessmen interviewed. A businessman identified as a "man of wide experience who had grown up in Middletown and is highly respected by the city" told the Lynds that ". . . . the two things he felt most upon returning to Middletown from a distant country were its prejudice and superficiality. 'These people are all afraid of something,' he said, 'What is it?' " [14] New stresses, added expectations, and lack of understanding or

[12] Robert S. and Helen M. Lynd, *Middletown: A Study in American Culture* (New York: Harcourt, Brace, 1929), p. vi.
[13] Lynds, *Middletown,* 32–34, 59–60, 84–87, 118–19, 120–30, 148–49.
[14] Ibid., 330, 493–95.

training in meeting them, left the Lynds' "sample" of Americans perplexed and unhappy. University of Chicago sociologists termed this type of situation "culture lag"; but they neglected to inform Americans like the inhabitants of Middletown about what they might do, beyond seeking a divorce, to alleviate their misery.

The most widely-read and influential historical work written during the 1920's, Charles and Mary Beard's two-volume *The Rise of American Civilization,* indicated that Americans *should* be frightened. In these volumes, the Beards repeated Charles' earlier contributions to the demystification of the Constitution, interpreting it in terms of an elite's desire for continued power in order to protect or extend material interests. They expanded this economic interpretation backward into colonial history and forward into the twentieth century. Their section on the Civil War, the "second American Revolution" that insured the triumph of industrialism, described a lusty "new bourgeois who spurted up into wealth and power with the ruin of the slave owners" in a manner reminiscent of Marx' and Engels' exuberant account of the bourgeoisie's rise in *The Communist Manifesto.*

Not only did the Beards observe (again recalling Marx and Engels) that ".... triumphant business enterprise. ... the system of acquisition and enjoyment, was calling into being its own antithesis—forces that challenged its authority and conditions that required a reconsideration of its laws and ethics. . . ;" but they suggested where this process was leading. History was repeating old patterns, the Beards declared. At the apex of every great civilization in the past, rich and enterprising businessmen devoted to commerce, industry, and finance had accumulated enormous power. They discussed Egypt, Babylonia, Persia, Carthage, and Athens—all dead civilizations—before embarking on a lengthy comparison between America and Rome. They described Rome "slowly changing into an empire while paying homage to its ancient constitution," by which time "the doom of all was at hand." And they referred to the United States as "this new Roman Empire," hardly an optimistic vision of the American future.[15]

Probably the most significant achievement of the academic intellectuals between 1912 and 1930 was their crucial role in the nearly complete repudiation of every scientific rationale for racism. Early in the twentieth century only a few humanitarians and scholarly skeptics doubted the premise that a hierarchy of races existed in the United States, with "Nordics" on top, recent immigrants from Southern and Eastern Europe far down but above migrants from Mexico and Orientals, and, at the very bottom, Negroes. By the late 1920's, prevailing opinion among intellectuals

---

[15]Charles and Mary Beard, *The Rise of American Civilization* (New York: Macmillan, 1927), 2 vols. Page numbers in this footnote are from the more widely distributed 1933 single-volume edition, II, 166–69, 542–44.

had been almost entirely altered. The change was not widely disseminated enough, however, to prevent passage of immigration restriction acts in 1921 and 1924, or to affect the course of judicial opinions concerning Negroes until later.

Again Boas and his students led the way toward undermining Victorian verities. Boas himself measured head forms and took other bodily measurements of recent immigrants and their children at a rate of up to 1,200 individuals a week, then reported "very striking and wholly unexpected results." In the American environment, the evidence showed conclusively, "far reaching changes" took place, demonstrating an unsuspected "great plasticity of human types." Boas' student Melville Herskovits came to similar conclusions after measurements of Negro migrants to the North. Other students and protégés of Boas destroyed one of the major weapons used by those who tried to make a case for Negro inferiority—the results of army and other intelligence tests. Supported by fellowships Boas arranged, Mead, Herskovits, social psychologist Otto Klineberg, and others demonstrated that the intelligence test scores of Negroes correlated closely with their length of residence in Northern cities. Negroes who had lived for long periods in the North scored higher than Southern whites.[16] By the late 1920's, an amazing number of influential social scientists had publicly testified to drastic changes in their opinions about race, a highly unusual form of action among mature scholars. As a consequence, textbooks and lectures were revised, journals reoriented, and books and articles announcing corrected ideas published.

Dramatic evidence of the shift in scholars' belief systems was provided by the difference between the 1913 and 1928 editions of the *Annals of the American Academy of Political and Social Science,* both devoted to the American Negro. The 1913 issue, entitled "The Negro's Progress in Fifty Years," dealt in general with achievements whites had induced among the somewhat retarded children called Negroes. Even Howard W. Odum, struggling for fair-mindedness, found himself obliged to repeat most popular racist myths, for example (p. 196): "Partly because of innate traits,

---

[16]Stocking, *Race, Culture and Evolution,* 163–80, Mead, "The Methodology of Racial Testing," *American Journal of Sociology,* 31 (Feb. 1926), 657–67; Herskovits, "The Racial Hysteria," *Opportunity,* 2 (June 1924), 166–68; "Some Effects of Social Selection on the American Negro," *Publications of the American Sociological Society,* 20 (1926), 77–80; "Some Physical Characteristics of the American Negro Population," *Journal of Social Forces,* 6 (Sept. 1927), 93–98; "Race Relations," *American Journal of Sociology,* 34 (May 1929), 1129–39; *The American Negro* (New York: Knopf, 1928); Klineberg, "An Experimental Study of Speed and Other Factors in Racial Differences," *Archives of Psychology* (1928). (Klineberg's earlier research is summarized in Klineberg, ed. *Characteristics of the American Negro* [New York: Harper, 1944], passim, in his *Race Differences* [New York: Harper, 1935], and in Boas to Klineberg, Feb. 6, 1928, Oct. 25, 1929, Papers of Franz Boas, American Philosophical Society, Philadelphia).

and partly because of home and race influences, the Negro children do not apply themselves to their work." Six black contributors, including Booker T. Washington and W. E. B. DuBois, wrote what consisted essentially of apologies for Negro deficiencies. Only the youngest black contributor, sociologist George Edmund Hayes, who had earned his Ph.D. from Columbia University the previous year, came close to demanding full equality for his race.

This situation was reversed by 1928. In the Introduction to that issue, its editor, University of Pennsylvania sociologist Donald Young, declared:

> Much has happened since 1913 to make it desirable that another volume be devoted to the relationships between the colored and white races in the United States. In fact, since that time students of race as well as laymen have had to discount or even reverse many of their theories concerning "trends" and "solutions" of Negro developments and "problems."

Then followed a series of articles by a wide variety of social scientists, none of which suggested the racial inferiority of Negroes and some of which asserted that such ideas were no more than myths. The most militant black scholars in the country offered a perspective not placed earlier before white scholars in such eloquent and concentrated form. DuBois typified their tone. After presenting what he called "a recital of the most barbarous examples of racism in the country's history," he complained that still, "... at the mere presence of a colored face, again and again our whole moral fabric fails and collapses. ... What is going to become of a country which allows itself to fall into such an astonishing intellectual and ethical paradox? Nothing but disaster." [17]

Among the more significant converts was Howard Odum. His 1910 *Social and Mental Traits of the Negro* mixed genuine sympathy for his wretched subjects with every racist cliché ordinarily applied to the mentality of blacks, but by 1928 he had changed his mind completely. Odum, the most influential social scientist in the South, thereafter devoted himself to encouraging and carrying out projects designed in large part to investigate, publicize, and alleviate the problems of Southern blacks. [18]

Other important converts in the same pattern were sociologists Carl Kelsey of the University of Pennsylvania and Edward Byron Reuter of the

---

[17] J. P. Lichtenberger, ed., *The Negroes' Progress in Fifty Years. The Annals of the American Academy of Political and Social Science,* 49 (Sept. 1913). David Young, ed., *The American Negro. Annals of the American Academy of Political and Social Science,* 140 (Nov. 1928), hereafter cited as *Annals, 1928.* Young's statement can be found in the Introduction, *Annals, 1928.* The statements by DuBois are from his essay "Race Relations in the United States," *Annals, 1928,* 6–10.

[18] Howard Odum, *Social and Mental Traits of the Negro* (New York; Columbia Univ. Press, 1910); "Standards of Development for Race Development," *Journal of Race Development,* 5 (1915), 364–83; *Rainbow Round My Shoulder: The Blue Trail of Black Ulysses* (Indianapolis: Bobbs-Merrill, 1928); Vance, "Odum."

University of Iowa. The conventional racism in their books published prior to 1920 changed to outright denials in books written during the subsequent decade that any evidence existed indicating the superiority of one race over another. Edward A. Ross, sociologist at Stanford and the University of Wisconsin, one of the more rabid racists early in the twentieth century, rewrote his popular text *Principles of Sociology* during the late 1920's. His new introduction proclaimed that the volume now incorporated "the chief findings of the cultural anthropologists," several of whom were quoted on the subject of race in the text. All general theories about race lacked scientific validity, he now asserted, and he suggested: "Giving school children the view of race differences common among anthropologists would do much to forestall race prejudice." [19]

Finally, even Princeton psychologist Carl C. Brigham, whose *A Study of American Intelligence* had served as the basic text for those who used the army World War I intelligence tests as evidence of "Nordic" racial superiority, recanted. In an article published in 1930 Brigham acknowledged: "Comparative studies of various national and racial groups may not be made with existing tests." He concluded: "In particular, one of the most pretentious of these comparative racial studies—the writer's own—was without foundation." [20]

As a result of the all but unanimous rejection of racism by the scholars most involved in the study of race, the ideas of Boas and his disciples thus became the conventional wisdom of intellectuals, insinuated by them throughout American society, especially through educational institutions and the higher courts. Symptomatic of this shift, a careful survey of scientists carried out in 1929 revealed that a mere four per cent still believed in the genetic inferiority of Negroes. Only nineteen per cent agreed even that Negroes *seemed* inferior. About half not only denied the existence of racial differences, but even the possibility of important differences based on race, tantamount to rejecting altogether the significance of race. [21] Thus, among those Americans with greatest influence over public opinion then and in the future, one of the basic concepts which had given distinction (and power) to

---

[19] Carl Kelsey, *The Negro Farmer* (New York: Jennings and Rye, 1903), esp. p. 3; cf. Kelsey, *The Physical Basis of Society* (New York: Appleton, 1923). Edward Byron Reuter, *The Mulatto in the United States* (Boston: Gorham, 1918); cf. Reuter, *The American Race Problem* (New York: Crowell, 1927), and *Race Mixture: Studies in Marriage and Miscegenation* (New York: McGraw-Hill, 1931); Edward A. Ross, "The Causes of Race Superiority," *Annals, American Academy of Political and Social Science,* 18 (July 1901), 67, 83–89 esp.; *Principles of Sociology* (New York: Century, 1930), rev. ed., esp. ix, 201, 206.

[20] Carl C. Brigham, *A Study of American Intelligence* (Princeton: Princeton Univ. Press, 1923); Brigham "Intelligence Tests of Immigrant Groups," *Psychological Review,* 37 (1930), 165.

[21] Charles H. Thompson, "The Conclusion of Scientists Relative to Racial Differences," *Journal of Negro Education,* 3 (1934), 494–512. Thompson had collected his data in 1929.

Victorian culture virtually disappeared as a respectable idea. The influence of popularizers of racist ideas, such as Lothrop Stoddard and Madison Grant, hung on for a while; but their opponents possessed weapons which soon placed outright racists outside the arena of civilized discourse among those who claimed to be educated and reasonable. Thereafter, their successors found themselves constantly on the defensive.

Literary intellectuals also bore deeply into the foundations of Victorian beliefs. The liveliest, largest, and perhaps most talented group of novelists, poets, playwrights, and critics in American history skillfully exposed the same faults emphasized by the academic intellectuals and added types of complaint. Influential works such as Sinclair Lewis' *Main Street* and *Babbitt* and Dreiser's *An American Tragedy* carried social messages which hardly differed from those of *Middletown, Coming of Age in Samoa, Patterns of Culture,* or *The Rise of American Civilization.* The novelists denounced materialism, pressure for conformity, shattered family life, a fragmented society, and the inability of American civilization to fill its members' needs or even to teach them what these were. Additional important strains made the literary critique of conventional American culture even more damaging—and interesting.

An example of certain of these added strains is provided by Van Wyck Brooks' *The Ordeal of Mark Twain.* According to Brooks, Twain—a satirist comparable in ability to the world's greatest writers—was emasculated as an artist and as a man by a Victorian society and its representatives totally unsympathetic with and afraid of great art. Brooks then suggested that American artists after World War I lived in a similar business-dominated atmosphere and urged them not to succumb to a fate like Twain's. Most hardly required the warning, but, as Sherwood Anderson wrote to Brooks, "You must realize what an inciter to flame in others you are."[22] F. Scott Fitzgerald, who felt that something inhibited the use of his full abilities, reacted with great alarm. Sent Brooks' volume by his editor Maxwell Perkins, who observed that it expressed ideas already stated by Fitzgerald, the novelist soon accused Perkins of attempting to censor his work in a fashion similar to the ordeal inflicted on Twain. Fitzgerald then marshaled all his artistic powers and wrote (and rewrote) *The Great Gatsby*[23]—the story of a man from the Midwest, like Fitzgerald and Twain,

---

[22]Van Wyck Brooks, *The Ordeal of Mark Twain* (New York: Dutton, 1920). The statement by Anderson was taken from William Wasserstrom, *The Legacy of Van Wyck Brooks* (Carbondale: Southern Illinois Univ. Press, 1971), 3.

[23]For Fitzgerald's reaction to Brooks' volume, see John Kuehl and Jackson Bryer, eds., *Dear Scott/Dear Max: The Fitzgerald-Perkins Correspondence* (New York: Scribner's, 1971), 30–31, 45–47, 138–39, 151–52. These incidents are placed in further perspective by Robert Sklar, *F. Scott Fitzgerald, The Last Laocoon* (New York: Oxford, 1967), 135–47, 151–52, 199–205.

who mistakes wealth and social position in the form of a beautiful woman ("with money in her eyes") for true happiness. Fitzgerald's (and Brooks') preoccupation with artistic concerns, although shared with certain social scientists, differentiated the general tone of the academic and literary critiques of American civilization.

Another strain of criticism, found only on the fringes of the academic community—in the writing of theologians Richard and Reinhold Niebuhr, literary historian Vernon Parrington, and perhaps Benedict, for example—consisted of pessimism about the possibilities of modern civilization, which applied to deficiencies traceable to Victorianism but went beyond, sometimes suggesting that Western civilization had taken a wrong turn centuries earlier. Fitzgerald's *Gatsby* contained traces of this element; but it emerged more clearly along with the themes already mentioned in T. S. Eliot's *The Waste Land*, Ezra Pound's *Cantos*, Ernest Hemingway's *The Sun Also Rises*, Eugene O'Neill's *The Hairy Ape*, Joseph Wood Krutch's *The Modern Temper*, William Faulkner's *The Sound and the Fury*, and in a peculiar Southern agrarian form, in *I'll Take My Stand*, a book of essays by twelve Southern writers.[24]

Defenders of Victorianism recognized the dangers of the intellectuals' revolt, especially its influence over the contents of books and the other media, the actions of urban middle-class citizens who tried to emulate Greenwich Villagers, and the opinions of students. Sinclair Lewis presented the most graphic portrait of this fear in his description of the desperate efforts made by Zenith's leading businessmen to end George F. Babbitt's private revolt and to force him to join the superpatriotic, anti-intellectual, Good Citizen's League.[25] The head of the National Civic Federation, the preeminent association of businessmen and a few conservative labor leaders dedicated to protecting traditional American values, wrote to William Howard Taft late in 1918 that, in combating domestic subversive doctrines, "It is not so much among the labor classes here that the work needs to be carried on, as among the so-called 'intellectuals,' the college men, teachers, editors, preachers, and even sentimental businessmen." In April, 1920, the same leader wrote to the head of the Rotary Clubs of America: "By means of insidious propaganda spread through the colleges, the churches, the newspapers and magazines, and all the media for influencing public sentiment, the idea has been taking hold in many important places that the present order of society is a total failure and ought to be abolished."[26]

[24]For a recent discussion of Ezra Pound's attitudes, see Hugh Kenner, *The Pound Era* (Berkeley: Univ. of California Press, 1971), esp. 301–17, 377.

[25]Sinclair Lewis, *Babbitt* (New York: Harcourt, Brace, 1922), p. 277.

[26]Ralph M. Easley, Chairman, Executive Council, National Civic Federation, to William Howard Taft, Sept. 18, 1918, Box 55; Easley to Arthur Woodward, April 1, 1920, Executive Committee File, Box 188, both National Civic Federation Records, New York Public Library.

*    *    *

Victorian culture, weakened by the subversive assaults of intellectuals, was attacked also by ethnic minority groups. The latter succeeded in reducing the British-Americans, chief bearers of Victorian culture, to merely another ethnic minority, though one which remained more powerful, in most respects, than others. The most effective, though not the most politically or financially powerful, of these groups was composed of black Americans. Blacks staked out moral claims that first disturbed the consciences and then affected the actions of influential white Americans. The intellectual sanction given to their claims by the evidence which discredited racist concepts made use of this moral leverage possible. Eventually, their powerful appeal to the national egalitarian and Christian ethos was bound to be reflected in statute law and in legal interpretations that would promote social change. "Eventually," however, seemed to lie well beyond the lifespan of rebellious blacks, and organized post-Reconstruction revolt began, in a polite fashion, early in the twentieth century.

Efforts openly devoted to improving the status of black Americans during the first three decades of the twentieth century—the Niagara Movement, the NAACP, the Urban League, journals such as *The Crisis, The Messenger, Opportunity*—all could be ignored safely by the vast majority of whites, despite the intelligence of the black leaders and the prominence and wealth of their white associates. Even the ideas of W. E. B. DuBois, perhaps the most significant in twentieth-century U.S. intellectual history, and the literature of the Harlem Renaissance hardly penetrated the consciousness of white Americans (with the exception of some intellectuals). However, to those whites who thought they knew the ordinary black American—the stereotyped loyal "darkie" servants of Victorian America—Marcus Garvey's enormous black nationalist Universal Negro Improvement Association provided varying degrees of surprise. Garvey himself, usually photographed in outlandish military or academic uniforms, was ordinarily dismissed as a joke or a charlatan. Accounts of his ideas written for whites vastly overstressed his statements about a return of some blacks to Africa and his unsound business ventures. Nonetheless, he claimed that his followers numbered in the millions; delegates to his conventions from UNIA chapters in virtually every state in America and scores of foreign nations packed Madison Square Garden. Lengthy parades of his followers included paramilitary units; his rhetoric included statements indicating a willingness to engage in race war. No other militant black organization had come close to Garvey's in size or geographical breadth, nor did rivals in that respect arise during the 1960's or 1970's. No other leader presented such a comprehensive program of black separatism, incorporating economic, religious, educational, artistic, and social elements. His organization's journal, *The Negro World,* was denounced by the Justice Department as ultraradical and banned as subversive throughout the Caribbean, Central America, and much of Africa. Fearful law enforcement agencies infiltrated the UNIA, accused Garvey of revolutionary objectives, harassed him, and arrested him for mail fraud connected with his organization's business ventures. These were intended to establish eventually a parallel separate black economy in the United States, an idea with which DuBois was sympathetic, despite his general distaste for Garvey.[27] Found guilty of fraud (almost certainly inadvertent), Garvey received a jail sentence, which was later commuted so that he could be deported to his native Jamaica. Garvey's concepts of black economic and social unity and separatism, however, implying an equality and a role for blacks which departed sharply from Victorian racial ideas, continued to attract respectful attention from thoughtful blacks in the United States, and throughout the world.[28]

Black nationalism, which aimed at cultural as well as economic pluralism—implying equality—posed black Americans' most serious challenge to the Victorian hegemony but not the only one. Raw, mass violence, and the threat of worse to come, helped force reluctant Americans to grant a measure of social, political, and economic equality to blacks. "Riots" which occurred in most major Northern cities during and after World War I surprised and alarmed those who thought that Negroes knew "their place," largely because blacks defended themselves fiercely, and even conducted attacks of their own. A commission appointed to study the most severe of these race wars, the five-day Chicago riot of July, 1919, after careful research attributed it basically to white racism and black segregation and poverty. A few of the suggested remedies were transformed into actions.[29]

In the field of music, blacks established considerable cultural autonomy. Black jazz and the related blues, spread mostly from the South, especially

---

[27] A. Mitchell Palmer, "Radicalism and Sedition among the Negroes as Reflected in their Publications," Report of the United States Department of Justice. *Senate Documents,* vol. 12, no. 153, 66th Congress, 1st Session, 1919, 161–87. On Garvey's effect, see Directorate of Intelligence, Home Office, Special Report No. 10, October 7th, 1919, "Unrest Among the Negroes" (marked "Secret"), File 811.4016/27, Justice Department Records. For DuBois's generally favorable attitude toward Garvey's plans, see W. E. B. DuBois, "Marcus Garvey" *The Crisis,* 21 (Dec. 1920, Jan. 1921), 58–60, 112–15.

[28] Individuals as diverse as Malcolm X, Stokely Carmichael, Elijah Muhammad, Kwame Nkrumah, and members of the Jamaican Rastafari cult have taken Garvey as a model. At present, the only available manuscript dealing with the UNIA which utilizes many recent interviews with members of Garvey's organization, and the multiplied number of issues of the *Negro World* and of UNIA records uncovered during the past few years, is Emory J. Tolbert, "Marcus Garvey and the Universal Negro Improvement Association in the West: 1914–1930," unpublished Ph.D. dissertation, Univ. of California, Los Angeles, 1975.

[29] Arthur I. Waskow, *From Race Riot to Sit-In* (Garden City, N.Y.: Doubleday, 1966) is the most recent survey of these battles. William M. Tuttle, Jr., *Race Riot: Chicago in the Summer of 1919* (New York: Atheneum, 1972) chronicles the dreary story of lessons unlearned from that event.

New Orleans, to the entire country during the first three decades of the twentieth century. The greatest musical impact came in the 1920's, with the development of the phonograph and radio industries, large-scale black migration to the North, and the vogue of the "new Negro." Jazz suffered severe dilution as it was adapted to every form of Western music. Black musicians were ridiculed as artistically impoverished primitives whose natural but potentially dangerous gifts for a hedonistic music and accompanying sensual dances were vastly improved by white assimilation. Much of the derision arose from acquired tastes; but a good deal carried nuances of fear for established status and for public morality.

The proposition that jazz and the blues constitute America's greatest artistic contribution to Western civilization has been advanced and defended ably. That idea had its proponents by the 1920's. It was a bit embarrassing and disturbing for those who thought of themselves as the custodians of American high culture to be informed by the celebrated visiting composer Igor Stravinsky in 1925 that "The music of the future will have to take it [jazz] into account, no matter what the tendency of the composer." Stravinsky clearly was not referring to the jazz of George Gershwin or Paul Whiteman. He told an interviewer in the United States: "In jazz you have something that sneaked in on us from an out-on-the-corner cabaret. . . . We don't like to admit it, but real music *has* such simple origins." The monopoly that Victorians had granted to Western symphonic forms and orchestral concerts as the highest artistic accomplishments in music thus was broken by a music with deep and distinctly black roots.[30]

During the 1920's, spokesmen for other ethnic groups became openly receptive to concepts of cultural pluralism similar to those that Garvey represented for blacks. Many of these people held crucial values in common with Victorians: in some cases because of assimilation, such as that of the "lace curtain" Irish, in others fortuitously, as in the case of Jews, who had been limited in much of Europe to urban, commercial life. However, most members of these groups continued in varying degrees to value their own cultural heritages. Furthermore, most American Victorians who encouraged propagation of their values refused to perceive acculturated "foreigners"—no matter how complete their apparent assimilation—as fellow Americans or fellow Victorians, in a fashion reminiscent of their attitude to the heathen converted by missionaries in foreign lands. Partly because of these reservations on all sides, and partly in defense against nation-wide Americanization

[30]Daniel Mason Gregory, "Stravinsky as a Symptom," *American Mercury,* 4 (April 1925), 465-68. The most valuable volumes on the development and spread of jazz are Gunthur Schuller, *Early Jazz, Its Roots and Musical Development* (New York: Oxford Univ. Press, 1968); and M. W. Dixon and John Goodrich, *Recording the Blues* (New York: Stein and Day, 1970).

campaigns, drives for immigration restriction, and the Ku Klux Klan, various types and degrees of separatism were advocated by Catholic and Jewish groups especially. These groups already maintained distinctive and separate religious and educational institutions. Their ranks included millions of people who had brought with them to the United States a heritage of resistance against oppression and full assimilation. Though not even the most dedicated Zionist or Irish nationalist advocated domestic programs nearly so comprehensive as Garvey's, Judah Magnes' Kehillah may have been moving in that direction when Magnes migrated to Palestine in 1922. Such pluralistic perceptions of United States society contradicted the Victorian ideal of assimilation.[31]

\* \* \*

The declining influence of the Victorian ethos was not entirely due to organized movements for cultural change. Possibly the most devastating assaults on Victorian culture were delivered at that vital point: "the home." This term encompassed not only the physical entity, of no small importance in itself, but also the family with its peculiar personal relations and complementary obligations. Those who valued that basic unit of Victorian society watched with despair as Americans tore it apart. Parents who placed personal fulfillment above devotion to spouse and children; the consequent skyrocketing divorce rate; the rapid rise of women's proportion in the work force; children who felt closer to their peers than to their parents—all delivered shattering blows to the primary Victorian haven against the world's vicissitudes. The process was hastened by feminists, who bore a special dislike for conventional patriarchal family arrangements. In 1925 the National Women's Party persuaded Congress to hold hearings on an equal rights constitutional amendment, in which Party spokeswomen made it plain that by equal rights they meant total equality.[32]

[31]The classic theoretical study of pluralism written during the 1920's is Horace M. Kallen, *Culture and Democracy in the United States* (New York: Liveright, 1924). The best recent exploration of the concept is Milton Gordon, *Assimilation in American Life* (New York: Oxford Univ. Press, 1964). See also Wilton S. Dillon, ed. *The Cultural Drama: Modern Identities and Social Ferment* (Washington: Smithsonian, 1974), much of the thinking in which is a step in advance of that found in Nathan Glazer and Daniel Patrick Moynihan, *Beyond the Melting Pot: The Negroes, Puerto Ricans, Jews, Italians and Irish of New York City* (Cambridge: Harvard Univ. Press, 1963). On the Kehillah, the most comprehensive treatment is Arthur A. Goren, *New York Jews and the Quest for Community* (New York: Columbia Univ. Press, 1970). A good sample of the recent literature on American ethnic groups is Patrick J. Gallo, *Ethnic Alienation: The Italian-Americans* (Rutherford, N.J.: Fairleigh Dickinson Press, 1974).

[32]Anxious male legislators let the debate be carried on chiefly by women. The long fight over an ERA between feminists demanding legal equality and a combination of female workers enjoying special privileges and middle-class women fearful of losing their special role in the family and society can be followed in legislative hearings. For example, see Committee on the

One consequence of women's changing role was a shift in generally acceptable sexual mores and behavior. This began with growing freedom to discuss sexual relations and proceeded to a stage at which all types of sexual activity outside of marriage increased significantly.[33] Greenwich Village nonconformists led the assault on prudery before the twenties; but the rising fees for F. Scott Fitzgerald's stories ($4,000 each from the *Post* by the late 1920's) serves as a barometer of the extent to which victory over that prudery was won throughout the country.

Meanwhile, within the business community, a traditional stronghold of Victorianism, tendencies clearly appeared during the 1920's which were transforming American civilization. Twentieth-century industrialization was led by corporations growing continually in size, differentiated internally in products and functions, and active over major portions of the earth. In most cases, a handful of companies increasingly dominated the nation's most important industries. The developing style among such firms—reliable continuity of product quality and/or service, personnel who could work smoothly with suppliers and customers—hardly required Victorian values. "Character" in the Victorian sense bore only the slightest relationship to the faceless efficiency of the interchangeable line and headquarters executives, sales engineers, and research scientists at most huge industrial companies. Damage to Victorianism caused by these corporations and others with a similar ethos was subtle, but lethal.

The rapidity and magnitude of corporate growth necessitated the development of immense managerial bureaucracies. These contributed to the enlargement of urban megalopoli, which provided the various services—including the suppliers, subcontractors, pools of talent, residences, retailers, and entertainment—these firms required. Rising productivity and real income created a sizable affluent middle class and encouraged an un-Victorian blatant hedonism, with businessmen using corporate expense accounts setting an envied example. Federal, state, and municipal governments assumed greater, more complex duties as this bureaucratization of business coincided with related societal changes. Bureaucratic agencies in each level of government were created to deal with problems arising out of the size of business firms and the impersonality of most of their decisions.

Judiciary, House of Representatives, 68th Congress, 2nd Session, *Hearing on H. J. Res. 75, Equal Rights Amendment to the Constitution, February 4 and 5, 1925* (Washington: GPO, 1925). All the women's professional journals opposed the ERA in the 1920's.

[33] Aron Krich, *The Sexual Revolution: Seminal Studies into 20th Century American Sexual Behavior* (New York: Dell, 1964, 1965), 2 vols., reviews research on this matter and reprints crucial sections of the most important monographs. Also see Carl N. Degler, "What Ought to Be and What Was: Women's Sexuality in the Nineteenth Century" *American Historical Review,* 79 (Dec. 1974), 1467–90; and James R. McGovern, "The American Woman's Pre-World War I Freedom in Manners and Morals," *Journal of American History,* 55 (Sept. 1968), 315–38.

An enlarged and specialized system of higher education brought together concentrations of teachers and researchers in various fields, requiring managerial structures of their own. Professionals organized themselves more thoroughly, and with tightened regulations. Those and similar events produced a society ever more bureaucratized, demanding increasingly for smooth operation a type of person resembling the new corporate managers, individuals quite different from the ideal self-righteous, "inner-directed" Victorian.[34]

The fate of the prewar progressive movement provided unmistakable evidence that Victorian authority no longer ran throughout the land. Those elements of progressivism intended by its middle-class leaders largely to preserve Victorianism failed. Progressive measures to inculcate Victorian values, symbolized by prohibition and attacks on prostitution, disappointed their proponents. Giant business corporations (frequently referred to mistakenly as "trusts") continued to grow almost without public control and to influence the whole society's development. Progressive social welfare measures hardly helped the poor, largely because most progressives placed their faith in moral appeals to adopt Victorian virtues. When the foundations of a welfare state were erected by the New Deal, most surviving progressive leaders opposed its creation.[35]

* * *

Soon after the Klan fell under the control of two public relations experts in 1920, that organization became devoted to the defense of old-fashioned Victorianism—though a rather simple version of it, and a rather sour defense.[36] The Klan's original hostility to "uppity" blacks continued, but it moved into the background as Klan representatives reported more pressing worries among the organization's broad potential constituency. An early tendency toward Reconstruction-type violence by Klan members, especially against violators of traditional mores in the South, practically ended after

[34]An immense literature on this topic was summarized by David Riesman, Nathan Glazer, and Reuel Denney in *The Lonely Crowd* (New Haven: Yale Univ. Press, 1959); and William H. Whyte, Jr., *The Organization Man* (New York: Simon and Schuster, 1956).

[35]Otis L. Graham, *An Encore for Reform: The Old Progressives and the New Deal* (New York: Oxford Univ. Press, 1967). An excellent brief analysis of the progressive crusade against prostitution can be found in Eric Anderson, "Prostitution and Social Justice: Chicago, 1910–15," *The Social Science Review*, 48 (June 1974), 203–28.

[36]I have included a more detailed account of the Klan's successes and failures in Stanley Coben, "The First Years of Modern America, 1918–1933," in William E. Leuchtenburg, ed., *The Unfinished Century* (Boston: Little, Brown, 1973), 255–356; and Coben "The Failure of the Melting Pot," in G. Nash and R. Weiss, eds., *The Great Fear* (New York: Holt, Rinehart and Winston, 1970), 144–64. Also see Kenneth Jackson, *The Ku Klux Klan in the City* (New York: Oxford Univ. Press, 1967); and Charles C. Alexander, *The Ku Klux Klan in the Southwest* (Lexington: Univ. of Kentucky Press, 1965).

the hooded order's money-hungry leaders discovered that a fortune could be made by promising to allay peacefully the widespread anxiety of Protestant Americans throughout the United States. Organizers, or "kleagles," most of whom possessed experience as professional organizers for fraternal orders or as evangelical ministers, traveled through the country following instructions to discover the exploitable fears of white, native-born Protestants by speaking to local ministers and newspaper editors. This form of "market research" showed that the Klan's white evangelical Protestant members and potential members suffered from almost the same concerns in every section of the United States. Support for traditional virtues and morality consequently joined opposition to those whose new power supposedly endangered these values: intellectuals and various ethnic minorities.

It rapidly became apparent, however, that the minorities, whose influence, practices, and ideas the Klan promised to defeat, already had occupied and consolidated their political hold on all major metropolitan centers. By the early twentieth century, cities not otherwise controlled by Irish politicians enjoyed the privilege of Irish district attorneys, judges, policemen, and other influential public servants. Jews had assumed positions of critical economic and social power. Klan leaders accused Jewish motion picture directors and producers, for example, of responsibility for movies subverting conventional ideas, and the Klan's charges were essentially correct.[37] These events coincided with the movement of millions of blacks to Northern cities. As a consequence, the millions of Klansmen, and those who would have joined had they dared—or if they had been able to afford the $10 initiation fee, $12 uniforms, plus dues—protected Victorian morality and the Victorian social status quo only at serious peril to their continued physical and economic well-being in the nation's most important cities. Huge Klan meetings in and near these cities were broken up by gunfire; parades of Klan members and supporters, when permitted, met motorists and gunmen intent upon murder. Police called to protect besieged or molested Klansmen almost invariably arrested Klan members on charges of disturbing the peace, inciting a riot, or violating specially adopted repressive ordinances. Widely distributed lists of Klansmen facilitated effective boycotts of their business firms, which realized suddenly their dependence on Catholic and Jewish customers and suppliers or, in some areas, on blacks or Mexican Americans as well.

New York's Irish Catholic mayor publicly ordered his police commissioner to treat known Klansmen as he would "Reds and bomb throwers," an open invitation to legalized murder, Klansmen complained.

[37]The best available survey of the subject is Norman Zierold, *The Moguls* (New York: Coward-McCann, 1969).

Mayor James Curley of Boston in inimitable emotional speeches, which included burning crosses as stage props, practically requested audiences to attack known Klansmen (which they did), perhaps accounting for the sparse Klan membership in that area. In Chicago, a racially "balanced" commission was appointed by the City Council to consider official policy toward the Klan, which had enrolled more members in Chicago than in any other city. The three-man investigative commission consisted of one Catholic, one Jew, and one black. Their report—quickly accepted—led to adopting legislation against secret societies and penalties for wearing masks in public. The report was sent to the Illinois state legislature, which took similar action. Expensive new Klan meeting halls exploded and burned to the ground in cities from Fort Worth, Texas, to Terre Haute, Indiana, and Portland, Maine, and in each case police were unable to discover the culprits. An editorial which appeared in every Klan newspaper throughout the nation asked pointedly, and plaintively: "Why are no offices of the Knights of Columbus destroyed?"

Klan leaders spoke publicly of helping to enforce prohibition legislation and laws against other "vices," and in rural areas they did. After a national Klan official suggested to a huge Chicago rally that the local Klan should be of future assistance in enforcing prohibition in that city, however, no action followed. An earlier "Christian" attempt at prohibition law enforcement in Chicago, led by a crusading Protestant minister, had ended with discovery of the minister's bullet-riddled body tauntingly near Al Capone's headquarters in nearby Cicero. Chicago Klansmen felt little safety in their large numbers or in their Christian righteousness when confronted with Capone's politically protected, ruthless private army. They helplessly left prohibition and other anti-"vice" law enforcement to state and federal authorities, who were overwhelmed by the task. In metropolitan centers like Chicago, New York (where Governor Al Smith encouraged the repeal of state prohibition laws early in the 1920's), Boston, San Francisco, and Milwaukee public pressure played a more important role than gangsters' bribes and violence in practically ending prohibition. To Americans of German, Italian, Spanish, Greek, Portuguese, Irish, Jewish, and Mexican ancestry, especially, laws interfering with consumption of beer, wine, and whisky were immoral—the opposite of Victorian beliefs (which should not be confused with furtive practice)—and these ethnic groups controlled most of America's largest cities. They were joined by lower-class blacks, most of whom greeted attempts to enforce Victorian morality with amusement, opposition, or apathy.[38]

---

[38]These events can be followed in the various Klan periodicals (the organization claimed over 90), which reported them with fair accuracy, compared to accounts in local newspapers. Most useful are *The Imperial Night-Hawk,* published in "The Imperial Palace," Atlanta, beginning

The Klan entered politics largely in self-defense, and enjoyed some temporary success, particularly in the smaller cities and towns of Indiana, Ohio, Illinois, Arkansas, Oklahoma, Oregon, and California. Police officials and "liberal" teachers were purged by victorious Klan slates. But Klan victories only served to unite those hostile to the organization's desire to return to the "old ways," and few Klan regimes lasted longer than a few years, some only until the quickest possible recall election. In the great American cities, their cause was hopeless.

Imperial Wizard Hiram Evans offered a candid evaluation of the situation: "The Nordic American today is a stranger in large parts of the land his fathers gave him. Moreover, he is a most unwelcome stranger, and one much spit upon." The blame, Evans felt, lay not only with un-American ethnic groups, but also with "de-Americanized intellectuals," who had sowed "confusion in thought and opinion" among the faithful. "The great mass of Americans of old pioneer stock" were, he acknowledged, ". . . very weak in the matter of culture, intellectual support, and trained leadership. . . . It makes it very hard for us to state our case and advocate our crusade." Evans concluded: "If the Klan should ever fail, it would be from this cause."[39]

The Klan and its upper-class counterparts had attempted to protect the dominance of Victorian culture in America. Their efforts foundered primarily for two reasons: potent groups within U.S. society rebelled against basic Victorian culture patterns, and the defenders themselves, hounded by intellectuals and faced with empirical evidence of societal change, lost much of their own confidence in the validity of the Victorian ethos.

Yet the powerful assaults upon Victorianism launched by intellectuals and other minority groups failed to replace crucial aspects of that culture with durable values, concepts, and institutions derived from their critiques. Feminists, for example, continue to argue among themselves about the merits of such solutions to their complaints as the comprehensive changes in family structure and functions suggested by Charlotte Perkins Gilman in 1898. Commenting on the recent thought and actions of black leaders, Harold Cruse complained in 1967: "Even today, the views of Washington vs. DuBois vs. Garvey are still being debated; but no one attempts to systematize the essential ideas of these pioneering leaders, for the Negro generations who came after these men can not hold a candle to their predecessors in intellect. The generation of Negro intellectuals born between

---

March 28, 1923; and *The Fiery Cross* (Indiana State Edition [Indiana had the largest Klan membership of any single state]).

[39] Hiram Evans, "The Klan's Fight for Americanism," *North American Review*, 223 (March 1926), 33–63. The essay is reprinted in Stanley Coben, ed., *Reform, War, and Reaction* (New York: Harper & Row, 1973), 217–32.

the two World Wars are, on the whole, an empty and unoriginal group." In a similar but more sympathetic vein, Paul Goodman attempted in 1968 to explain the consequences of the intellectuals' deficiencies: "There is no persuasive program for social reconstruction, thought up by many minds, corrected by endless criticism, made practical by much political activity. . . . The young are honorable and see the problems, but they don't know anything because we have not taught them anything."[40] Perhaps the greatest contribution scholars in American studies can make to this topic is to explain why viable new cultural syntheses eluded those who participated in the ferocious and considerably successful assault on Victorian culture.

[40] Harold Cruse, *The Crisis of the Negro Intellectual* (New York: Morrow, 1967), 333–34, also see 330–31, 564–65; Paul Goodman, *New York Times Magazine,* Feb. 25, 1968, quoted in Christopher Lasch, *The Agony of the American Left* (New York: Knopf, 1969), viii, a valiant attempt to explore the questions raised by Goodman.

# CONTRIBUTORS

GEOFFREY BLODGETT, Professor of History at Oberlin College, is the author of *The Gentle Reformers: Massachusetts Democrats in the Cleveland Era* (Cambridge, Mass., 1966), and has published biographical articles on Frederick Law Olmsted, the novelist Winston Churchill, Ida Tarbell, and Charles Evans Hughes, among others. His current research interest is conservative reform in the gilded age.

RICHARD D. BROWN is Professor and Chairman of the Department of History, University of Connecticut. He is the author of *Modernization: The Transformation of American Life, 1600–1865* (New York, 1976) and *Revolutionary Politics in Massachusetts: The Boston Committee of Correspondence and the Towns, 1772–1774* (Cambridge, Mass., 1970 and New York, 1976).

STANLEY COBEN, Professor of History at the University of California, Los Angeles, is the author of numerous books and articles in American history, including *The Development of an American Culture* (New York, 1968). Mr. Coben is at present completing a book dealing with changes in American culture during the 1920s.

DEE GARRISON is Assistant Professor of American History, Livingston College, Rutgers University. She is the author of several articles on librarianship and women's history, and is currently completing a history of the public library and a biography of Elizabeth Gurley Flynn.

DAVID D. HALL, Professor of History at Boston University and Director, American and New England Studies Program, has written extensively on the seventeenth century. He is presently at work on a study of Victorian intellectuals and their cultural politics. (See also, "The Politics of Culture: The Writer in a Young Democracy," *Barnard Alumnae,* January 1976).

DANIEL WALKER HOWE is Associate Professor of History at the University of California, Los Angeles. His publications include *The Unitarian Conscience* (Cambridge, Mass., 1970; winner of the Brewer Prize) and *The American Whigs* (New York, 1973). He is now writing a book on the political culture of the Whig party.

CLAUDIA D. JOHNSON is Assistant Professor of English at the University of Alabama. She has published articles in *American Literature, Studies in Short Fiction, Cresset,* and *American Quarterly.* She has co-authored, with Henry E. Jacobs, *An Annotated Bibliography of Shakespearean Travesties, Burlesques, and Parodies* (New York, 1975).

D. H. MEYER is Associate Professor of History at the University of Delaware. He is the author of two books, *The Instructed Conscience* (Philadelphia, 1972) and *The Democratic Enlightenment* (New York, 1975), as well as several articles. Mr. Meyer is now working on a book concerning "The Moral Universe of William James."

GREGORY H. SINGLETON is Assistant Professor of History at Northeastern Illinois University. His publications include "The Genesis of Suburbia: A Complex of Historical Trends" in *Urban Affairs Annual Review* (1973) and "Fundamentalism and Urbanization: A Quantitative Critique of Impressionistic Interpretation" in *The New Urban History* (1975). Mr. Singleton is presently at work on a book treating WASPs as an ethnic group.

MORRIS J. VOGEL, Assistant Professor of History at Temple University, is at work writing a history of the hospital as a social institution.

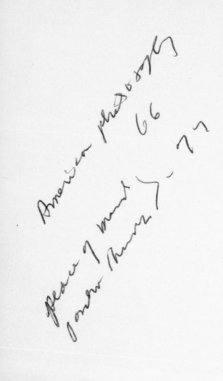